HARD WORK AND A GOOD DEAL

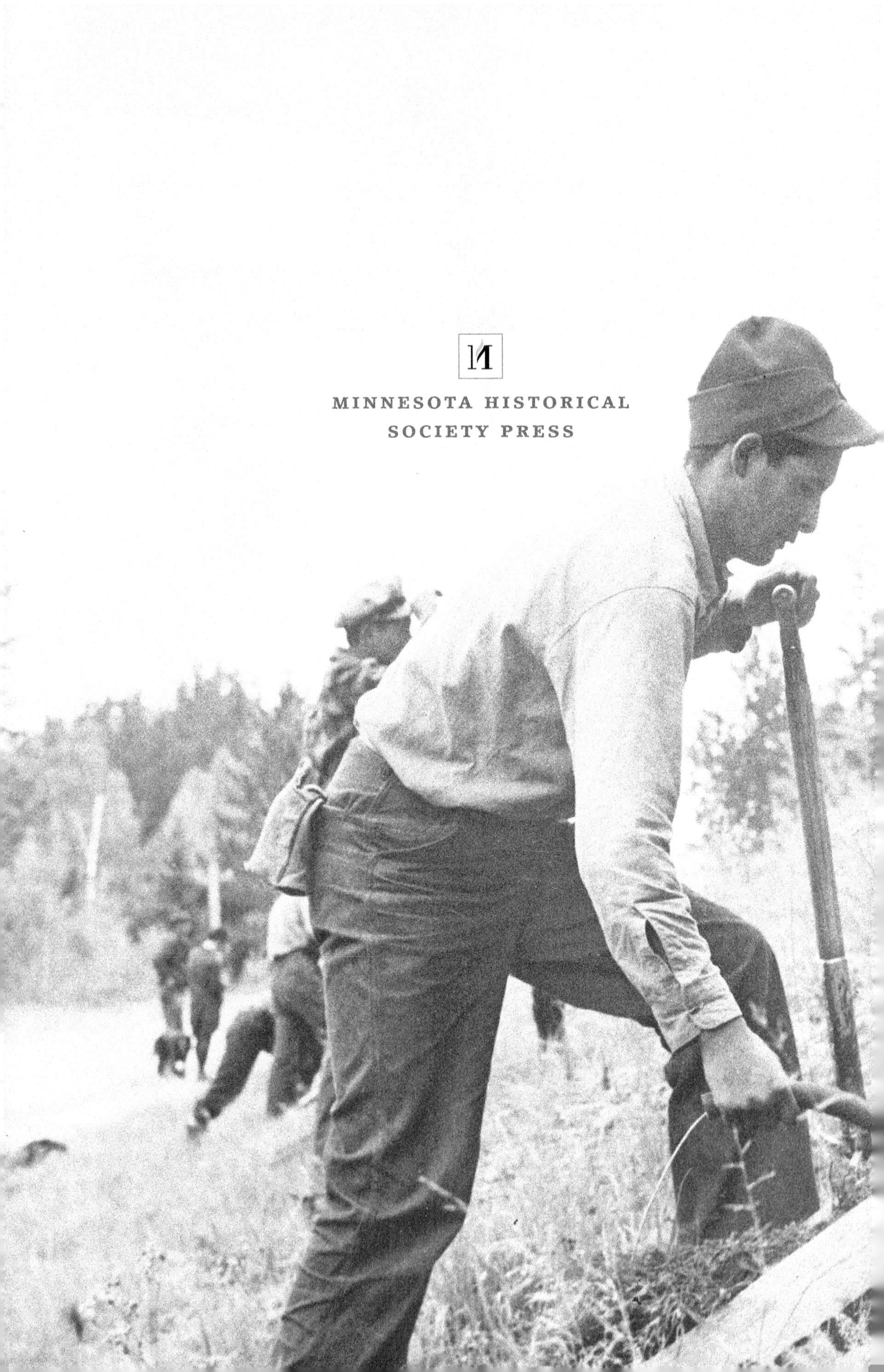

MINNESOTA HISTORICAL
SOCIETY PRESS

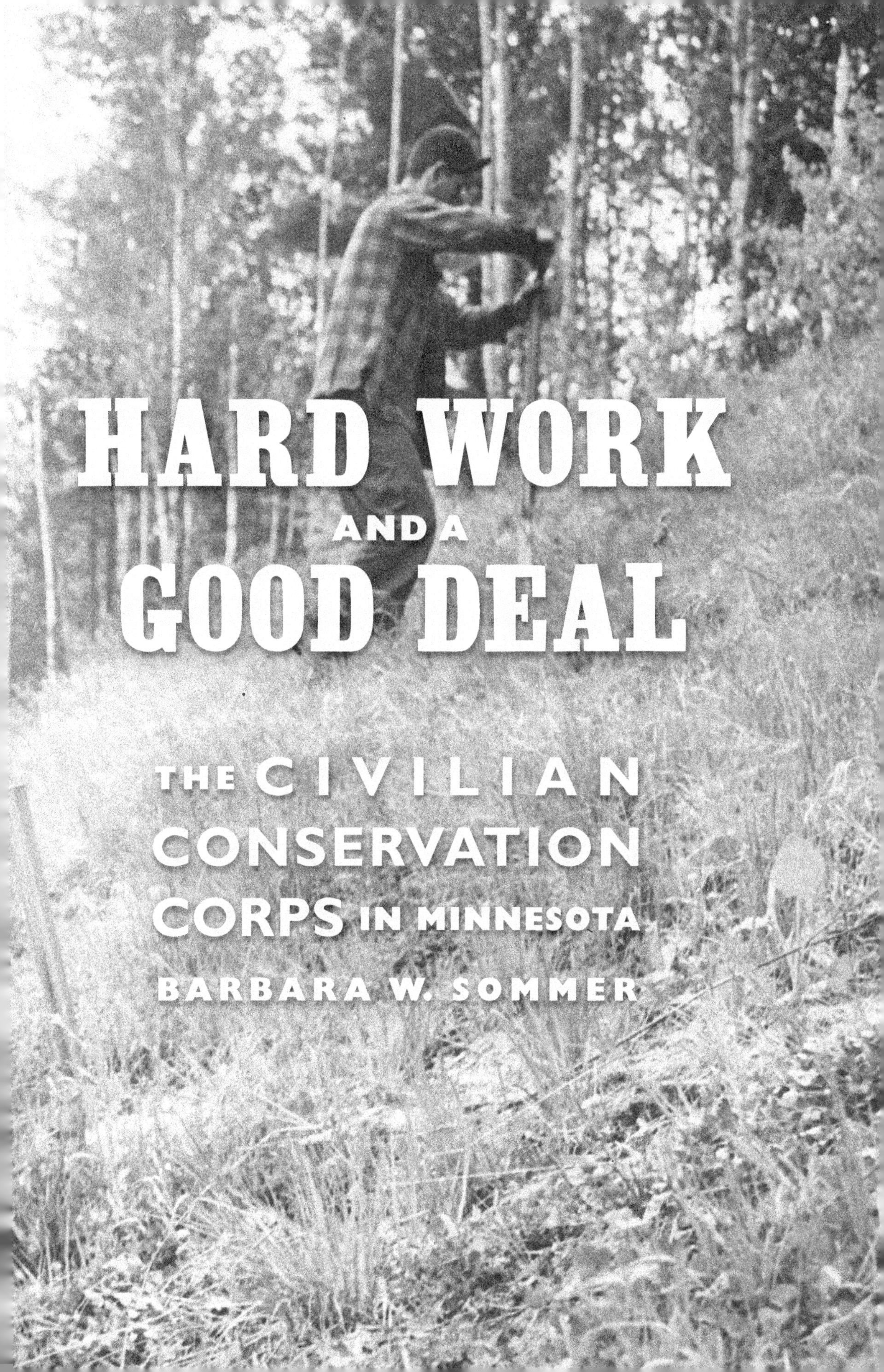

HARD WORK AND A GOOD DEAL

THE CIVILIAN CONSERVATION CORPS IN MINNESOTA

BARBARA W. SOMMER

mnhspress.org

The Minnesota Historical Society Press is a member of the Association of University Presses.

Manufactured in the United States of America

10 9 8 7 6 5 4 3 2 1

∞ The paper used in this publication meets the minimum requirements of the American National Standard for Information Sciences—Permanence for Printed Library Materials, ANSI Z39.48-1984.

ISBN: 978-0-87351-612-9 (hardcover)
ISBN: 978-0-87351-735-5 (ebook)
ISBN: 978-1-68134-234-4 (paperback)

LIBRARY OF CONGRESS CATALOGING-IN-PUBLICATION DATA
Sommer, Barbara W.
Hard work and a good deal : the Civilian Conservation Corps in Minnesota / Barbara W. Sommer.
p. cm.
Includes bibliographical references and index.
ISBN-13: 978-0-87351-612-9 (cloth : alk. paper)
ISBN-10: 0-87351-612-5 (cloth : alk. paper)
1. Civilian Conservation Corps (U.S.)—Minnesota—History.
2. Conservation of natural resources—Minnesota—History.
I. Title.

S932.M45S66 2008
333.76'1509776—dc22

2007029043

Front cover: CCC enrollees take a break in Chippewa National Forest.
Courtesy Chippewa National Forest
Jacket design: Cathy Spengler

CONTENTS

This book is dedicated to the more than 77,000 enrollees who served in Minnesota's 148 Civilian Conservation Corps camps and to the work project administrators, camp administrators, Local Experienced Men, and others who were a part of the Civilian Conservation Corps in the state.

Note: Although popularly known as the Civilian Conservation Corps, or CCC, this program's first official name was the Emergency Conservation Work Program, or ECW. The name was not officially changed until June 1937, but because the program was then and still is generally referred to as the Civilian Conservation Corps, the author has chosen to use that name throughout the book.

ACKNOWLEDGMENTS

Writing and publishing a book is both an individual and a collaborative process. Many people have tirelessly supported and assisted in this book's development, answering questions, providing information, tracking down photographs, and helping with all the tasks that are part of the process. Edward P. Nelson has been involved from concept through publication. His depth of knowledge was helpful at every turn, and his guidance and insight and support are gratefully acknowledged. Thank you to Harvey Richart and the members of Chapter 119 of the National Association of CCC Alumni for support of the project from inception through publication.

The Minnesota Historical Society's grants program provided funding to collect some of the interviews. Members of the Minnesota Historical Society staff always were ready to answer questions and help locate information. A special thanks is due to Robert "Skip" Drake. Also to Ruth Bauer Anderson, Deborah Miller, James E. Fogerty, Susan Roth, and Ann Regan and to Shannon Pennefeather, whose editorial skills are greatly appreciated. Thanks also to Steve Harsin and Scott Kuzma at the Iron Range Research Center, who helped track down information and photographs from the CCC collections. Vic Ruhland, formerly of the Natural Resources Conservation Service, provided information about the history of soil conservation in the state. Patricia Maus of the Northeast Regional Research Center in Duluth was an excellent resource, as was University of Minnesota archivist Lois Hendrickson. Thanks to Keith Matson of Chippewa National Forest for his very helpful review of the camps list and to Walter Okstad of Superior National Forest for being available to answer questions regardless of when I called. Mary Nordeen at Chippewa National Forest searched for photographs, as did Deborah Rose of the Department of Natural Resources. Bromley Griffin, formerly of St. Croix State Park, provided information about the park's CCC history. Mary Halbert and the members of Chapter 33 of the National Association of CCC Alumni were very helpful and are owed many thanks. Thanks also to the National Association of CCC Alumni (NACCCA) and the Minnesota Conservation Corps (MCC).

Others who lent their assistance include Arnold Alanen, Carol Ahlgren, Donald Wilson, William Marshall, George Poch, Richard Cameron, Kathy Kainz, Elizabeth Bright, W. H. Raff, and Douglas Seefeldt. An outstanding thank you to Gwenyth Swain, whose editorial and writing skills helped find and develop this publication's voice—of extraordinary importance when working with oral histories. And thank you to my family for their support: Anna and Nathan Sommer Lux, Erik Sommer, and Karin Sommer. The final and very heartfelt thanks is for my husband, Lawrence J. Sommer, without whose support this work would not have been done.

The publication of this book was supported, in part, by the Minnesota's Greatest Generation Project of the Minnesota Historical Society.

HARD WORK AND A GOOD DEAL

PART I
THE CCC TAKES SHAPE

INTRODUCTION: THE QUIET CHANGE

In 1933, a quiet change began in Minnesota and elsewhere across the country. One governmental program—part of an "alphabet soup" of New Deal programs started by President Franklin Delano Roosevelt in response to the Great Depression—offered hope to young men and teenage boys. Hope was what these men and boys needed most of all in the dark days of the Depression. But the Civilian Conservation Corps, or CCC, also gave them a steady paycheck and meaningful work.[1]

Whether you know it or not, you've probably seen traces of the CCC's work in Minnesota. The legacy lives in the warm stone used in the Lakeview Refectory at Gooseberry Falls State Park in northeastern Minnesota—and in countless other buildings constructed by the CCC across the state. It stands in the red pine trees planted on state-owned lands by men and teenagers of various walks of life, of various ethnicities, who were part of the CCC. The legacy lives in southeastern Minnesota, where the CCC implemented contour farming techniques still in use today. And perhaps most importantly, the CCC remains a vivid and vital part of the memories of men and boys who took part in the program. Few in the CCC would have called their work "revolutionary," but they knew it was special. Enrollee Harvey Richart put it this way: "What the CCCs accomplished will never again be equaled. It made our lives for the rest of our time." Another man, in a case of classic Minnesota understatement, said simply, "It was a good deal."[2]

CCC enrollees from a camp in Rabideau, Minnesota, take a break from their work in the Chippewa National Forest. Rabideau is one of the few remaining intact CCC camps in the United States. It was listed on the National Register of Historic Places in 1976 and designated a national historic landmark in 2006.

This book takes its title in part from that CCC enrollee's words. Within these pages, you'll find countless other quotations from oral histories. An oral history is a primary source document—similar to a letter or a diary—that is the result of an interview with someone who witnessed or participated in a historical event. The oral history interview is conducted to preserve and collect information about the past. Its goal is to leave for future researchers a first-person view of history.

The oral histories used in this book, all of which are available to researchers, shed light on history from the perspective of the men and boys of the CCC. Conducted in 1982, 1983, and 1994 with former enrollees, camp educators, administrators, army personnel, and others, these interviews tell us what it was like to be in the CCC. The quotations used are as faithful to the original interviews as possible, preserving speech patterns and even feelings—loneliness, humor, camaraderie, pride, frustration. Perhaps more eloquently than any other historical document, these oral histories tell us how the CCC affected the people involved. When combined with other sources, they help us more fully understand this part of Minnesota history.

Hard Work and a Good Deal is a celebration of the people of the CCC and of the work they left behind. It's also a backward glance to an era when—faced with a monumental crisis—both the federal and the state governments nurtured hope. Today, more than seventy years later, vestiges of that hope remain in tall trees, conservation farming techniques, stone buildings, and even simple walking paths—all started by the CCC and all part of the state's enduring landscape.

1: WHY WE NEEDED THE CCC

At first, Minnesotans didn't know they needed the ccc. Even before Minnesota became a state in 1858, people were drawn to the area's rich natural resources. Tall stands of trees, good soil, and navigable rivers beckoned. The state gradually built an economy based on farming, logging, milling, and mining.

By the 1920s, large and small farming operations were spread throughout southern, central, and western Minnesota. Some farmers were even planting on cleared forestlands up north. Along with producing wheat, corn, and other grains, farmers raised hogs and cattle. In southeastern counties, dairy farmers made milk production an important part of the state's economy.

Minnesotans looking for work outside of farming could generally depend on other industries, such as milling and logging, for jobs. But while logging operations in northern Minnesota still employed many men, by the 1920s they were winding down as lumber companies moved to the forests of Montana and the Pacific Northwest. That's not to say Minnesota workers had no other choices for jobs: flour milling and other industries had also developed in the state, particularly in the main population centers of Minneapolis and St. Paul.

In Minneapolis, General Mills (the former Washburn Crosby Company) was developing enduring brands such as Gold Medal flour, Wheaties, and

Bisquick. A friendly woman by the name of Betty Crocker answered questions about cooking and even offered advice on the radio. The company's main Minneapolis rival, Charles Pillsbury's flour-milling operation, had helped turn "Mill City" into a national leader of food production—and into a center for jobs.

Across the Mississippi River in the state capital of St. Paul, industries such as brewing provided employment. Schmidt's Brewery and the Hamm's Brewing Company were among the nation's largest—so successful, in fact, that in the 1930s the families of both companies would become victims of notorious kidnappings for ransom.

Industrial jobs in Minnesota were not isolated to the twin cities of Minneapolis and St. Paul. Up north on the Iron Range, the mining industry was hungry for workers to dig up some of the world's richest iron ore. Mines employed 18,000 men during World War I, and although numbers dropped somewhat after the war, iron ore production held steady in the 1920s. Ships owned by steel companies carried the ore from the Duluth harbor, through the Great Lakes, to eastern steel-producing centers.[1]

While the state's farmers, loggers, millers, brewers, and miners helped harvest and process natural resources, yet another industry was developing. With the rise of improved roads and automobiles, the "Land of 10,000 Lakes" was fast becoming a tourist destination, and tourism was providing even more jobs in the state.

But well before the stock market crash of October 29, 1929, signs of stress had appeared in Minnesota's economy and job market. The state was rich in businesses and industries based on natural resources. Growth, however, had put increasing strain on these resources. Throughout the state, signs of wear and tear were showing. Logging in northern forests left millions of acres of land practically barren. Elsewhere, particularly in the southern and western parts of the state, farming practices led to soil erosion that in turn polluted once-clear rivers and lakes. With greater dairy farming in southeastern Minnesota and increased demand for dairy products, many acres of marginal land, not suited for agricultural development, had been put into production.

Minnesota wasn't the only state to find itself in a precarious situation. On the Great Plains, erosion resulting from poor land use—combined with sustained drought—would eventually create the "Dust Bowl" in what came to be popularly known as the Dirty Thirties. Throughout the country, poor land and water use were sapping resources, and people were beginning to discover that nature had definite limits. Crop prices, which began falling in the years after World War I, made it a challenge for farmers to break even. Earning a profit was becoming a more and more elusive goal during the agricultural depression of the 1920s.

In Minnesota, many farmers were barely hanging on while others lost or abandoned land even before the Great Depression. In some areas of southeastern Minnesota, the market value of land fell by one-third between 1914

A float illustrating the devastating effects of soil erosion takes part in the Wykoff, Minnesota, Booster Day Parade on April 6, 1937.

and 1934. Average yields of corn, barley, wheat, clover, and timothy declined, too, as the land began to show signs of strain from overfarming.[2]

Heavily logged areas in the north also were under stress by the late 1920s. At that time, the lumber industry was under no obligation to restore lands to a useable state after harvesting timber. Much of this cutover area was left bare, too poor to support agriculture and too grim to attract tourists.

These fissures in the state economy would grow dramatically wider with the coming of the Great Depression. The Depression's impact wasn't immediate, however, nor were its initial effects felt uniformly across Minnesota. After the stock market crash, for many people life just went on. They went to work, sent their children to school, kept up their homes and gardens, and put their savings in the local banks.

Herbert Hoover, president during the first years of the Great Depression, was a successful engineer and popular leader. He believed in letting the country work its way out of its difficulties. The federal government might offer leadership, Hoover believed, but it should not actively intervene. Even when faced with the stock market crash and the ongoing effects of the post–World War I agricultural depression, Hoover looked to the nation's business, banking, and industrial leaders to sort things out. It wasn't until late in 1930 that he came to realize the situation was worse than he'd thought. A year after "Black Friday," as October 29, 1929, came to be called, banks across the United States began collapsing at the rate of ten a day, setting off waves of bank panics as people scrambled to remove their savings while they could. With this, the country began to slide into a period of economic instability that would eventually plunge countries around the world into economic depression.

By the early 1930s, the Depression's full effects were settling over Minnesota and other states. What people saw, among other things, was an unprecedented rise in joblessness. In Minnesota, unemployment rates in 1932 hit 29 percent—even higher than the national average. On the Iron Range, that figure rose to 70 percent. Iron ore production, which had averaged 33 million tons a year in the 1920s, dropped to 2.2 million tons in 1932, and employment at the mines fell to fewer than 2,000 men. That year, 86 percent of Minnesota's industries reported operating at a loss, with pulp and paper, machinery and metals hardest hit.[3]

Many future CCC enrollees vividly remember those early years of the Depression. John Rabuze talked about his father, a blacksmith, who was laid off from his job in the mines. Although he found work for the village of Buhl "off and on," sharpening tools at ten to fifteen cents apiece, everyone knew this wasn't enough to support a family. Eino Lahti said his father worked for the mining company for "years and years and years, and then, of course, he lost his job." Lahti knew there wasn't much in any "line of work, and the pay wasn't that good" for himself either. Nick Radovich, a young man already living on his own, worked for Republic Steel for three years, in 1928, 1929, and 1930. "In 1931," he said, "it was getting to be part-time, and in 1932, there was no work at all."[4]

Wages and agricultural prices fell precipitously. P. J. Halloran, an army sergeant who would be assigned to the CCC, described a situation common to many: "[My parents and grandparents] worked all year, produced a crop, and then, when they sold it, they weren't able to pay their feed bills." Rather than sell corn at too low a price, many farmers kept the crop and burned it for

Most northern Minnesota forests were logged in the late nineteenth and early twentieth centuries. This cutover forestland, with tree stumps still visible, shows the effects of intensive logging near Tower, 1901.

fuel during the winter. In 1931, dairy farmers' income was one-fourth of what it had been two years earlier, and by 1935, as many as 18 percent of the state's farmers were receiving some form of aid. In an attempt to raise prices by stopping the shipment of food into cities, some Minnesotans joined in the Farmers Holiday Association strike in 1932. The strike failed, although it did draw attention to conditions farmers faced.[5]

Those conditions were grim. More and more farmers were losing their land to foreclosure. Some landowners, unable to pay their taxes, abandoned their land, adding it to the growing tax delinquent rolls. At the end of 1930, over 6.8 million acres of land in Minnesota were tax delinquent; in 1933, one-seventh of the state's land area fell into this category. The farmers of northern Minnesota, many of whom had tried to plant on cutover forestland, were hit especially hard. By the early 1930s, three-fourths of the tax delinquent property in Minnesota was on logged-over areas in the northern part of the state.[6]

For many Minnesotans, whether they were farmers or not, any financial cushion they might have had before suddenly disappeared. During the Great Depression, at least 320 state banks and 58 national banks located in Minnesota closed their doors. Claude Darst remembered it this way: "The banks went broke, and [my father] lost all his money. In fact, [my parents] were quite wealthy, and they lost it all. It didn't make any difference whether you were rich or poor: when the banks went broke, everybody was treated the same."[7]

While many would later say they didn't know they were poor during the Depression because they had enough to eat, others vividly remembered hunger. Reinhold Holmer said, "I was going to reach for that second slice of bread, and my mother didn't say anything. But she raised her finger. And I understood: we needed something for the next meal." Claude Darst admitted, "I didn't know how I was going to eat from day to day." Paul Sersha, too, described living close to the edge: "Anytime we could make a nickel, we did. I had a paper route. Any money that I got, my mother and I went to Eveleth and got flour and things. And we had a garden and a few calves and hogs and chickens. That's the way we kept alive."[8]

Many men who would later enroll in the Civilian Conservation Corps were teenagers during the early years of the Great Depression. They sat idle in record numbers—one in four was unemployed. Those who did find jobs were often underemployed and working for the lowest wages in decades. Some, including Claude Darst, were homeless for a time:

> *I dropped out [of high school] because I was taking care of myself. . . . One of my sisters went with my grandparents, and one went with my aunt and uncle. My mother went to Rochester and worked for two dollars a week, and, quite frankly, I was left standing on the streets. . . . I got a room and I had this little job, fifty cents a day, delivering milk to a couple of schools, pasteurizing it and stuff. Then I had an appendectomy, and when I got back to work, I didn't have my job anymore because the buttermaker let his nephew have it. Things were just rough.*[9]

Clarence Johnson was a little luckier: he had a job, "sort of like a WPA [Works Progress Administration] job," remodeling the armory in Austin. But when that ended, he had to find more work and didn't know where to turn. Raymond Noyes remembered that even though his father was one of the first welders in Duluth, he could find only part-time work and then "his business just went down to nothing." Putting a human face on the numbers, he said, "It was so degrading during the Depression for a man not to have employment. I had a brother and sister besides myself, mother, and father. Five of us in the family. And, from day to day, we wondered where our next meal was coming from."[10]

Precise figures are hard to come by for 1932, when local and county governments were responsible for families in need, but just one year later as many as 137,000 Minnesota families were on relief, as welfare was then called. For many, the very act of signing up for relief was the ultimate humiliation. People prided themselves on being self-sufficient, in taking care of themselves. To admit publicly the need for help was a last resort. As Ernest Anderson remembered it, children would drop out of school to earn money if it meant keeping the family off relief. Ernest's father ran a little business in Chisholm, "making stuff to eat, you know. That is all it was." The Depression changed things: "I left school in the eleventh grade, just like most everybody else. I could have made it through twelfth grade easy. I was pretty good at school. But it was tough times, you know. And I had to help my dad."[11]

Michael Sanchelli, who also left high school during the Depression, said, "The local governments did start a relief plan, [but] it was more a pain in the neck than relief." Sanchelli vividly recalled picking up food provided under the relief program in his St. Paul neighborhood: "We had to go to the old Hamms residence on Gable St. right above on the east side of Swede Hollow. [You] would get a grocery order. Now when I say grocery order it wasn't what I would call groceries. It was dried prunes, dried apples, apricots and peaches, dried navy beans, sometimes a can or so of corn, peas, or string beans. [An] . . . order for my family went into one large bag. That was for the month!" Worse, from Sanchelli's standpoint, were the clothes offered by relief agencies: "You were a marked individual when you put on a pair of pants that you got from the relief places; welfare gray, starchy, some company must have made a million pair and sold them to the government."[12]

Allen Conkright remembered his family's struggle to stay off relief: "My dad wasn't around. My mother was a proud woman. She never applied for relief and never went on it that I know of." When he was in high school, his mother fell behind on her light bill, so he went to the municipal electric, light, and water plant and "worked it out. Dug ditches, put in water pipes, and the like. My mother was alone with four kids."[13]

Despite many people's best efforts to remain self-sufficient, however, payments to the needy in Minnesota rose as conditions worsened. Across the country, millions of families were faced with little or no means of support. Many would lose everything in what one historian calls a "roaring tornado

Children hold signs demanding jobs and food during a Workers Alliance demonstration in St. Paul on April 21, 1937, at the height of the Depression.

that ripped the financial heart out of the country." As the Depression worsened, two men were vying for the job of president of the United States of America. In essence, they brought two sets of ideas to the ballot box. During the early years of the Great Depression, President Herbert Hoover stayed true to his long-held political beliefs, encouraging business, banking, and industrial leaders to help turn around the economy. When this didn't work, he began to think the unthinkable for a politician of his background and beliefs: he suggested using direct government action. Hoover's suggestions, however, either were not accepted or were not fully implemented.[14]

New York governor Franklin Delano Roosevelt was running against the incumbent president. Roosevelt had ideas he thought would help the economy. When he accepted the Democratic Party's nomination in the summer of 1932, Roosevelt said, "I pledge you, I pledge myself, to a new deal for the American people." The set of federal government reforms and programs Roosevelt pledged in this "new deal" was drastic and potentially controversial.[15]

And the CCC was to be a part of it.

2: WHAT WAS THE CCC?

In November 1932, Franklin D. Roosevelt defeated Herbert Hoover to become president of the United States, taking the oath of office on March 4, 1933. In his inaugural address, as another bank panic raged, he said, "The only thing we have to fear is fear itself." Roosevelt found himself the leader of a nation in a precarious economic state. Determined to put people back to work, he pushed through a series of legislative reforms that, as a group, became known as the New Deal.[1]

Roosevelt's primary purpose in developing the New Deal was immediate economic recovery. His was an activist approach to federal government policy. Although Franklin Roosevelt (a Democrat) was from a different political party than his distant cousin, former president Theodore Roosevelt (a Republican), the two shared certain beliefs. Both held that the federal government should place public interest over private interests, that unfair economic practices should be rooted out, and that government should have a role in providing economic security.

FDR, as the new president was popularly known, drew on these views as he began to develop New Deal programs. He went to work immediately, and the intense activity that followed—from the opening of a special session of Congress on March 9 until its closing on June 16—came to be called the "Hundred Days." In that short span of time, the Roosevelt administration passed the Emergency Banking Act—which closed insolvent banks and restructured remaining ones—along with other wide-ranging legislation, including help for farmers, unemployment relief, reform of the securities market, and regulation of industry. Representing an interventionist and activist approach to government, New Deal programs would become controversial as time passed. But in 1933, they were welcomed as a way to begin to deal with the country's problems.[2]

Of all the "alphabet soup" programs to emerge from the New Deal—the AAA (Agricultural Adjustment Administration), CWA (Civil Works Administration), FERA (Federal Emergency Relief Administration), FHA (Federal Housing Administration), NRA (National Recovery Administration), PWA (Public Works Administration), WPA (Works Progress Administration)—the CCC was unique. Officially known as the Emergency Conservation Work Program, or ECW, it almost immediately became popularly known as the Civilian Conservation Corps, or the CCC for short. Another popular nickname for the program—"Roosevelt's Tree Army"—illustrates how closely it was linked in the public's mind to the newly elected president.[3]

Roosevelt dropped hints about the CCC even prior to his election. In his acceptance speech for the Democratic presidential nomination in July 1932, he promised to support "a definite land policy" to fight "a future of soil erosion and timber famine. . . . In doing so, employment can be given to a million men." He called the idea "the kind of public work that is self-sustaining" and said he had "a very definite program for providing employment by that means."[4]

More than any other New Deal program, the CCC was most completely Roosevelt's idea, one he would discuss with his staff just hours after taking office. In essence, the CCC reflected Franklin Roosevelt's "lover's passion" for conservation, the management of natural resources for long-term public benefit. While today people often think of conservation as environmentalism, or protecting existing resources, at the time of the CCC it focused on preserving and scientifically managing resources for practical use and economic purposes. As a young man, Roosevelt had absorbed many of these ideas from Gifford Pinchot, the innovative chief forester and founder of the U.S. Forest Service under President Theodore Roosevelt. FDR believed so strongly in the value of conservation that he wished to make his own mark in the field, but in ways that went beyond simple preservation of land.[5]

The CCC also grew out of FDR's early interest in developing relief programs to meet conservation needs. As governor of New York before he became president, he had tried this approach in a reforestation and unemployment relief program. Roosevelt also was aware of forest service relief programs instituted in California and Washington. When he became president, he was ready to develop a conservation work relief program on a national scale.

That readiness contributed to another defining quality of the CCC: it grew from an abstract idea into a real, working program with incredible speed. On March 9, just five days after he took the oath of office, Roosevelt met with the secretaries of agriculture, interior, and war, his budget director, the U.S. Army judge advocate general, and the solicitor of the Department of the Interior to outline a plan. He wanted to put five million young men to work on conservation projects. Roosevelt asked the group to write a bill for his plan as quickly as possible. The group went to work and sent him their first draft that same evening. The president then asked the secretaries of war, interior, agriculture, and labor—the federal agencies that would be most affected by his idea—to discuss plans to make it happen. They worked on the draft, preparing it to go to Congress for a vote.

In a public address on March 21, 1933, the day the bill was sent to Congress, Roosevelt called the program by its popular name, the Civilian Conservation Corps. He also formally defined its mission: it was a temporary program designed to put people back to work. Its purpose was to provide employment on conservation projects—in forestry, erosion and flood control, and parks—for needy, jobless young men between the ages of eighteen and twenty-five. Congress approved the concept but requested several changes, which were made before a revised bill was sent back on March 27, 1933. On March 31, ten days after the bill was first sent to Congress, lawmakers passed the Emergency Conservation Work Act. The act appropriated funds for the "dual purpose of relieving unemployment and promoting conservation of natural resources." On April 5, Roosevelt signed Executive Order 6106, the "Relief of Unemployment through Performance of Useful Public Works," which established the Emergency Conservation Work Program (later known as the CCC). It also named the program's director—labor organizer and FDR supporter Robert Fechner—ordered the secretaries of agriculture, war, labor, and interior to appoint representatives for an advisory council, and established $10 million in a treasury fund to get the program started.[6]

On April 6, less than a month after the idea was first discussed and only thirty-three days after Roosevelt took office, the first enrollees were accepted into the CCC. The first camp, Camp Roosevelt, was established at Luray, Virginia, the day after that. With the creation of the advisory council and the appointment of a director and assistant director, the CCC's basic structure was in place.

As a federal program, the CCC was unusual. Although a well-defined entity in the minds of the public, it was, in fact, a cooperative effort among a number of existing agencies. The Department of Labor, working with state employment and relief agencies, oversaw enrollment. The War Department, through the U.S. Army, handled camp administration, including transportation of enrollees to camp, physical conditioning, camp construction, and day-to-day operations. The Departments of Agriculture and Interior ran the conservation work programs. (Specifically, forest service personnel developed and supervised conservation projects for federal and state forest camps, while soil conservation service personnel were in charge of work programs at soil conservation camps. State park personnel, guided by National Park Service policies,

President Franklin D. Roosevelt speaking in Rochester, Minnesota, on August 8, 1934. Many local CCC enrollees remembered forming President Roosevelt's honor guard for this visit, during which he drew attention to the need for intensive conservation work in the severely eroded southeastern part of the state.

directed work programs at state park camps.) When needed, other departments, such as commerce, treasury, and navy, also were involved.[7]

The CCC has been described as the program charged with the responsibility for "a thousand conservation tasks which had gone too long unperformed." During the CCC years, conservation in the United States was still struggling to take hold. Conservationists focused on several major programmatic areas—water use, flood control, forest management, land management for hunting and fishing, and control of soil erosion. Minnesota's CCC program would work in all of these areas, restoring and stabilizing national forests, developing and expanding state forests, building a state park system, controlling flooding, and introducing soil conservation measures on agricultural lands in the southern part of the state. Work developing migratory bird refuges and aiding the state Bureau of Biological Services, although not as extensive, helped fulfill conservation goals for management of hunting and fishing habitat.[8]

The CCC was never a big organization on the state level or nationally. In Washington, total office personnel never topped more than forty or fifty people. Although there were several attempts to make the program permanent, including one in which its name was officially changed to the Civilian Conservation Corps, all were unsuccessful. The CCC, like most other New Deal programs, remained temporary, a short-term measure to put people back to work during a difficult time.[9]

Long after the Great Depression, the ccc was often confused with the WPA (Works Progress Administration), but the two New Deal programs were quite different. The WPA was authorized later than the ccc, in April 1935. WPA work was broadly based—from building roads to sewing clothes—while the ccc kept its focus strictly on conservation. Although the WPA, too, was designed to put the unemployed back to work on public projects, participants were generally heads of households, and thus older than those in the ccc. The WPA sometimes paid better than the ccc, but it didn't provide full-time, forty-hour-per-week employment. And the WPA put women to work, something that never happened in the ccc, where most enrollees referred to themselves as "boys" long after the program had ended and the boys had grown into men.

Some of the rules and goals of the ccc might seem paternalistic today. The program was designed to pay enrollees one dollar per day to live in camps and work on land and water conservation projects. But the men would be allowed to keep only five to eight dollars of their monthly income. The remaining twenty-two to twenty-five dollars were sent to designated dependents—usually the enrollees' parents back home.

ccc director Robert Fechner adopted an often fatherly tone when he spoke of the organization, calling it "a practical school where young men in their teens and early twenties are taught how to work, how to live and how to get ahead." Still, enrollees were never coddled. They were expected to work for the five to eight dollars of pay that they could keep. "One of the fundamentals of the CC program," Fechner wrote in a 1939 article, "is that enrollees put in a full five day, forty hour week whenever the climatic conditions permit. This is done in the belief that the work discipline and training acquired by enrollees on the job and through the normal routine of orderly camp living represents the best training and preparation for useful citizenship that we can offer."[10]

The logo of the ccc. Although popularly called the Civilian Conservation Corps from its earliest days, the official name of the program at its founding in 1933 was the Emergency Conservation Work Program. The name changed to Civilian Conservation Corps as part of federal legislation in 1937. ccc funding ended in 1943, although all Minnesota camps had closed by 1942.

The view was paternalistic, to be sure. But it speaks to the importance of work as a means of maintaining self-respect, a major theme of the Great Depression years. By and large, the young men who joined the ccc had no objections. Earl Krause, who enrolled in both a forest and a state park camp, reflected this when he said, "Well, [President Franklin D. Roosevelt] was the best [president] we ever had. He got things done. He took a lot of kids off the street and made men out of them." Kenny Johnson, an enrollee in a soil conservation

Running the ccc was a group effort. As enrollee Arthur Pryor put it, "In camp the clean-up and stuff belonged to the army, but out in the field that was the forest service." Army personnel managed the camps, while work agencies (including the forest service, among others) oversaw conservation projects. This photo taken at the Big Lake state forest camp in 1934 shows army and work program personnel. Front row, left to right: Joe McGrath, foreman; Curly Garres, engineer; Randolph Brown, education advisor; Russell Trengrove, camp work superintendent; Reed E. Davis, company commander, U.S. Army; Harold Halbrisen, second in command, U.S. Army. Back row, left to right: Don Burcalow, technical forester; Leo Smith, fire warden; George Wilson, foreman; George Santerre, foreman; and Dr. Royal Paine, company physician.

camp, found a job and pride at the same time: "President Roosevelt started the ccc to put young men to work, and we did a lot of real good work, lasting work."[11]

That work started quickly after Roosevelt signed the bill creating the ccc. The president set the seemingly impossible goal of enrolling 250,000 young men and having them all working by July 1, 1933. Young Minnesotans, eager for work, would help the ccc meet and quickly exceed that goal.[12]

In Minnesota, as in other states, setting up the ccc and getting it running was a shared responsibility. Recruiting enrollees fell to F. M. Rarig, state director of public relief, and C. S. Rondestvedt, supervisor of ccc enrollment for the state relief agency, while the army set to work organizing camps. The Minnesota ccc army headquarters was at Fort Snelling in St. Paul under the command of Brigadier General D. L. Stone.[13]

On April 5, 1933, the same day President Roosevelt signed the executive order establishing the program, Captain Morrill W. Marston of the Third Infantry stationed at Fort Snelling was given special duty to begin formation of Company 701 with ten enlisted men, the first ccc company in the state. The seven in the number meant Minnesota was in the Seventh U.S. Army Corps area—along with Arkansas, Iowa, Kansas, Missouri, Nebraska, North Dakota, and South Dakota—and was run from headquarters in Omaha, Nebraska, under command of Major General Frank McCoy.[14]

The Seventh Army Corps area was assigned a goal of setting up 155 camps, broken down as follows: Arkansas, 28; Iowa, 16; Kansas, 7; Minnesota, 61; Missouri, 16; Nebraska, 5; North Dakota, 7; and South Dakota, 15. Each state also was given an enrollee quota or goal. Minnesota's quota of 6,000 enrollees was calculated using a ratio of state to total U.S. population—at the time Minnesota had about two percent of the country's population.[15]

Having a quota did not mean a state could immediately participate in the ccc; each state had to devise appropriate conservation projects first. Although the U.S. Army ran the camps in which enrollees lived, the work agencies—including the state and national forest services, the soil conservation service,

ccc Director Robert Fechner, appointed by President Roosevelt in 1933, is seen here with two Minnesota officials—Harold Lathrop of the State Parks Division on the left and Grover Conzet of the Forestry Division on the right—shortly after speaking at a national meeting of state park representatives at Itasca State Park on June 6, 1939. This visit to the state would be Fechner's last: he died in 1939 and was succeeded by his assistant, James J. McEntee, who ran the ccc until funding ended in 1943.

the national and state park systems, and others—developed and supervised conservation tasks. Initially, work in Minnesota focused narrowly on forested and cutover land in the north and eroded land in the southeast. But once the state demonstrated its need for conservation work and its ability to recruit and employ large numbers of enrollees, the reach of ccc projects widened and Minnesota's quota was relaxed.[16]

For administrative purposes, army leaders divided Minnesota into four subdistricts. Three of these were in forest areas: the East Superior Subdistrict headquartered in Two Harbors, the International Falls Subdistrict headquartered in Hibbing, and the Chippewa Subdistrict headquartered in Cass Lake. The Southeastern Subdistrict, in Rochester, was in an area of widespread soil erosion.[17]

During the hectic days of ccc organization in Minnesota, no one kept track of the first camp to be established. Gegoka on McDougall Lake in the Superior National Forest was probably the first, being formed on May 7, 1933. Within ten days, the Bena, Caribou, Halfway, and Pike Lake/Pike Bay camps opened. The first state forest camps, formed between June 10 and 13, 1933, were Sullivan Lake, also known as Camp Charles, and Side Lake, both of which operated continuously for eight years, and Owen Lake. The first state park camps were Scenic State Park, Camp Ripley, and Lake Itasca, all established between June 21 and 29, 1933. Several soil conservation camps,

Brigadier General David Stone (third from left) was commander of the Minnesota ccc army headquarters at Fort Snelling in St. Paul. Here he is shown with members of the Minnesota district's flight team, probably around 1937.

including Caledonia and Houston (both in Houston County), were established within a day or two of one another in June 1933.[18]

Within the first full year of operation, Minnesota's ccc met its goal of sixty-one camps: twenty-four state forest camps, twenty-four federal forest camps, ten soil erosion camps, and three state park camps. By August 1933, the state had more than double the enrollees allowed in its first quota, with 12,200 men at work. Nationally, by July 1, 1933, more than 1,300 ccc camps had been established and the president's original goal of 250,000 enrollees had been met in full. Because demand for enrollee positions was so great, the national goal was increased to 300,000, the first of several expansions that would be made. That increase included minority involvement; on the average, ten percent of the ccc population was African American.[19]

Enrollees at the Seagull camp, ca. 1938. The state's most remote ccc camp, Seagull was located in northern Minnesota at the end of the Gunflint Trail.

Minnesota made quick work of setting up camps and meeting quotas for numbers of white enrollees. But while the state's ccc did recruit significant numbers of Native Americans (in a separate program begun in June 1933), it consistently fell short in enrolling African Americans. As the ccc developed, it wasn't uncommon for states with well-documented conservation work needs to see their quotas relaxed—as was eventually the case in Minnesota. But while more and more whites in the state enrolled in the ccc, Blacks found it harder and harder to get a foot in the door.

The original legislation creating the ccc contained a nondiscriminatory clause stating that "in employing citizens for the purposes of this Act, no discrimination shall be made on account of race, color, or creed." These words—the work of Representative Oscar DePriest, the only Black member of Congress at the time—were carried through each ccc funding bill. But the ccc was never fully able to translate the idealism of the words into action. This failure became one of the main criticisms of the ccc at the time and continues to be a source of questions today.[20]

Many New Deal leaders were in favor of fully carrying out the antidiscrimination clause, among them Harold Ickes, the secretary of the interior. But setting up and running ccc camps was the responsibility of the U.S. Army, which had a strict segregation policy. During the ccc years, following army policies, Black enrollees either were kept in separate camps or, early on and especially in states with low Black populations like Minnesota, were given separate quarters, away from whites, in "mixed" camps under the direction of white officers. Minnesota was not alone in failing to make the promise of the DePriest clause real. But controversy over that failure was intense in the state.

CCC director Robert Fechner was squarely behind the program's discriminatory practices, although he did not see them as such. "I am satisfied," he said in a 1935 letter, "that the negro enrollees themselves prefer to be in companies composed exclusively of their own race." He went on to define the CCC's policy: "This segregation [in the CCC camps] is not discrimination and cannot be so construed. The negro companies are assigned to the same types of work, have identical equipment, are served the same food, and have the same quarters as white enrollees." Further, he said that during his many visits to Black camps, he had "never received one single complaint."[21]

Leaders of Minnesota's Black community were not long in pointing out the unfairness of CCC policy. Spearheading the response was Charles Washington, executive director of the Twin City Urban League. Washington took up the cause in the spring of 1936, as fewer and fewer Minnesota Blacks were accepted into the CCC, firing off letters to the U.S. Department of Labor, the Minnesota Relief Agency, and the Seventh Corps area headquarters. In his correspondence, he pointed out that in Minnesota, white and "colored" boys attended school together, played sports together, and had, as a result, "developed a fine spirit of tolerance and understanding." Any discrimination against

Do Your Buying with Merchants Listed in Your Newspaper

MINNEAPOLIS SPOKESMAN

That which is great and splendid is not always laudable, but whatever is laudable must be great.—Selected

VOL. 5, NO. 6 MINNEAPOLIS, MINN., FRIDAY, SEPTEMBER 23, 1938 SINGLE COPY FIVE CENTS

MINNESOTA CCC CAMP BOYS SENT SOUTH

Citizens Will Fight Transfer of Minnesota CCC Boys to Missouri

Quartet to Sing

Race's Only Congress Member Principal Urban League Dinner Speaker

Gets License

October Bride

Business and Professional Announces Sumner Field Housing Project Information

Joshua T. Munroe, Mpls. Resident 30 Years, Dies

The Minneapolis *Spokesman* focused attention on the plight of African American enrollees from Minnesota sent to "Jim Crow camps" in the South beginning in 1937. The cultural climate of northern states differed significantly from that of the South; parents were understandably concerned when they learned their sons would not remain in Minnesota. Despite a massive campaign by the Twin Cities Urban League and other community leaders, the decision to attach African American enrollees from Minnesota to companies in other states was upheld.

These enrollees probably are members of Company 1728, stationed at the Temperance River camp near Tofte, ca. 1933. Reflecting the army's segregationist policies, Company 1728, formed in the state of Missouri, was composed entirely of Black enrollees, with white officers.

Black Minnesota enrollees would be seen, as he put it, as a "violation of the spirit of the entire program."[22]

Controversy intensified when, midway through the program, some Black Minnesotans in the CCC were forcibly sent to join all-Black units in other, traditionally southern states. The Minneapolis *Spokesman* and the St. Paul *Recorder*, newspapers edited by Cecil Newman, carried in 1937 an editorial titled "We Don't Want Our Boys Sent South," in which Newman decried the situation as "an injustice that will not stand in the face of widespread and proper protest." Then, in the fall of 1938, an order came down requiring all Black enrollees in Minnesota camps to report to an all-Black camp in Missouri or face administrative discharge. No more Blacks, the order continued, were to be admitted to Minnesota camps. Charles Washington found out about the order only when enrollees telephoned him as they were being moved through the Twin Cities by train on their way to Missouri. Washington said later, "We found that those boys were to some extent browbeaten into agreeing to go." The news made another banner headline in the *Spokesman* and *Recorder* newspapers: "Minnesota CCC Camp Boys Sent South." The *Spokesman* protested the transfer as "a vicious move to send our boys into states which subscribe completely to Jim Crow traditions," concluding that the "colored people of this state and their friends are going to fight the C.C.C. camp thing to the finish."[23]

Fight on they did, sending more letters, keeping the issue alive in the press, and at times successfully pushing through the enrollment of small numbers of Blacks. But national forces were stronger than the local protest.

While the Urban League's campaign earned support from elected officials including Governor Elmer A. Benson and senators Henrik Shipstead and Ernest Lundeen, the CCC administration and the army kept most qualified Black enrollees out of the program and sent those few who did succeed in enrolling to camps in other states. CCC director Fechner and other administrators restricted the ability of Blacks to enroll in the CCC, forcing them into a limited number of all-Black companies. Army policy was often cruelly blunt, as in a telegram sent to the Minnesota Relief Administration from the Seventh Corps area in Omaha: "No colored enrollees will be needed." These attitudes remain a source of pain and controversy—underscoring the differences in experiences between Black Minnesotans and others in the CCC.

Less controversial was the CCC's program for American Indians. Shortly after the founding of the CCC, commissioner of Indian Affairs Charles J. Rhoads recognized the program's potential for Native Americans and requested that an Indian division be formed within the CCC. His successor, John Collier, carried out that request, establishing the Indian Emergency Conservation Work program (IECW) under the Department of the Interior, Office of Indian Affairs. The IECW went into effect on June 19, 1933, becoming one of the first pieces of New Deal legislation to directly benefit Native Americans.[24]

Amos Owen, a Mdewakanton Dakota from the Prairie Island community, described it this way: "They had this Civilian Conservation Corps that the Department of the Interior put out. That was for everybody—they could work on the reservation. They had jobs, such as road repairs and stuff like that. It gave everybody employment. It kept the married families working. The money wasn't much, but a dollar went a little farther way back then."[25]

A CCC-ID crew works on the Mille Lacs Indian Reservation, ca. 1938.

When the popular name Civilian Conservation Corps began to catch on, the IECW became known as the Civilian Conservation Corps–Indian Division (CCC-ID). The program differed in significant ways from the CCC. Camps were run through the Bureau of Indian Affairs (BIA), not the U.S. Army. The CCC-ID's age range was more flexible, being open to all men aged seventeen and older and in good physical health who were enrolled members of a tribe. As with the CCC, men were recruited, but through local, tribal agencies.[26]

CCC-ID administration was organized by districts and reservations. In Minnesota, part of the Lakes State Region, participation was coordinated through the Consolidated Chippewa Indian Agency, the Red Lake (Chippewa) Indian Agency, and the Minnesota Sioux Indians at Pipestone. The Consolidated Chippewa agency served the six Minnesota Chippewa Tribe reservations: Fond du Lac, Grand Portage, Leech Lake, Mille Lacs, Nett Lake (Bois Forte), and White Earth. The Red Lake agency served the Red Lake Band of Chippewa, and the Minnesota Sioux agency covered the Pipestone, Prairie Island, Upper Sioux, Lower Sioux, and Prior Lake communities and reservations in central and southern Minnesota.[27]

The CCC-ID was a New Deal program, but it can also be seen as part of a larger reform movement taking place in the 1930s. On June 18, 1934, Congress passed the Indian Reorganization Act, also known as the Wheeler-Howard Act. Its purpose was to "conserve and develop Indian lands and resources; to extend to Indians the right to form business and other organizations; to establish a credit system for Indians; to grant certain rights of home rule to Indians; to provide for vocational education for Indians; and for other purposes," beginning a process of reversing federal policies of a century or more.

As Edmund Jefferson Danziger, Jr., has described it, it reversed "allotment, Americanization, and assimilation policies."[28]

The CCC-ID was created during this period of change, and its design was influenced not only by the stated needs of the CCC—providing work to unemployed men on conservation projects—but also by the reform movement. In particular, CCC-ID programs were not always standard conservation work programs. Leaders developed work programs that supported community and tribal cultural history, heritage, and needs while also promoting concepts common to the CCC.

A group of African American enrollees plants trees during the early years of the CCC, before policy shifted and Blacks were removed to camps outside the state.

Whatever their cultural heritage, Minnesota's CCC enrollees did needed work, work that left a lasting impression on the state. The majority of CCC undertakings in Minnesota were forest projects, most in the cutover areas of northeastern Minnesota, where enrollees helped develop and enlarge state and national forests. Soil erosion control projects, another major work project category, helped prevent erosion in southern Minnesota, especially in the hilly southeastern areas. State park development and construction projects, the state's third major CCC work project category, helped create the park system Minnesota has today.

Not discounting the impact the CCC had on the state's landscape, it had even farther-reaching effects on the men and boys who joined. Each one of them had a story to tell—of why they joined, of their emotions when they enrolled, of how hard they worked, of the accomplishment they felt, and of how welcome the money they sent back home was.

3: WHO JOINED MINNESOTA'S CCC?

Minnesota's ccc enrollees were much like those in other states. Juniors, or "boys," made up the largest category. Enrollment guidelines stated that each had to be among the "needy unemployed," unmarried, between the ages of eighteen and twenty-five, a citizen of the United States, and physically fit for manual labor.[1]

As the program got up and running, some administrative changes were made. On April 22, 1933, less than a month after its organization, the ccc expanded to employ Local Experienced Men (LEMS). These were the local foremen and the artisans, stonemasons, and craftsmen who helped oversee specialized work programs. Hired to work in the camps, they were allowed to live at home and did not have the same age or marital restrictions as enrollees. They also earned more money. On May 23, Roosevelt issued an executive order allowing needy World War I veterans to enroll in the ccc; he set a limit of 25,000 men and noted that veterans also would not be held to the age or marriage restrictions of junior enrollees.

If it were possible to construct a typical Minnesota enrollee, his story would sound something like this: "Jack Smith" was nineteen years old in the late summer of 1934, the oldest of seven children. His father was a blacksmith and subsistence farmer who had been out of work for two years. His mother took in washing when it was available. Without the little food they raised themselves, Jack and his family already would have been forced to leave their home. As it was, they were wondering how they were going to make it through the coming winter.

When Jack heard about the ccc from the county relief officer, he thought it sounded like a chance to help his family. He signed up and was accepted for a standard six-month enrollment period. In October, having been assigned to work at a state forest camp in northern Minnesota, he received his first monthly paycheck—thirty dollars. Of that, twenty-five dollars was sent to his family and he kept five dollars. His mother wrote him several weeks later to say that the money had helped buy groceries as well as shoes for several of the younger children and that, with money coming in every month, the family hoped to be able to stay on the farm through the winter.

"Jack Smith" is not a real person, but his story is based on information collected during oral history interviews. The typical ccc junior enrollee was between seventeen and nineteen years old. He had completed eight years of schooling, was about ten pounds underweight, and was five feet eight inches tall. He was one of six children, typically of white parents, and either had never worked or had been without work of any kind for six months. He stayed in the ccc up to twelve months, ate fifty cents' worth of food a day, gained ten pounds, and grew half an inch. Alfred "Irv" Nelson described the average enrollee as a "pretty scared" kid. Most, he said, were a lot like him: "I was probably seventeen years old. I had never really been away from home before for any time at all."[2]

New enrollees were accepted into the program four times a year: in January, April, July, and October. Enrollments lasted six months. At first, enrollees could rejoin for just one more period, for a total of twelve months in the ccc. In 1934, during severe drought conditions, the national enrollment goal was raised to 350,000 men; in 1935 it was again enlarged to 600,000 men. In order to meet these larger goals, the upper age limit for junior enrollees was increased from twenty-five to twenty-eight years and enrollees were allowed to remain in the program for three six-month enrollment periods, or one and one-half years, rather than just two enrollment periods. The high point of ccc enrollment was reached in the summer of 1935, when over half a million men were signed on nationally.[3]

By 1937, as the economy began to improve, eligibility requirements were changed once more. Enrollees no longer were required to be in need of relief or welfare but simply "unemployed and in need of employment." Age limits were changed again, and enrollees were allowed to reenlist for four full enrollment periods, or up to two years.

Using the language of the military, enrollees *enlisted* in the ccc and when they left they were *discharged*. If they left in good standing, they were given an honorable discharge. Enrollees who broke the rules faced the possibility of a dishonorable discharge. Some enrollees left for other reasons, most often because they found camp life to be difficult. In those cases, just as in the army,

A CCC company leaving Fort Snelling for the Superior National Forest, 1933

they were classified as absent without leave (AWOL). Enrollees had their own way to describe going AWOL. Michael Sanchelli recalled a conversation on the subject: "I heard one man say to a teenager, 'I thought you were up in the forests.' The teenager replied, 'I went over the hill. . . .' *Going over the hill* was the term used for leaving the camp for good without authorization." The names of AWOL enrollees were sent to their local recruiting agencies, and if the men did not return in fifteen days, they were dishonorably discharged. Nationally, 7.3 percent of enrollees received dishonorable discharges; in Minnesota, the rate was 1.6 percent. Most enrollees left the CCC for other jobs. If a job did not work out, they were eligible to reenroll in six months.[4]

During processing, enrollees identified who would receive the twenty-five dollar monthly allotment. Knowing of the need in their families, most designated their parents. By 1939, when the Great Depression began to lift and the number of needy families declined, enrollees were allowed to keep more money each month, but most still asked that their families receive the dependents' allowance.[5]

Enrollment and pay differed slightly in the CCC's Indian program. Interested men filled out an "Application Blank for Enrollment CCC-ID," giving name, number and age of dependants, and tribal enrollment status. After being accepted, each man filled out a "Personal History Card," identifying his occupation, a relative to contact in case of emergency, and the person who would receive the largest, or dependent's, share of the monthly paycheck.[6]

CCC-ID enrollees were free to return home when needed and were not required to live in camps or to sign up for a fixed enrollment period. Boarding camps were similar to army-run CCC camps, but the CCC-ID also had mobile camps and designated work areas run by enrollees who lived at home.

Enrollees living in camps earned the standard CCC monthly pay scale. Those who lived at home earned $2.10 per day for a maximum of twenty days per month.[7]

As with the CCC, the state's CCC-ID program had an enrollment quota. With a Native American population of 11,077, including 5,691 men, Minnesota's first CCC-ID quota in 1933 was for 400 enrollees. The state had the same quota as Wyoming, falling between California at 350 and Oklahoma at 440. The quota remained in this range throughout the program.[8]

Young Black Minnesotans did not have the same opportunities as Native Americans in the CCC-ID or as whites in the CCC. Although the legislation creating the CCC specified that it was to accept enrollees without regard to "race, creed, or color," in reality few Blacks were accepted for enrollment, this despite obvious need in the community, where unemployment figures were often listed as twice the national average. For the first several years of the CCC, leaders of the African American community in the Twin Cities recruited members informally and worked to keep steady the number of Black enrollees, which fluctuated between twelve and twenty-four men per enrollment period. Paul Wood, a forest camp enrollee, remembered the situation:

> *I went into the CCCs in July of 1934. There were twelve of us, maybe more. The African American citizens around here [St. Paul] had been agitating because they weren't accepting any black enlistments. They agitated and agitated. I guess the CCCs started a year or so before that, but there was agitation to let some of the blacks in. Finally, when the enlistment was opened, we were actually recruited, informally recruited, by some of the older people. We had this opportunity, so they wanted us to go in. Some of the discussions that our elders had with the powers that be related to the fact that maybe they would send us south someplace or something like that. They wouldn't go for that. We were going to stay right where we live, in this state. They couldn't get rid of us going south. They had to find someplace for us here.*

Of course, eventually African American enrollees were sent south to fill slots in all-Black companies.[9]

When the CCC first started in 1933, word spread fast about the new federal conservation program that offered jobs. People were looking for work, and jobs for the young men targeted by the CCC were few and far between. Many people, such as Allen Conkright, a Kansas enrollee who served in a Minnesota forest camp, found out about it in the newspaper. In the Twin Cities, newspapers serving the state's Black community, such as the Minneapolis *Spokesman,* ran articles with headlines like "Boys Who Want to Attend CCC Should Register." Some newspapers ran articles encouraging World War I veterans to enroll through the Veterans Administration in Minneapolis. People heard about the CCC on the radio or by word of mouth from relatives and friends.[10]

In the CCC's early years, the "relief" requirement was considered a stigma similar to that accompanying "welfare," causing a fair amount of confusion. The CCC was clearly a work program, an important distinction for the enrollees. Many commented on the role of relief agencies in recruitment. Nick Radovich, an enrollee at a forest camp, remembered relief agents contacting his friends and asking them to sign up. Clarence Johnson found out about the program when he went to the local relief office in the courthouse.[11]

During the first years of the operation, when need was the greatest, there were as many as five applicants for each open position. Steve Bartek remembered his father working three days a week to support seven children, and "not everyone was even home then." But, he said, "after I went to sign up, I didn't hardly get in because everybody didn't get in that signed up. It was kind of a deal that you had to be really poor."[12]

Nick Radovich also almost was not accepted:

> *They were taking kids when they started the CCC camps. Most of them to begin with were from relief families. There were fifty kids that went from Hibbing. I didn't have a call to go, but I went with a friend of mine. I was going to try to get in. They were accepting these people that needed it the most. I don't know how they decided. I wasn't working either, [but] I didn't make it. I started home, and I got halfway and [my friend] George came running to beat the band. He said a couple of guys dropped out and I should go back there quick. He wanted me to go with him. We chummed around together. So I ran back, and they took me. I got in.*[13]

Minnesota met its original recruitment goal easily. During the winter of 1933–34, enrollment dropped slightly, but the state still had 10,260 men serving in the CCC on November 30, 1933. This number included 6,351 people from Minnesota and 3,909 people from other states in the Seventh Army Corps area. Of the Minnesota total, 4,956 were juniors or boys, 493 were World War I veterans, and 902 were Local Experienced Men (LEMS).[14]

Clair Rollings, a Minneapolis native who taught school in Cromwell, Minnesota, before becoming an educational adviser at the Winnibigoshish and Rabideau camps, shared his impressions of early enrollees: "The first two hundred enrollees in Company 708 came largely from the Iron Range with a few from the Twin Cities and other villages and farms throughout Minnesota. ... They were hungry, broke, some were poorly clothed, some had dropped out of school, and a few had gotten into mischief, largely because they had no gainful work to do." Enrollees came from a wide variety of backgrounds. A 1935 report for a forest camp noted several had "reformatory records." But that didn't matter: if they met the standard requirements for admission, they were accepted.[15]

Many juniors or boys compared enrolling in the CCC, especially during the early years, to enlisting in the army. As far as Michael Sanchelli was concerned, the CCC was "army uniforms, army food, and army regulation." When friends urged him to join up, he first reacted this way: "'Boy,' I thought to myself, 'are these guys nuts! It's like joining the army.'" This view didn't stop Sanchelli from enlisting himself.[16]

After getting in, new enrollees reported to the recruiting office nearest their homes. From there, they were sent to Fort Snelling in St. Paul for review and processing. At Fort Snelling, they received physicals and shots, were administered an oath of enrollment, and were given clothing, bedding, and other personal items. A two-week training course prepared them for the conservation work they would be doing; after completing it, they were assigned to camps.

The physical was a big step for some; it was administered to enrollees in both the CCC and the CCC-ID programs. Enrollee Raymond Noyes remembered that not everyone could pass but that people were given as many breaks as possible. Steve Bartek, a forest camp enrollee, discovered that the minimum weight requirement was 107 pounds. "I was not quite heavy enough," he recalled later. "I was about two pounds short. So they told me to go and drink water. I kept drinking water and drinking water. I never found out how close I got, but they let me in."[17]

Army doctors in the CCC (and nonmilitary doctors in the CCC-ID) gave enrollees typhoid and smallpox vaccinations. Not surprisingly, some of the most vivid descriptions of the enrollment process involve these immunizations. Allen Conkright described it this way: "They gave us shots. Yes indeed, they did. We were all dressed like we were born, no clothes, going through the lineup. One guy, right ahead of me in line, he had an aversion to shots or nee-

Enrollees were issued seasonal clothing. Many Minnesota enrollees remembered the army's summer clothes schedule didn't always match the chilly weather up north. Enrollees in summer clothes are from the Lovelis camp; those in winter issue (page 35) are from the Gegoka camp.

dles. They stuck that needle in his arm, and he just blacked out." Alfred "Irv" Nelson, an enrollee at the Rabideau camp, remembered the shots, too: "They gave us shots for everything, and I think it was always with a square needle."[18]

Black enrollees remembered their stay at Fort Snelling not so much for the pain of shots at the physical but for their first contact with the army's policy of segregation. At the fort, Black recruits stayed in separate barracks and sat at separate tables in the mess hall. Paul Wood remembered: "They would come visit us, and we could go visit them. Segregation was in the actual sleeping quarters and in eating."[19]

After the physical, all enrollees were issued the items they would need for their time in the CCC. Raymond Noyes continued the story: "Then we were supplied all our clothing, our bed linens, such as blankets, sheets, and pillowcases. We were given quite a large selection of clothes, like two pairs of shoes, underwear, jackets, caps, mitts, and whatever you might need to wear." The distribution did not always run smoothly. Clothing initially came from a collection of leftover World War I uniforms. Alfred "Irv" Nelson remembered that "nothing fit on the first issue of clothing. It was two sizes either too big or too small."[20]

Eventually, army officials got everything sorted out, making sure each enrollee got two sets of army-issue work clothes, a dress uniform, two pairs of shoes, woolen blankets, sheets, a pillow, three pairs of socks, two hats, two pairs of underwear, a laundry bag, a trunk, a shaving kit, and personal items. After the World War I surplus uniforms ran out, enrollees received denim work shirts and denim pants. When clothes or shoes wore out, enrollees could turn in the old ones for new items.

Originally, CCC-ID enrollees were not issued clothing at all. In November 1933, as work projects continued into the winter months, CCC-ID leaders asked Director Robert Fechner to provide a clothing allowance. Despite misgivings about the cost, Fechner approved the request. CCC-ID enrollees did not receive uniforms, not surprising since the Bureau of Indian Affairs—and not the U.S. Army—ran the camps. Instead, they were issued one pair of trousers, one denim work jacket, two pairs of denim overalls, two work shirts, two pairs of underwear, four pairs of socks, one pair of shoes or boots, one pair of rain boots with liners, and two pairs of gloves or mittens with liners—the total cost not to exceed twenty dollars. These clothes had to be returned—or paid for—by enrollees if they left the CCC-ID before the end of a standard enrollment period.[21]

In both the CCC-ID and the CCC, clothing was issued for either summer or winter work. Winter wear included a heavy overcoat and mittens, while summer clothes included a raincoat. When the seasons changed, enrollees turned in one set of clothing for another, although the CCC's schedule did not always coincide with the true dates of winter or summer in Minnesota, particularly up north. Many enrollees remembered spring weather that did not warm up fast enough for them to be comfortable in summer clothes right away.

Everyone in standard CCC camps, not just enrollees, had to wear a uniform. Clair Rollings described them: "Army personnel wore regular army uniforms with full insignia. Foresters wore green forest service uniforms, and enrollees were provided regular army Class A G.I. [surplus World War I] uniforms, for dress, without insignia, and army fatigues, without insignia, for work. The educational advisor wore civilian clothes until late in the CCC program, when he was required to wear a dark green uniform resembling that of the forest service." In 1938, President Roosevelt, seeking a more up-to-date image for the CCC, ordered new dark green dress uniforms for administrative personnel.[22]

Hilding Johnson, a camp educator, shows off his CCC uniform, ca. 1938.

After processing, CCC enrollees were formed into companies of about two hundred men and given their camp assignments. Each camp housed one company. Minnesota enrollees usually were sent to Minnesota camps, although some found themselves in California and other western or southern states. And Minnesota camps sometimes included enrollees from Missouri, Kansas, Nebraska, and other states in the Seventh Army Corps area.

The stay at Fort Snelling for processing was eliminated in 1937. From then through the end of the program, enrollees applied directly to the company commander of a camp or to the local recruiting office for permission to join the CCC. After being accepted, they were given a camp assignment and were sent straight to the camp, where physicals, shots, and the oath of enrollment were administered and where they were given their training. Edward Schubert remembered this experience. He

Company 704 forms ranks at the Halfway camp. Companies generally were made up of two hundred men, although numbers sometimes dropped toward the end of enrollment periods.

signed up and then "just waited right at the Forestry Office. . . . They just said, 'Wait here and the truck will pick you up.' . . . My mother knew that I was going, and I told her when I left, I said, 'Now I don't know if I'll be back today or not. We'll see what happens.' . . . Of course, if I didn't come back for lunch, she knew I was gone."[23]

However they enrolled, most of the men and boys who joined the CCC or CCC-ID in Minnesota were glad for the chance to work. Clarence "Ole" Allen had passed the civil service test in 1929 to work as a forest ranger; by 1933, he was on indefinite layoff. Ernest Spry, from the Grand Portage Indian Reservation, picked "spuds" for farmers. With all ten members of the family working, they earned three dollars a day, "but they were long days." After that, he worked for a farmer in northern Minnesota at a dollar a day "until there was nothing more to do."[24]

In Minnesota, as elsewhere, those who were lucky enough to be employed often worked for reduced wages. Bernard Penner, who would become a Local Experienced Man (LEM) in the CCC, was laid off from his job at the Ford plant in St. Paul: "They shut down entirely, from Model A to Model T." Already married, he supported his wife and himself by mowing lawns, washing windows, and pumping gas until he got a job for thirty-nine cents an hour painting the roofs of Pure Oil stations in the Twin Cities. As he said, "It was groceries."[25]

The CCC and CCC-ID gave Bernard Penner, Ernest Spry, and others like them the chance to work and help their families. The next step came when they headed out to camp.

4: A HOME AWAY FROM HOME

The CCC was established so quickly that camps were not actually ready for the first enrollees. The flurry of activity at Fort Snelling was followed, at least at first, by a trip to an empty site. The neat and orderly army-style camps that people came to associate with the CCC simply did not exist.

When the program began, conservation officials—usually forestry, parks, and soil conservation personnel—identified the top priority conservation project areas in the state. Then they worked to get permission from landowners, private and public, to turn over centrally located plots of land for each camp.

Throughout the CCC, staff followed certain criteria in choosing camp locations. Camps needed to be within twenty-five miles of identified work sites and on high ground (wherever possible) with water and good road access. Officials inspected possible camp locations to find the best sites. Early on, some camps were on private land leased from the owners, but due to cost issues this policy was not regularly used.

J. C. "Buzz" Ryan, a forester at the Sullivan Lake camp in northern Minnesota, described setting up one of the first camps in the state:

Roosevelt was elected in the fall of '32, and right after the first of the year we started getting letters out of [the state forestry office] in St. Paul planning on some of these ccc camps. We didn't know what we were going to do or what form they were going to be. They called on us rangers to figure out if we could handle camps. Then the letters started coming from St. Paul, telling us to look up sites for these camps and have them inspected.

One night, about one o'clock at night, I got a call from G. M. Conzet, who was [Minnesota] director of forestry, and he said [he was] going to send the first company of cccs out of Fort Snelling to a state camp. They were going to be sent up to Cusson, but something had come up and [he couldn't] send them there. I [told him] . . . I'd had [everything] inspected. He said [he was] going to send me the camp. He called back the next morning and wanted to know where to send them. [I said] 'Send them to Brimson on the Iron Range Railroad.' We talked it over a little bit, and he said, 'You get ready. Hire all the trucks and buses you can. We'll have a company there tomorrow morning.'

The next morning, at six o'clock in the morning, a twelve-coach train arrived with a whole company of cccs. They'd been paid their first payday in St. Paul just before they left. When they all rolled out of the coaches, every bottle of pop and every candy bar and everything eatable in the little store in Brimson was bought.[1]

This scene was repeated across the state and across the country as the first ccc camps were established. Setting up a camp was not easy. Arriving at the sites, forest camp enrollees found fields or clearings in the woods stacked with boxes waiting to be unpacked. Army-issue canvas tents, used as temporary barracks, waited to be set up—thirty-six tents per camp. Nick Radovich remembered his first day. After riding twenty-three miles through the woods in the back of a truck in the drizzle and rain, "we got out there, and here was this piece of land. There was swamp and stumps and trees and everything else, and we had to pitch in and clean out the brush and take out the stumps. Some guys were lucky and they didn't have a stump, or some guys had big stumps that they had to work like heck to get it all out and cleared. We got the fence up. We set up our fuel ranges for the kitchen and all that stuff. When we got them all up, we would sleep in these tents."[2]

Getting the tents up and the stoves working was the first order of business. After that, enrollees, sometimes with help from unemployed men in the area, began building the camps. Webster Sterba, a student at the University of Minnesota's School of Forestry, wrote in June 1933 of the process as it was just beginning: "I believe very few of [the camps] have been actually completed. It seems that shower baths and possibly electric lights will be among the luxuries." Enrollees worked fast, especially in northern Minnesota, wanting to get things closed in before winter. E. V. Willard of the state Department of Conservation sent a telegraph to the U.S. Forest Service in September 1933 outlining progress: "Construction work on all state forest camps about seventy percent complete with half completely built." By winter, the first forest camps in Minnesota were completed and enrollees were working on conservation projects.[3]

A temporary mess tent provides open-air cooking at the new Cut Foot Sioux camp.

Early state park camps had the same construction schedule, with commanders using enrollees and local workers to help build them. Camps often were located in out-of-the-way areas with few job opportunities. Cecil Levin, superintendent of the Jay Cooke State Park camp in northeastern Minnesota, offered this assessment: "During the period of construction in camp, a sizeable crew of local carpenters and helpers were employed. Some of these men had not worked for months. The benefits to the communities from which these men came are quite obvious. Such action also helped to raise public morale and created a better feeling between camp and community." Camp commanders often bought construction materials from local businesses for the same reason.[4]

For the first two years of the CCC, Minnesota's soil conservation camps were on a different schedule than were forest and state park camps. They operated as temporary tent camps, staying open from spring to fall. When they closed, their enrollees went to year-round camps for the winter. Even with this temporary status, enrollees had to work hard to set up the camps. Claude Darst, assigned to the Houston camp in southeastern Minnesota, remembered pulling out cornstalks from his tent site. Beginning in 1935, when soil conservation camps became year-round facilities, they were built according to the same army construction standards as forest and state park camps.[5]

CCC-ID camps were set up in much the same way. The first CCC-ID camp in Minnesota was at Nett Lake, with the closest post office at Bois Fort. Nett Lake opened on July 16, 1933, and would eventually house up to 125 enrollees at the main camp and at three mobile camps attached to it. But the first

Early ccc camp buildings generally were made of wood (logs or plywood) with either palisade exteriors, such as that used at the Side Lake camp (top left), or tar-paper coverings, as at the Cut Foot Sioux camp (top right). After several years, the army began to develop portable camp designs. An example is shown here at the Plainview camp, ca. 1940.

enrollees arrived to find a bare site. Construction was complicated by government regulations for purchasing building materials. Enrollees had to live in tents for months as the foreman tried to straighten things out. A cook/mess hall was built, but construction of other buildings dragged on. Winter soon came, with early snow and below-zero temperatures. After reviewing the situation, Minnesota district staff made several administrative changes, and the camp was at last completed. Even with the delays, it cost only about $8,500 to build, less than the average for ccc camps during the first years.[6]

Early camps were built of logs or plywood with palisade or tar-paper exteriors. Enrollees and local men often sawed lumber on the spot at portable sawmills. By November 1933, during the second enrollment period, the army began standardizing ccc camp construction. The cost of building the early camps was relatively high at $18,000 to $20,000 apiece, especially since they were designed to be used only as long as there were approved conservation work projects in the area.[7]

As a cost-saving measure, army personnel began experimenting with portable building designs in 1934, adopting them as the ccc standard on July 26, 1937. Buildings in portable camps rarely had foundations and were constructed with bolts so they could be taken apart and reassembled. But unlike more permanent sites, these camps generally cost less than $5,000 to build. Although it took twelve railroad cars followed by one hundred truckloads to move the building pieces, adding another $5,000, this still represented a major cost savings.[8]

ccc camps looked and operated like military bases, not surprising since they were run by the U.S. Army. The average camp had about fifteen buildings: four or five barracks, a mess hall and kitchen, agents' quarters (for forestry, park, or conservation agents), officers' quarters, a headquarters building, a storehouse, a welfare building, a dispensary, a school building, a recreation hall, a lavatory and bathhouse, a latrine, and two small service buildings.[9]

Camp design was utilitarian and functional. Harley Heegard remembered the Lovelis camp near Park Rapids: "The rec hall was on one end, the kitchen was on the other end. There were four barracks on the east side, and I believe there were three more over on the addition on the west side. The lawn was kept nice: they policed the lawn every day for cigarette butts and candy wrappers and stuff like that." The buildings were as comfortable as the enrollees could make them. Edward Schubert, an enrollee in a state park camp, remembered "the only place you had to sit in the barracks was your bunk or your footlocker. That was it. There was no other furniture to speak of." Each barracks had between forty and fifty army-issue bunks or cots, uninsulated walls, and wood or coal stoves for heat.[10]

Sergeant P. J. Halloran described the barracks in a portable camp: "There was nothing in the barracks itself. The barracks were prefab. They were bolted together. There was no insulation whatsoever on the inside. We got two-by-fours on the outside walls. At each end there were stoves; they were

Enrollees pause while cleaning the barracks at one of the two Gooseberry Falls State Park CCC camps.

made of two fifty-five-gallon barrels. We mounted them on top of each other, and we burned wood. There were double bunks, metal double bunks, military bunks, and we made military bed."[11]

The barracks leader slept on a bed near the door. Raymond Noyes said of his barracks: "We would alternate: one person's head would be towards the aisle, and the next person's head would be towards the wall. Then we had a one-gallon empty can with sand in it for putting our [cigarette] butts in. Nothing could be thrown on the floor. The floor had to be kept clean." John Cackoski never forgot the ritual of cleaning: "One thing I remember about the barracks was that you could start sweeping the floor from one end, [and] you never had dust at the other end. There was space between the boards on the floor, and all the dust went down."[12]

Wind and snow came through cracks in the walls and floors of the barracks. Enrollees remembered waking up many mornings covered with frost. If the weather was too cold, one or two enrollees were assigned to keep the stoves going all night. Some barracks had coal stoves, as Victor Pope remembered: "Some places, they burned only wood. We burned only coal. We had an old black round stove. And it had to be shiny, too. We had to shine it up. We had some black stuff we had to put on it, and then we had to use a heavy brush. When they shined, you could pretty near see yourself in it. We had to keep them shiny all the time." Hot stoves in wooden buildings led J. C. "Buzz" Ryan to comment: "The stoves [in the barracks] all had this tin around them so they wouldn't catch fire." Others remembered a pail of water, frozen on cold nights, or maybe a bucket of sand that, as Raymond Noyes said, could double as a place to put cigarette butts.[13]

Camps used gas lanterns or candles for light until the army supplied them with one or two 32-volt lighting plants, later increased to 110-volt plants. William J. Fraser, a civil service mechanic working for the CCC, remembered how this worked in the remote camp locations:

> *My territory covered an area from Sandstone to the Pigeon River on the North Shore and along Highway 1 from Finland to Ely and then along the Echo Trail to Orr, and from Cusson to Lake Kabetogama. . . . The light plants were Fairbanks Morse single-cylinder engines, usually three of them, which*

charged batteries in glass cells. These were 32-volt systems. About half of the camps were supplied with this type of electrical power. The other plants, as I recall, were Koehler plants with continental engines which generated 115 volts. Remember, this was before the days of rural electrification.[14]

Following standard army design, ccc camps had many common characteristics. A flagpole stood in front of the administration building. A bulletin board for memos, flyers, and other camp items was centrally located, and enrollees like Clarence Johnson knew that "anything new that happened around the camp was always posted there." Gravel paths or boardwalks connected the buildings, although at least one camp in northern Minnesota had tarred walkways. Enrollees outlined flower beds and walkways in stone, painting the stones white as part of beautification projects. Commanders held camp beautification competitions. The Good Harbor camp at Grand Marais was one winning example, named outstanding company and camp in the Seventh Army Corps area during the second enrollment period. Signs went up at the camp entrances to let everyone know.[15]

Most camp commanders also had regular maintenance schedules, important since the camps were not designed or built to be permanent installations. They generally had an expected life span of four or five years. Anything older than five years was considered an "old camp," often in need of major repairs.[16]

Companies worked hard to maintain high standards, vying for recognition at state and regional levels. A sign at the Side Lake camp proclaims that Company 717 was honored as the best company in the Minnesota District.

Although Nett Lake was part of the CCC-ID, its history of improvements and maintenance includes just about everything that could happen at a CCC camp. Nett Lake required constant upkeep and maintenance. Its three original barracks from 1933 housed about fifty enrollees each. But in May 1935, one barracks building was moved to a mobile site, so camp leaders requested funds for enrollees to help build a new one. In addition, the camp light and water system burned down early that year. During the summer of 1935, enrollees helped build a fireproof building for the new light and water system, construct the replacement barracks, put up a new fence at the approach to camp, lay gravel on the grounds, construct a new garage, and develop an athletic field. The camp ordered athletic supplies, including baseball equipment, which was "seriously needed by our enrolled men" in both the main camp and its mobile site.[17]

With this work completed, Lake States district camps supervisor J. H. Mitchell expressed concern in September 1935 about the camp recreational building. While it worked well for activities such as indoor tennis, dances, movies, and large meetings, there was "no quiet nook . . . for reading" or for enrollees to gather for social reasons, Mitchell wrote to the commissioner of Indian Affairs. If men wanted quiet time, the only available place was on the cots in the barracks, where the lighting was poor. Mitchell requested that the hall be remodeled to address these concerns. The reply, several weeks later, said that although camp costs had now reached about $14,000, work should begin so that one of the barracks would be temporarily remodeled to include a reading room.[18]

By 1937, enrollees could stop using their temporary reading and meeting place because they had finished work on a new recreation center with an arts and crafts shop. The shop portion of the building included woodworking equipment and "ample carpentry and other tools." At the building's other end was a lounging and reading area. The space in between housed the camp assistant's quarters, the canteen, and the camp library. The next construction project put enrollees to work replacing the mess hall, which had burned on Christmas morning in 1938.[19]

All the work done to maintain and develop Nett Lake camp didn't go unnoticed. When Norman W. Scherer, a Lake States district official, visited in 1936, he described it as having a "very striking" appearance, with "the most noticeable features [being] the brick chimneys and the fact [that] the buildings are all painted [gray with white trim]. Some work has been done toward a beautification program which is to be highly commended."[20]

Although Minnesota CCC-ID administrators regularly expected the Nett Lake camp to run out of conservation work projects, by 1939 it was six years old and still operating. Not surprisingly, the camp was in need of more repairs. Scherer estimated it would cost about $7,000 to bring the camp up to "first class condition." Instead, he recommended building another camp and moving Nett Lake operations to it. The new Nett Lake camp, located close to

Entrance gates offered visitors their first introduction to CCC camps. Often ornate, gates were constructed by enrollees. This example is from Camp Buckboard.

the post office in Gheen, opened on February 12, 1941, in time to serve a hot noon meal to everyone.[21]

Even with all the regulations and standards that had to be followed in building and maintenance, individual camps often took on a unique look. Most CCC camps had elaborate gates or entries with signs identifying them by name and number. The recreation halls and the officers' quarters often had large, native-rock fireplaces. Ernest Anderson described a feature of the Kabetogama Lake camp, which he called the "best camp" in the whole system: "It was made so you didn't have to go outside at all, to go from one barracks to another or to the rec hall or the administration office . . . or to the forestry or army headquarters. I think that was the only camp in the organization that was that way." Steve Bartek described another camp: "I remember that our camp [Side Lake] was the only one that had blacktopped streets. They did that, [camp commander] Captain Wipf and Doc Badger; they started to pave and blacktop that Number 5 going up north. We had a deal with the contractor to give so much old army clothes and stuff like that. Somehow we got all the sidewalks blacktopped and driveways blacktopped. We had a wonderful place!"[22]

Staff members and enrollees worked together to make each camp efficient and—to some extent—distinctive. A typical CCC camp commander was

Camp libraries and reading rooms often were quite comfortable, as this photograph of the Bayport camp's reading room, ca. 1940, shows.

usually a first lieutenant or captain from the regular army or the reserves. He was responsible for running the camp and for taking care of the enrollees when they were not working on assigned conservation projects. Several noncommissioned officers assisted the commander in this work; they included a second-in-command, a doctor, company sergeants, clerks, and cooks. Work agency personnel at the camps included superintendents, engineers, construction assistants, mechanics, and foremen. Local Experienced Men (LEMS) were hired for specific needed skills and, as Don Burcalow said, for their "knowledge of the particular [work] area." They also often served as foremen for work crews.[23]

The cost of running a CCC camp was between $900 and $1,000 per enrollee per year. This figure included pay, clothing, food, shelter, administration, supplies, and equipment. The average camp housed about two hundred enrollees, as many as twenty-five army personnel, and about thirty work agency staff. Usually, twenty-five enrollees took on assignments to help run the camp, serving as mess stewards, storekeepers, clerks, educational advisor assistants, hospital and dining room orderlies, cooks (including one baker), mechanics, blacksmiths, warehouse workers, tool dressers, machine operators, and truck drivers. Others helped as conservation project leaders and assistant leaders, which meant a raise in pay of up to twenty dollars a month. Other jobs for enrollees—including barracks leaders, wood crews, and KP (kitchen patrol)—were also vital to camp organization.[24]

The camps were self-contained units. Camp doctors handled common illnesses in the infirmary, sending the more severe cases to hospitals in nearby towns. Enrollees got dental treatment either in the camp or from an area dentist. Quick to find nicknames for almost everything, enrollees soon dubbed the army "mother," because it fed, clothed, and sheltered them.

The commander determined to what extent a camp would be run like a military base. Some commanders were strict, while others ran more relaxed outfits. Enrollee Allen Conkright described the differences in commanders at the Big Lake forest camp near Cloquet: "We had to come out in the morning for the raising of the flag, stand at attention. And retreat, the same thing, in the evening, lowering of the flag. We went through that for a while; then it was abolished. We had regular army officers, West Point men, at first. After that, we got the reserves coming in." At the Cusson forest camp, LEM Pete Trygg remembered his regular army camp commander as a stickler for rules: "We had to lace our shoes right to the top, tie a bow knot on them, and have them stand by the bed. . . . When you put them on you had to unlace them again. . . . I thought that was crazy." Side or spike camps, which weren't run by military officers, were not as strict. Remembering this, forest camp enrollee Willard Nelson commented, "the best memories are of the side camps."[25]

Because of the army's role in CCC camp administration, some Americans wondered if the CCC was, in fact, a quasi-military program, meant to prepare

Local Experienced Men (LEMS) were hired "because of their knowledge of the particular area," according to forester Don Burcalow. They also helped train enrollees and direct their work. This group of LEMS poses in front of the Mille Lacs Lake highway wayside camp office in 1940.

ccc camps were administered by U.S. Army personnel. This group, at the Side Lake camp, includes Captain William Wipf, left, who commanded the camp and saw to it that all streets and sidewalks there were paved.

enrollees for eventual enlistment in the armed forces. But this was not the case. The army, initially reluctant to be involved in the ccc at all, basically provided a ready-made process for operating the camps and for getting the program up and running as quickly as it did. It can safely be said, however, that the "boys" of the ccc learned much about military discipline—and many would later enlist when the United States entered World War II. The men of the ccc and their military commanders also learned a great deal about how to move people and facilities quickly over long distances, a skill essential to war but also to moving camps to ever-changing conservation work areas.

The ccc-ID never came under the same criticism—of being intended to increase military readiness—because it did not have the same military flavor as the main ccc program. ccc-ID camps were run through the Bureau of Indian Affairs, and overall administration was organized by districts and reservations. A coordinating officer supervised all ccc-ID activities in a district, including off-duty activities such as recreation and education. The reservation superintendent, working with the camp manager, was responsible for the ccc-ID on the reservation. George Morrison, a high school student summer enrollee in the Grand Portage camp, remembered: "The camp was not run militarily like white ccc camps. [It was] a little more free. They were disciplined, but not overly so." Although Native Americans also enrolled in Minnesota's ccc camps, most entered the ccc-ID.[26]

Along with the camp at Nett Lake, the ccc-ID operated a large camp at Grand Portage along the North Shore of Lake Superior. Consolidated Chippewa work crews lived at home or in mobile camps at Cass Lake, Grand

Portage, Lake Vermilion, Mille Lacs, Nett Lake, White Earth, Nay-tah-waush, and Fond du Lac. Each site employed between ten and sixty men. Camps on the Red Lake Reservation included Unit 1, also called Camp 1, Ponemah Camp, and Camp 4. Camp 1, open by October 1, 1933, housed ninety enrollees in an old logging camp. Project work crews for the Lower Sioux Agency at Pipestone were based in Eggleston, Shakopee, Morton, Granite Falls, and Pipestone. In 1940, each Lower Sioux Agency unit had between four and fifteen enrollees. During the summer of 1937, eighteen Sioux from Sisseton, South Dakota, also lived and worked at the Nett Lake camp, but most CCC-ID enrollees working in Minnesota came from within the state and completed work projects on their own reservations.[27]

Relationships between camps and the surrounding communities were not always easy, particularly at camps with large Black populations. During the first year of the CCC, several full companies of Blacks from other states in the Seventh Army Corps area did conservation work in Minnesota. Company 1728 from St. Louis, Missouri, for example, was sent to the Temperance River camp near Tofte along the North Shore of Lake Superior in 1933. U.S. Army Reserve officers, including Captain G. R. Eggleston, company commander, ran the camp. This all-Black company served two enrollment periods in Minnesota. While there, among other things, members put in the stonework along Highway 61 at the Temperance River. Shortly after the company arrived at the Temperance River camp, the Tofte town board passed a resolution stating that people in the community were not "accustomed to live near

African American members of Company 1728 faced hostility from the community when assigned to the Temperance River camp on the North Shore of Lake Superior near Tofte in 1933. The company was reassigned to a soil conservation camp in Missouri in 1934.

any colored race" and asking that the camp be moved "further back in the interior or any other place where local whites will not object."[28]

When Company 1728 returned to St. Louis in the summer of 1934, a company of white Minnesota enrollees took its place. This pattern repeated itself in other Minnesota ccc camps, becoming more restrictive in both mixed camps and those with all-Black companies. ccc policy was slowly making itself clear both locally and nationally. All-Black companies or large groups of African American enrollees less than full company strength would no longer be sent to states like Minnesota with small Black populations. And states unable to recruit a full two hundred–member Black company would more likely send Black enrollees to all-Black camps in southern states than send enrollees to mixed camps in-state.

All-Black units were not the only ones to encounter suspicion and hostility in nearby communities, especially during the ccc's early years. Many enrollees remembered signs in store windows saying "No Dogs or ccc Allowed." P. J. Halloran, an army sergeant assigned to forest camps, described the situation: "There was a social stigma attached to the fact that you had gone in. . . . Wearing that uniform, when I walked in [to a business], I was very conscious of the comments that were made at certain times."[29]

Many camps celebrated major anniversaries, such as the founding of the ccc, with open houses for guests from surrounding communities. This May 1940 invitation is from the Badoura camp.

A young North Dakota woman provided additional insight. Before the Great Depression, she said, her community had been filled with "good-hearted . . . helpful" people. But now, she told her diary, it was overrun with "lallygagging sidewinders"—a "tribe" of city boys in the nearby ccc camp. To her, the enrollees were "different." She considered them unwelcome outsiders who, through their work projects, meddled inappropriately on the land in her area. As she put it, "After all the changes the government is making, it isn't home to me anymore."[30]

To promote good will and overcome local resistance, camps bought some supplies locally, hired local men for start-up projects, and eventually hosted open houses. Company 717 at the Side Lake camp, for example, sent out invitations in the fall of 1940 to members of the Kiwanis, Rotary, Lions, Knights of Columbus, and Elks clubs in Hibbing and Chisholm, the two towns nearest the camp, as well as to the general public through the *Hibbing Daily*

Tribune and the *Tribune-Herald* of Chisholm. Over two hundred people attended, and many took home copies of a special edition of the camp's newspaper that described Side Lake and its work.[31]

At open houses, enrollees gave visitors tours—which usually ended with free dessert and coffee in the mess hall. One enrollee, a cook's helper, proudly remembered being asked for his recipe for pineapple upside-down cake by several women visitors. Such programs and visits often resulted in complimentary articles in local newspapers and helped reduce friction between camps and nearby communities.

Minnesota camps also hosted national leaders. In June 1936, CCC director Robert Fechner visited several northern Minnesota camps, including the Gooseberry Falls State Park camp, the Good Harbor forest camp at Grand Marais, and the Grand Portage CCC-ID camp. On June 6, 1939, some months before his death, Fechner returned to the state to speak at a national meeting of state park administrators and visit the World War I veterans' camp at Itasca State Park. After Fechner's death, enrollees commemorated his last visit with a metal plaque: "In Memoriam, Robert C. Fechner, 1876–1939. First Director of the CCC from 1933–1939. Mr. Fechner Visited This Camp, June 6, 1939. Tablet Placed by Members of CCC Company 1785, World War Veterans." They attached it to a stone at Pine Ridge Campground in Itasca State Park, where it may still be seen today.[32]

During the CCC's years of active operation in the state (from 1933 to 1942), Minnesota averaged fifty-one camps per year. The high point of Minnesota CCC activity came during the summer of 1935, when the state had 104 camps housing approximately 18,500 enrollees. It ranked ninth in the country at the time for the number of camps operating in a state.[33]

But the greatest tributes to CCC camps aren't to be found purely in numbers. They rest in the words and memories of CCC enrollees. In honor of the fourth anniversary of the program, celebrated on April 4, 1937, one such enrollee, Easton Hance, wrote a poem. "Seeing Four Years of the CCC," while reflecting Hance's pride in the Big Lake camp near Cloquet, also aptly described a typical CCC camp through the eyes of one of the "boys."

SEEING FOUR YEARS OF THE CCC

April fourth has come and gone
And people came miles to see
Just what had been accomplished
In four years of the CCC
They found a very modern camp
That eight score boys call home
Which they will always remember
Where ever they may roam

There have been lots of changes
In this camp of ours
We've gone from tents to barracks
And have worked many hours
To make it what it is today
And much better it will be
For we are all proud of our camp
After four years of the CCC[34]

. . .

CCC and CCC-ID Camps in Minnesota, 1933–42

5: LIFE IN THE CCC

Reactions to life in a ccc camp varied from one enrollee to the next. Sergeant P. J. Halloran's first impression was that it was "lonely and desolate and cold as hell." John Cackoski said, "As far as camp was concerned, you couldn't beat it. It was ideal for people that were out and on the streets, didn't have a place to go. They got good clothes, warm clothes, and wasn't too bad living quarters."[1]

During the early years of the ccc in Minnesota, Black enrollees had their own unique experience of camp life. Initially, efforts were made to comply with the DePriest clause by allowing Blacks to serve in their home states even if this meant assigning them to white camps—in contrast with later actions that removed African American enrollees from Minnesota camps entirely. From their first contact with the ccc, Black enrollees were affected by the army's segregation policies. The first Blacks were sent to forest camps in northeastern Minnesota, arriving at all-white camps. Up to fifteen African Americans might be assigned to live in camps with white enrollees, but often numbers were much smaller. Blacks lived and ate in separate quarters, mixing with whites mainly when performing conservation work. Despite the separation of races, the army considered such camps to be "nonsegregated" or "mixed." But enrollees recognized the experience for what it was. Paul Wood described the situation at his camp: "We were assigned to our quarters,

Enrollees had differing views on camp life. Some, such as John Cackoski, took particularly positive standpoints: "As far as camp was concerned," he said, "you couldn't beat it." Itasca State Park Camp, 1934.

which were segregated. There was space behind one of those long barracks buildings, and behind that there was a partition with a door and twelve bunk beds and a potbellied stove. That's where we went; that's where they put us. It was similar to the other arrangements [for white enrollees]. The only thing is that it was segregated. The washrooms were forty to fifty feet behind the barracks. There was no discrimination in the washroom."[2]

Alfred Williams remembered similar conditions at the Northern Light camp: "[The officers] were all white. We had our own barracks. The white kids had their barracks. When we went to the mess hall to eat, the black fellas sat at our table and the white fellas sat at their tables."[3]

Camp life was carefully structured, and enrollees of all racial backgrounds were expected to follow the rules. The day usually began with reveille, followed by roll call, a flag-raising ceremony, and breakfast. After breakfast on weekdays, enrollees reported for conservation work projects. They worked a seven-hour day with time out for lunch and for morning and afternoon breaks. Returning to camp, they had free time before and after dinner. Bed check at the end of the day made sure everyone was accounted for. Saturday mornings were times for inspections, vehicle maintenance, and other camp cleanup work. When these tasks were complete, enrollees stayed in camp, went into town on a pass, or took one of the two trips home they were allowed during each enrollment period.

Many years later, when Fred Ranger, an enrollee at several forest camps, was asked about the weekday work routine, he described it this way:

> *I [drove] a truck. . . . The foreman comes with the guys [enrollees], and they get in the truck. I shut the [truck] gate and put the canvas down, and the foreman tells me where to go [for the work project that day], and we bring them there. From there he shows me where to park. I make a fire for the guys and hand out tools. At about eleven o'clock, I'd go back to camp, get the coffee and their sandwiches . . . four sandwiches apiece. I come back and put the coffee by the fire so it keeps warm. After they're gone, I'd put everything back together . . . and [they'd] come back around 3 or 3:30 PM, [and] I'd drive them home.*

John Buskowiak, an enrollee in a soil conservation camp, remembered the lunches served at the work sites: baloney or summer sausage sandwiches with cake or cookies for dessert.[4]

At the beginning, the camp food allowance was thirty-five cents per enrollee per day. This was raised to between forty and fifty cents per enrollee per day toward the end of the CCC program. Typically, the company commander and cook purchased the food, and the cook and his helpers prepared it. When asked about their memories of life in the camps, enrollees almost always commented on the food. Eino Lahti said of the food at his forest camp, "It was beautiful. I never ate so good in my life. The food was good." During a one-month period, enrollees at the Day Lake forest camp north of Grand Rapids ate 2,868 loaves of bread, 4,500 pounds of potatoes, 1,800 pounds of sugar, 292 pounds of butter, 510 dozen eggs, 2 tons of meat, 1,400 pounds of flour, and miscellaneous amounts of fresh and canned fruits and vegetables.

"The food was beautiful," enrollee Eino Lahti said. "I never ate so good in my life." Food in CCC camps was served family style, as shown in this image of a mess hall set up for a meal, probably at a state park camp.

They washed it all down with 3,559 pints of milk. The menu for October 27, 1934, at the Big Lake forest camp near Cloquet was typical:

Breakfast: fried eggs, fried bacon, dry cereal, coffee, bread and butter, sugar

Lunch: boiled hot dogs, boiled potatoes and gravy, sauerkraut, rice custard, coffee with cream and sugar, bread and butter

Dinner: hamburger balls, mashed potatoes and gravy, fried hominy, coleslaw, cocoa, bread and butter.[5]

Enrollees also commented on the food served in the CCC-ID camps. An Oklahoma Indian woman, sent to Nett Lake to take inventory of agency property and describing herself as a "terribly finicky" eater, remembered the food at the camp was very good. There were complaints during one period about beef stew being served every day for months at one of the Nett Lake mobile camps, but this was soon corrected. George Morrison, when asked to define the differences between the CCC and the CCC-ID as he remembered them, said, "Indian camps were special in the sense they had better food. They had very excellent meals and an abundance of food."[6]

A CCC-ID enrollee looks over his instructor's shoulder at the Nett Lake camp's cooking school. A pie and loaves of bread, examples of food served in the camp, are visible in the lower left-hand corner.

Most enrollees grew taller and stronger under the influence of decent food, and lots of it. Harvey Richart, an enrollee at a state park camp, said, "Some of the boys got pretty husky." At a soil conservation camp, Claude Darst remembered "some of the people taking the food and throwing it on the wall and calling it 'pig's food.' But when you're talking about cooking for two, three hundred people, you can't please everybody. It was good wholesome food." When there was not enough food, enrollees complained or refused to work, as they did at Wanless, a forest camp near Schroeder, in 1934. William Kraklau described the enrollees taking the situation into their own hands at a forest camp located at the end of the Gunflint Trail along the North Shore of Lake Superior: "Seagull could have been run better. The food was pretty bad for awhile, and there wasn't much of it, either. The camp commander was selling it. We had a couple of food riots. We had some guys who had done time at St. Cloud [State Penitentiary], and they knew the ropes. Finally, we wrote Washington[, DC], and somebody came and investigated, and then things were a little better."[7]

For holidays, especially Thanksgiving and Christmas, enrollees got special meals. Articles in camp newspapers, building on nostalgia, sometimes described ccc holiday meals as being like "mother used to prepare." Thanksgiving dinner in 1936 at the Caledonia soil conservation camp in southeastern Minnesota is just one example, consisting of fruit punch, celery, olives, dill pickles, roast turkey and dressing, giblet gravy, candied sweet potatoes, mashed potatoes, cranberry sauce, asparagus tips, lettuce salad with French dressing, Parker House rolls with butter, bananas, grapes, apples, nuts, candy, mince pie, pumpkin pie, Neapolitan ice cream, mints, wafers, and coffee. Christmas dinner in 1934 at the Sawbill forest camp near Tofte along the North Shore of Lake Superior was vegetable soup, roast turkey, mashed potatoes, brown gravy, baked sweet potatoes, lettuce with French dressing, creamed cauliflower, sliced tomatoes, celery, rolls and bread with butter, plum pudding, mincemeat pie, coffee, sugar, milk, candies, nuts, and assorted fruits. Liquor was not allowed in some camps, though enrollees often got a bottle of beer with a holiday meal.[8]

"Peeling spuds." As in the army, enrollees in the ccc were frequently assigned kitchen patrol (KP). Many remember peeling vats full of potatoes—just as these members of Company 702 are doing at the Bena camp.

When enrollees came down with communicable illnesses such as strep throat, measles, or chicken pox, there were few ways to stop disease from spreading. Often the best option was to quarantine the infected camp until the disease had run its course. Most CCC camps were quarantined at least once.

Whether they thought the food was good or not, enrollees helped with the preparation. Paul Sersha learned to peel a garbage can full of potatoes in two hours at his forest camps. Joe Baratto described the routine at another forest camp: "It wasn't bad, but you wash a lot of dishes and kettles and had to keep it clean. The mess sergeant, he kept you on the ball. You had to clean and scrub the mess hall and scrub the tables. You had to clean the refrigerator and the big walk-in cooler. He kept everything clean. It had to be clean." This was more than an arbitrary rule. The Fernberg forest camp near Ely had a typhoid epidemic in 1936 because of lack of proper procedures for cleanliness. At least three people died before the situation was corrected.[9]

When major illnesses or injuries did occur, the camp doctor was there to handle them. Reuben Berman, one of the first Minnesota reserve army medical officers to serve in the CCC, remembered spending the year after his internship at the Cusson forest camp earning two hundred dollars a month as a camp doctor. He lived in town near the camp on a monthly budget of fifty dollars, saving the remainder of his salary for his three-year residency at Minneapolis General Hospital.[10]

Most camps dealt with epidemics or outbreaks of diseases at one time or another. Because the only way to control some diseases at the time was to keep healthy people away from sick ones, a camp was put under quarantine when its enrollees came down with contagious diseases such as mumps, scarlet fever, diphtheria, or measles. Signs at the camp entrances notified visitors if a camp was under quarantine. Camp administrators also worked hard to keep accidents to a minimum, but when they did occur, they were handled either at the infirmaries or, for more serious cases, at hospitals in nearby towns.

Following standard army procedures, camp commanders made sure every part of the camp—not just the kitchen and mess halls—was kept clean and orderly through regular inspections. Arthur Pryor, a forest camp enrollee, remembered, "They'd blow the bugle at six o'clock [in the morning]. We'd get up, clean up, and make your bed for inspection." Eino Lahti described inspections at his camp this way:

[Captain Wipf's] inspections came on Saturday mornings. You had to mop the floors and clean everything up and dust and make the beds and every-

thing else. [Then] the [enrollees in the] barracks that got the lowest rating would have to stay in camp for the weekend. The rest could go on leave. Everybody really worked. I never was subjected to barracks inspections or anything in my military service as I did in the ccc camp. You had white glove inspections. He'd come in with white gloves on, and he'd reach up in the rafters and make sure there was no dust on these things and all that. You had to make your beds a certain way. He would bounce a quarter on it. If it bounced, it was good. If not, you had to re-make it.

John Ek commented, "We got inspections, surprise inspections, health inspections. That was the military part. They were strict, of course, because they were trained that way."[11]

Many enrollees remembered barracks inspections by army personnel at ccc camps, as shown in this undated photograph. "We got inspections, surprise inspections, health inspections," recalled John Ek. "That was the military part. They were strict, of course, because they were trained that way."

Enrollees usually had time to themselves on late weekday afternoons and evenings and after inspection on weekends. During these periods, many attended classes and other educational programs at the camps.

A formal education program was not originally part of the ccc. On May 9, 1933, as the first camps were being organized, Director Fechner authorized forestry and vocational classes, modeling them on classes for enlisted men in the regular army. Forest Service staff taught the forestry classes, and army personnel taught the vocational classes. On November 22, 1933, an official ccc Office of Education was formed, under army direction. And in 1937, education and training formally became a part of the ccc when provisions for both were included in that year's funding bill.[12]

Classes were offered at ccc camps in everything from literacy and high school equivalency to vocational training. Enrollees pursue studies in the education program at the Maple Lake camp, ca. 1940.

Nationally, the ccc education program had nine deputies, one for each of the U.S. Army Corps administrative areas, all reporting to the ccc director of education. In Minnesota, district advisors reported to the Seventh Corps area advisors. Camp educational advisors reported to the district advisors. Beginning in 1937, when enrollees were sent directly to the camps, orientation became another camp activity, the responsibility of the educational adviser.

Although orientation varied from camp to camp, it usually included regularly scheduled meetings covering such subjects as conservation, civics, sanitation, and safety. Enrollees were also allowed to take up to ten hours per week of general education and vocational training. Educational programs increased in quantity and quality. In 1937, a schoolhouse was suggested as part of the camp layout, and camps that didn't already have a building set aside for education were encouraged to build one.[13]

Allen Conkright remembered "the educational advisor had classes for just about anything you wanted to do" at his forest camp near Cloquet. Forester Don Burcalow said the classes he taught had good turnouts, not surprisingly, because "there was nothing else to do, no TV in those days."[14]

Clair Rollings described the educational program at Rabideau, a forest camp near Blackduck:

> *As a qualified high school instructor, I was able to teach such basic and practical courses as English, math, public speaking, et al. My assistant taught spelling, typing, etc. Foresters taught some on-the-job instruction*

and field experience. One forester specialist taught ornithology or bird study. The camp doctor taught personal hygiene and first aid. One of the forester's wives, a music instructor, helped develop a good enrollee band. The clarinet player had played a year with a good St. Olaf College band. One person on the trumpet and one on the piano also had a year or more of music training in college. At the end of one and a half years of training, the Company 708 band became quite good and was in demand for local events.[15]

Enrollee Alfred "Irv" Nelson remembered this program as well: "It was a very well-equipped school—it wasn't the best of everything, but it was very good. The boys spent a lot of evenings there and Saturdays and Sundays, leisure hours. The school was equipped with woodworking tools, typewriters, motion pictures, projectors. They showed a lot of educational pictures in teaching and forestry classes, woodworking classes, diesel engines, mechanics. There was a Junior Audubon Club. They even had garden clubs during the summer." True to the mission of the CCC, educational films in forestry camps focused on conservation themes of the period, with titles such as *From Seed to Sawmill* and *Fighting Forest Fires*.[16]

Camps close to towns sometimes organized programs with local public schools to give enrollees who had not finished high school a chance to earn a diploma. The Lanesboro soil conservation camp and Lanesboro High School had a program for enrollees to take classes and graduate from the high school. Some camps became college centers, offering enrollees who were high school graduates additional opportunities.[17]

Educational advisers were encouraged to offer vocational classes using camp equipment whenever possible, and LEMs often were asked to teach classes in specialized subjects. Camp forester J. C. "Buzz" Ryan, commenting on the educational programs fifty years later, said, "Many of the boys . . . credit the education they got in the camps for the jobs they have. We had one particular boy . . . [now a] retired lieutenant colonel from the air force. He thinks he would never have gotten any place if it wouldn't have been for the education program we had in the CCC camp."[18]

CCC enrollees arrived with a wide range of educational backgrounds. Some had finished high school or had completed several years of college. Some had not finished eighth grade. Others could not read or write. Many camps, especially after 1937, expected illiterate enrollees to join reading classes. Raymond Noyes remembered, "They built a beautiful education building at Gooseberry, and they tried to teach a number of classes. Some men didn't know how to read or write, and they tried to have small group classes where they would get them so they could read and write." Nationally within the CCC, between 85,000 and 110,000 enrollees became literate.[19]

Safety classes also were organized through camp educational programs. Allen Mapes, an enrollee in several forest camps, said, "we did not wear hard hats," but safety regulations were appropriate for the time. Many enrollees completed first aid certification. Camp leaders were proud of safety records and routinely posted on the bulletin board information about safety procedures and the number of accident-free days.[20]

Many camp newsletters or newspapers also grew out of CCC education programs. The national newspaper of the Civilian Conservation Corps was *Happy Days,* but most camps also published their own newspapers with names such as *The Broken Mirror, Dusschee Creek Ripples, The Big Lake Breeze, The Side Lake Star, The Deer Lake Echo, The Lone Wolf,* and *The Veteran's Voice.* Designed to promote "camp spirit," these publications included stories, often written by enrollees. Camp publications also featured information about everyday events, names of enrollees who were leaving and those who were new in camp, and news about upcoming events. Information about camp mascots, safety tips, and inspirational comments often also found their way into the pages of the camp paper. Jokes poked fun at the CCC, the camps, the weather, the food, camp commanders, enrollees, and anything else enrollee-journalists could think of. Editorials sometimes gave advice and encouragement. One such editorial, in *The Broken Mirror* from Company 723 at the Lewiston soil conservation camp on October 18, 1937, ended with these thoughts:

> *What are your aims in life? Are they worthy of your hard work and concentration? Or are you just shooting aimlessly, not knowing where you are going to hit but just close your eyes and hope you hit it lucky? You know when it comes to getting the better things out of life there is no such thing as luck. You can't hope to shoot here and there and fall into something that you want. Those things are earned only by setting a goal and shooting straight for it until that goal is attained. They are worked for and sweated for, sometimes at great cost, and sometimes even at the cost of heartbreak.*
>
> *CAN YOU DO IT? REMEMBER TO AIM STRAIGHT, SHOOT STRAIGHT, AND DO NOT BE SIDETRACKED!*

In January 1937, *The Once Over* from Company 717 at the Side Lake forest camp, north of Hibbing, ran an editorial along the same lines titled "Learning in Our Changing World While in the CCC's." It ended with the admonition: "A chance like this comes along only once in a lifetime. MAKE THE BEST OF IT." Some camps also had enrollee-run radio stations to "let Mr. and Mrs. Minnesota know what the CCC's are all about."[21]

Education—through classes and newspapers—continued to be an important part of the CCC until the country began to move closer to war in the early 1940s. In 1941, Luna Lake forest camp administrators tried to develop a high school program working with school officials in Chisholm, the nearest town at fifteen miles from camp. But the plan failed because the camp's gasoline allowance couldn't cover enrollee transportation between camp and school. When education classes could be held, they increasingly focused on defense work, as at Lanesboro, where the 1941 educational program included an "excellent National Defense Training course taught in town involving blacksmithing, welding, and general metal work."[22]

Throughout the CCC years, Indian Division camps also had education programs. These became better organized in 1937 when the CCC-ID determined that education should take priority over welfare and recreation. The program responded to the very real needs of Indian communities, in which many enrollees could not read or write in English and only about half had a fourth-grade education.[23]

The CCC-ID developed its own national magazine called *Indians at Work,* which became one of the most well-known and well-respected publications of the New Deal era. In Minnesota, program leaders concentrated on providing classes at the Nett Lake and Grand Portage camps for enrollees, regardless of age, who were lacking an eighth-grade education. The Red Lake CCC-ID ran an extensive educational program, including vocational education, at the Red Lake High School. On many reservations, public school staff and WPA instructors came in to teach classes in English, beginning science, arithmetic, spelling, history, and grammar. In 1941, more than one hundred Minnesota CCC-ID enrollees received their graduation certificates in a ceremony with a commencement address given by the president of Northland College in Ashland, Wisconsin.[24]

Spending time in a CCC or CCC-ID camp wasn't all work and hitting the books, though. Enrollees had fun. They played sports, hiked, swam, fished, watched movies, and attended dances, either in camp or at the nearest resort or town.

Enrollees often made their own entertainment. Here, some of the "boys" ham it up at Cut Foot Sioux camp, ca. 1935.

ccc enrollees got to know one another and played practical jokes, most often when a group of new boys arrived in camp. Following army tradition, new enrollees were called "rookies." Each camp had its own routine, but ccc rookies nearly always underwent some kind of initiation. Some were sent out in the woods with a sack and a lantern to hunt "snipe." Others were dispatched to the supply room for striped paint, left-handed monkey wrenches, or elbow grease. Their beds were short sheeted, their pants run up the flagpole, their shoes nailed to the floor. Steve Bartek remembered the forest camps he was in: "When we first started and we got in the camp, they always try to break you in, call you 'rookie.' They would say, 'Go down there and bring that shoreline up.' There were lots of gimmicks like that. Trying to break them in and stuff. 'Go see if you can push that flagpole [down]: it is a little too high. See if you can bring it down.' So you'd go up there and start grabbing that flagpole."[25]

Once in camp, enrollees often gave one another nicknames. Allen Conkright remembered some of them: "Cue Ball, Cue Ball with Hair. Almost everybody had a nickname. Sadie Brooks. Ruthie Hollister. Eldon 'Seldom' Smart." Edward Schubert noted:

> *I didn't have a nickname. My brother-in-law—he was not my brother-in-law at the time, but he became my brother-in-law later—he was a very stern-looking person, and he had the name of "Stoneface." Another fellow, a friend of mine who was in camp, kind of a rough sort of a character, he got the name of "Goon." Another kid who was fighting all the time got the name of "Tiger." Another one who was a little bit owly and growly all the time, they named him "Cinnamon," after a bear. A lot of fellows wound up with nicknames, and it stuck with them for a long, long time.*[26]

Some leisure activities—such as sports—were well organized. When in camp, enrollees played baseball, softball, basketball, and hockey, and they had boxing and wrestling meets. Camps formed teams for sports and competed with one another for championships. John Cackoski realized right away how important sports were:

> *When I joined the CCs, I was in the rec hall in Virginia [Minnesota] with my buddy. We played basketball together in high school. We were standing, talking about how we were going to go out West. Then across the floor came the lieutenant from the ccc camp at Side Lake. He and the sergeant walked right toward us. And my buddy said, "Oh no, we're going to Side Lake." And that lieutenant come over to us and told us we were going to Side Lake. And we knew why: because we played basketball, and he was looking for basketball players. He got himself a good team.*

The Side Lake camp team won the state ccc basketball tournament two years in a row.[27]

Some camps also played against city teams. Clarence Johnson said of the Big Lake forest camp at Cass Lake: "We had a pretty good baseball team. [Company] 720 won the district championship that year. They had a fellow there called Doc Appids. Almost anyone around Bemidji or Nymore would

Organized sports—here, the baseball team at the Grand Portage CCC-ID camp—were an important part of camp life.

remember him because he was a terrific hitter and a pretty good pitcher. This baseball team played other camps; they had just like a World Series of today. At the end of the year, the champions would get together and fight it out. And 720 came up that year with the championship."[28]

Joe Baratto remembered the baseball team at the Cut Foot Sioux forest camp near Deer River: "Each camp had a ball team that was picked from the best players who would then make the team. Like our team. After you played all the camps, we played Deer River, the city team. When you came to the final, you started playing each other, and we won the championship up there in baseball. We beat a Kansas City outfit at Cass Lake. When we beat them, we had to play the championship Indian team. We beat them, too. We won every year. We had a good club." In 1937, the basketball team from the Grand Portage CCC-ID camp played in the North Shore League against other area CCC camps and towns. They won the North Shore League championship and were presented with a silver cup along with a bronze statue for "superb sportsmanship."[29]

Some camp sports were more casual. Depending on the season, enrollees went skating, ski jumping, fishing, sledding, swimming, and hiking. Edward Schubert liked hiking at his state park camp: "You could go out walking anytime you wanted to, if you wanted to walk. We explored a lot, really. Mostly it was looking for deer and whatever else we could find." In the winter, enrollees raided bear dens and brought back cubs as camp mascots.[30]

Recreational pursuits at ccc camps spanned the gamut from pole-vaulting (at the Halfway camp) to snowshoeing (at the Rabideau camp). African American enrollees visible in the background of the pole-vaulting photo indicate that this image was taken early in the program, when Blacks still served within the state's borders.

"In camp, we had accordions," said John Cackoski. "We always had music. . . . We had some guitars. We had one guy with a saxophone. I used to sing with them." Enrollees from the Isabella and Deer Lake camps show off their musical skills.

Although there were organized programs in camps, John Cackoski echoed many enrollees' comments about free time: "Recreation, you had to make your own." His hobby was woodworking:

In the evening, they had classes. I was handy with a knife. I started making picture frames out of wood. First, I just made a few for myself. I had a foot-locker. I painted the top of it myself. Then, when I made these picture frames, I varnished them and sat them up on a stump to dry. . . . The doctor come in and looked them over. He asked me if I'd sell them. I sold every one—he bought every one. The captain bought one for the desk in his office. I made quite a few after that, and every one I made, I sold. . . . I used to go in the woods and pick special trees, soft to carve. Made them out of that. They were nice; nice looking.[31]

Music was also an important source of entertainment in camp. Lorenz R. Lindstrom, a forest service camp supervisor, wrote to his girlfriend about "trying to get our concertina player to give us a few songs before we go to bed." John Cackoski said, "In camp, we had accordions. We always had music. It was Slovenian music, mostly. The ones who had the accordions were Slovenians, mostly. We had some guitars. We had one guy with a saxophone. I used to sing with them. That's where I learned some Slovenian songs." Godfrey Rawlings, an African American enrollee in a forest camp, remembered "one fellow, they called him 'Slim.' He was from the Deep South, and he picked a banjo. He used to play the banjo at night, and we'd sit around and sing the blues and things like that."[32]

Some music came over the airwaves. Robert Engstrom, an LEM at a forest camp, remembered, "the radio was all you had. I used to listen to Wayne King every night at 11 o'clock from Chicago." Other programs came through, too. Lorenz R. Lindstrom wrote to his girlfriend after listening to Jack Benny on the radio: "He's good tonight."[33]

Camps had movies and organized dances. Allen Conkright remembered, "We'd have a company dance down at the pavilion. I drove to Duluth and picked up (oh, I liked that!) a whole truckload of girls. I never had such a good time in my life." John Cackoski described going to dances at his camp: "We walked in [to a dance], and all the CCs were on one side of the room and the girls were on the other side. We come in, we didn't sit with the boys: we sat with the girls. I know one guy, he got married to the girl he met when he was in the CCs."[34]

When there were dances in nearby towns, truckloads of enrollees attended. Clair Rollings remembered the excitement of "those Saturday nights at the local resort" near his CCC camp:

Here enrollees from three or four camps gathered to compete for the attention of the local girls at the dance. Enrollees from one or two nearby camps were from Kansas. They were the "foreigners" who had to be kept away from the nicest-looking girls at all costs. One night, fights became more frequent and more violent than usual and eventually developed into a real old-

> *fashioned lumberjack brawl. Officers in charge were pushed to the limit to stop fights and keep order. Big Clem from Company 708 was half dragged outside the hall and attacked by four or five enrollees from Kansas. Two or three of the attackers spent the next day or two in the camp hospital. Big Clem was a young giant about six feet five inches tall and liked nothing better than a good fight.*[35]

Individual cars were not allowed, but, in violation of camp rules, those enrollees lucky enough to have cars sometimes hid them nearby. Edward Schubert remembered that "we went home every weekend. There were cars around the camp. No one was supposed to have a car. Usually cars were parked a half mile out from camp." Joseph Franzinelli described the setup: "Come Friday night, if you had someplace to go and if you weren't a trouble-maker, they'd give you a three-day pass, and you'd take care of yourself. One or two of the guys would have a little car ducked out there in the woods. Come the weekend, six guys would ride home. They'd come back and hide the car because the captain [camp commander] would not allow any." Enrollees knew the rules, but also how to get around them.[36]

Not all enrollees were included in the fights or the fun, however. U.S. Army segregation policies kept African American enrollees apart from others. Paul Wood, an African American at a forest camp, said, "Then, occasionally they'd have a dance and we weren't invited. Everybody was invited but [the African American enrollees]. I spent most of my time in the barracks or out playing basketball or football or something like that."[37]

For movies in the recreation hall, Black enrollees were assigned seats slightly apart from the rest of the camp population. Paul Wood had earlier broken the color barrier as a high school basketball player in St. Paul. Faced with barriers in the CCC, he confronted his camp commander:

> *I went right to his office. I went alone. I asked him why we had to be segregated in the movies. He said it was his order. I said in the state of Minnesota we have a statute that forbids segregation. He said, "You're in the army now, and where the army is concerned, it takes precedence over everything except what is considered civilian authority." I had [also] gone to the first line of command, the sergeant. He was a Minnesotan. He was very embarrassed. He said he couldn't do anything. I told him I was going to see the captain. He advised me not to do that, tried to throw a scare into me. I could get a dishonorable discharge. They used that.*

In spite of Wood's efforts, enrollees remained segregated during movies. And even with the sergeant's warning, Wood received his honorable discharge from the CCC in 1935.[38]

African Americans found their own fun in CCC camps. Formal social events—following army policy—excluded Blacks. But enrollees sometimes challenged that policy at informal gatherings. Godfrey Rawlings hosted a party open to all in the segregated end of his barracks at a forest camp:

I loved to play pool. I threw a party because everyone had to put up two dollars that entered a pool tournament. And there were quite a few that entered the pool tournament. It's a form of elimination. I won the pool tournament. The money that was put in to enter the tournament was given to the person that won. So I went to the PX [canteen] and bought a case of beer. And I took it back to my barracks. . . . My mother had sent a box of goodies for me. I'll never forget them. A couple of cans of sardines, a ring of baloney, a ring of liverwurst, a box of graham crackers, a box of white crackers. There was bananas and oranges and some candy. This was a neat box. Boy, was I glad to get that. So I brought out the box. . . . We had a good old party in there.[39]

CCC enrollees of all ethnic backgrounds had little money. Payday was once a month. At the designated time, enrollees lined up to sign for the money they were allowed to keep, with the remainder of what they earned going to their designated dependents. Most enrollees had only what they were given each month on payday. Vernon Butcher, a forest camp enrollee, said, "We got thirty dollars a month. Twenty-five dollars of it went home. Five dollars saved with you to buy smoking tobacco or haircuts. Of course, five dollars went a long way in those days." Each camp had a canteen that sold candy, soft drinks, cigarettes, beer (if allowed), and personal items to enrollees. Ralph Halbert remembered of his camp's canteen, "nothing was more than a nickel."[40]

Camp canteens were popular places. In 1940, during a one-month period, the 250 enrollees and support personnel at the Day Lake forest camp near Grand Rapids bought 2,256 candy bars, 1,784 bags of smoking tobacco, 1,284 packages of cigarettes, 2,784 bottles of soda pop, 1,736 ice cream bars, 972 pints of ice cream, 272 bars of soap, 198 boxes of soap flakes, and 157 cans of shoe polish. Items for the canteen were purchased in Grand Rapids, Deer River, and Bovey, helping support the local economy in these northern Minnesota communities. In turn, canteen profits helped pay for furniture for the recreation hall, magazines, books, movie projectors, athletic equipment, and washing machines. Minnesota enrollee E. K. "Bud" Mallory, while serving in forest and soil conservation camps, developed a canteen design that was used in camps in Seventh Army Corps states.[41]

On Sundays, depending on how far away the nearest town was, enrollees could go in to church. Nondenominational services also were held in the camps, with the CCC providing one chaplain for eight camps. Milford Humphrey, a lay preacher from Grand Marais, served as chaplain for camps along the North Shore of Lake Superior. He said the army was "always cooperative" in getting the enrollees to attend. "They didn't insist on the boys going to the services, [but] if there was a super-interested officer in charge, he would do extra duty to get the boys out for services."[42]

Enrollees were sometimes asked to take on special community service tasks on top of their regular work, such as helping hunt for lost people. E. K. "Bud" Mallory remembered doing this at the Land O'Lakes forest camp. The most unusual case occurred in 1935, when his company helped hunt for kidnap victim Charles Ross, a millionaire greeting card manufacturer from Chicago, Illinois, who, according to reports, had been brought to Minnesota. Mallory and several others found his body in the woods near Outing where his kidnappers had left him.[43]

Except for holidays and special occasions, enrollees had few days off and were expected to put in a full day's work. The boys took their work seriously. Enrollee Matt Anzelc, using an army term for slacking off, said of the work ethic that pervaded his camp: "Everybody worked and worked hard. You didn't see any goldbricking." Some pretended to be sick, but Eino Lahti described what would happen in these situations: "This is where you find a typical army hospital thing, a dose of castor oil when you first went in [to the infirmary]. And that would cure you of whatever you had, or if you were going to be goldbricking, you didn't really want to go back to the [camp] hospital."[44]

The Sullivanite, the newspaper for the Sullivan Lake camp, published a short poem written by an enrollee stressing the commitment most felt toward their work:

ODE TO A GRIPER

If you wish to gripe
Thou scandal-hound
Do it when
No one's around[45]

Whether he griped or not, no one in the ccc ever forgot the main reason why he was in camp—to do much-needed conservation work in forests, on soil erosion, or at state parks. The basic outlines of that work in the state of Minnesota are covered in greater detail in the next three chapters.

PART II
THE WORK OF THE CCC

Gifford Pinchot, who oversaw the establishment of the U.S. Forest Service in 1905, helped make the public aware of the term *conservation* and of the importance of preserving natural resources. He is seen here in his office, ca. 1910.

Christopher Columbus Andrews, shown here at Itasca State Park around 1915, was an early proponent of the conservation of natural resources and scientific forest management in Minnesota.

INTRODUCTION: MINNESOTA'S CONSERVATION FOUNDATIONS

By the time the ccc was founded in 1933, Americans were beginning to recognize the need to care for natural resources. This concept was not new. As early as the 1820s, writers, artists, and intellectuals such as Ralph Waldo Emerson, Henry David Thoreau, George Catlin, and James Fenimore Cooper proposed saving natural resources for the sake of beauty alone. In 1864, George Perkins Marsh helped turn the focus in a different direction with his book *Man and Nature*. Marsh started a new movement to preserve remaining resources. He advocated using modern techniques to manage natural resources so they could be enjoyed by the public and so that they might also create some economic benefit.

Under the leadership of President Theodore Roosevelt in the early 1900s, Americans learned of what was, for the first time, being called *conservation*. Gifford Pinchot, Roosevelt's chief forester and a progressive who believed in Marsh's idea of scientifically managing resources, was among the first to use the term *conservation* in discussions of natural resources. Pinchot served as the main architect of government-led conservation during Roosevelt's administration. He oversaw the establishment of the U.S. Forest Service in 1905 and popularized the idea that effective forest management should provide "the greatest good for the greatest number." In other words, natural resources such as forests should be efficiently managed and used in ways that benefited all people.[1]

While Pinchot was introducing conservation ideas in forestry, John Muir was gaining national attention for his writings on the need to preserve open space for the public good. In particular, Muir championed the creation of a system of national parks. Yellowstone, the first national park, was established in 1872, with Sequoia and Yosemite following in 1890, but many more parks took shape in the early 1900s with the rise of the conservation movement. These national parks had a dual mission of conserving open spaces and landscapes while providing for enjoyment and attracting visitors. Muir's more idealistic preservationist views conflicted with Pinchot's more practical utilitarian beliefs, but both worked to conserve and protect the country's natural resources.[2]

Conservation ideals were applied in forestry and in the creation of national parks early in the 1900s, but interest in soil conservation followed more slowly. Dr. Hugh Hammond Bennett, a former chemist in the U.S. Department of Agriculture, had been speaking out for decades about the causes and types of soil erosion and the need for scientific soil management. His work attracted little attention until the country moved closer to the

Dust Bowl era. With Bennett's 1928 bulletin, *Soil Erosion: A National Menace,* people finally started to listen.[3]

In a dramatic move as conditions continued to worsen, Bennett managed to delay important testimony before Congress in 1935 until a major dust cloud reached the capitol. As the dust cloud settled over Washington, DC, Bennett gestured out the windows and declared, "This, gentlemen, is what I am talking about"—and convinced the lawmakers of the need for a permanent government agency to address soil erosion and related issues. With this, the Soil Conservation Service (SCS) was established in the U.S. Department of Agriculture. Bennett developed several soil erosion experiment stations around the country, including one at La Crosse, Wisconsin, which would help provide leadership for Minnesota's CCC soil conservation work.[4]

Before the SCS was established, the Soil Erosion Service (SES) was formed as a temporary agency in the U.S. Department of the Interior. Organized on August 24, 1933, it oversaw early CCC conservation work. In Minnesota, this coordination began when regional director R. H. Davis transferred Herbert Flueck, Minnesota's first soil conservationist and first SES soil conservation work program administrator, to Spring Valley, Minnesota, in 1934. In 1937, as the permanent USDA soil conservation program continued to grow, the Minnesota soil conservation coordinator's office opened in St. Paul with Flueck as acting state coordinator. The next year, Minnesota CCC project management was consolidated under the Faribault project office, where it remained through 1942. The Department of Conservation Division of Drainage and Waters approved all soil conservation projects.[5]

The conservation ideals of Pinchot, Muir, Bennett, and others guided much of the work of the CCC. In Minnesota, others helped to shape and promote conservation of natural resources. During Minnesota's early years, as throughout the country, people showed little interest in conservation. Legislators established Minnesota's first state park, Itasca, in 1891 and the first state forest preserve, Pillsbury State Forest, in 1900, but the state did little to administer or manage these lands, and conservation laws of the day didn't effectively protect natural resources.[6]

Christopher Columbus Andrews—a decorated Civil War veteran, attorney, and former U.S. ambassador to Sweden and Norway—helped change that, particularly in the area of forest conservation. Andrews, already interested in scientific forest management, learned more about reforestation projects and policies while in Scandinavia. He quickly realized that similar policies could help back home. In Minnesota, Andrews helped found a state tree nursery and several state parks, encouraged the legislature to set aside land for forest reserves, and supported expansion of the state forest service. He also led efforts to create Minnesota's two national forests—the Minnesota National Forest in the north-central part of the state (which became the Chippewa National Forest in 1928) and the Superior National Forest, located in northeastern Minnesota between Lake Superior and the U.S.-Canadian border.[7]

In all his work, Andrews supported sustainable and managed use of forests. Forests, he believed, should occupy land unsuitable for agriculture. Cutting or harvesting trees should be allowed, but annual cutting should not exceed annual growth. Resources should be continually renewed through reforestation. These ideas were not initially popular in Minnesota, where the public had grown accustomed to years of clear-cutting in northern forests. But by the 1920s, influenced by national policies and guided by Andrews, the Minnesota legislature began to develop a stronger system of land, forest, and water management.[8]

At the urging of Governor Floyd B. Olson, also a strong conservationist, the legislature enacted laws that reorganized the Department of Conservation (DOC) in 1925 and again in 1931. (This department is the forerunner of today's Minnesota Department of Natural Resources.) Olson's commitment to conservation was clear: "Commercial exploitation in the past has despoiled our forests, marred our landscapes, and dissipated our resources. It has robbed our people of the greater part of their heritage of natural resources. Let us guard what is left diligently and zealously." Under Olson's leadership, for the first time Minnesota had a Conservation Commission and a Department of Conservation with specific areas of responsibility: forestry, game and fish, drainage and waters, and lands and minerals. William T. Cox became the first commissioner of Conservation. Grover M. Conzet was named director of the Division of Forestry in 1924 and ran this division throughout the CCC years. These men practiced Pinchot's governing tenet of forest management—the best use for the most people. They shared Andrews's conservation beliefs and would use these principles to guide forest conservation work for Minnesota's CCC.[9]

Support for soil conservation in the state began slowly gaining ground in the 1920s and early 1930s. In 1931, Frederick J. Alway, head of the Soils Division at the University of Minnesota's Institute of Agriculture, identified a number of measures that could be used to help keep soil in place. These included terracing, strip cropping, contour farming, general revegetation, check dam construction, tree plantings on steep slopes, and using lime to de-acidify soil and encourage cover crops such as clover and alfalfa. Minnesota's newly reorganized Department of Conservation worked with the university to encourage use of these procedures on Minnesota farmland, although little headway was made until the CCC began its work.[10]

Minnesota in 1933—at the time of the CCC's creation—was a state in grave need of conservation work. The northern part of the state originally was covered with forests of white and red pine interspersed with stands of spruce, fir, aspen, and birch. But most of the forests had been logged, leaving behind bare, rocky acreage covered with thin soil. This cutover land was poorly suited for agriculture. Farms on cutover land were failing in record numbers, and 35 percent of the land was tax delinquent. Although some leaders recognized the need to replant forests on this land, the state simply didn't have the

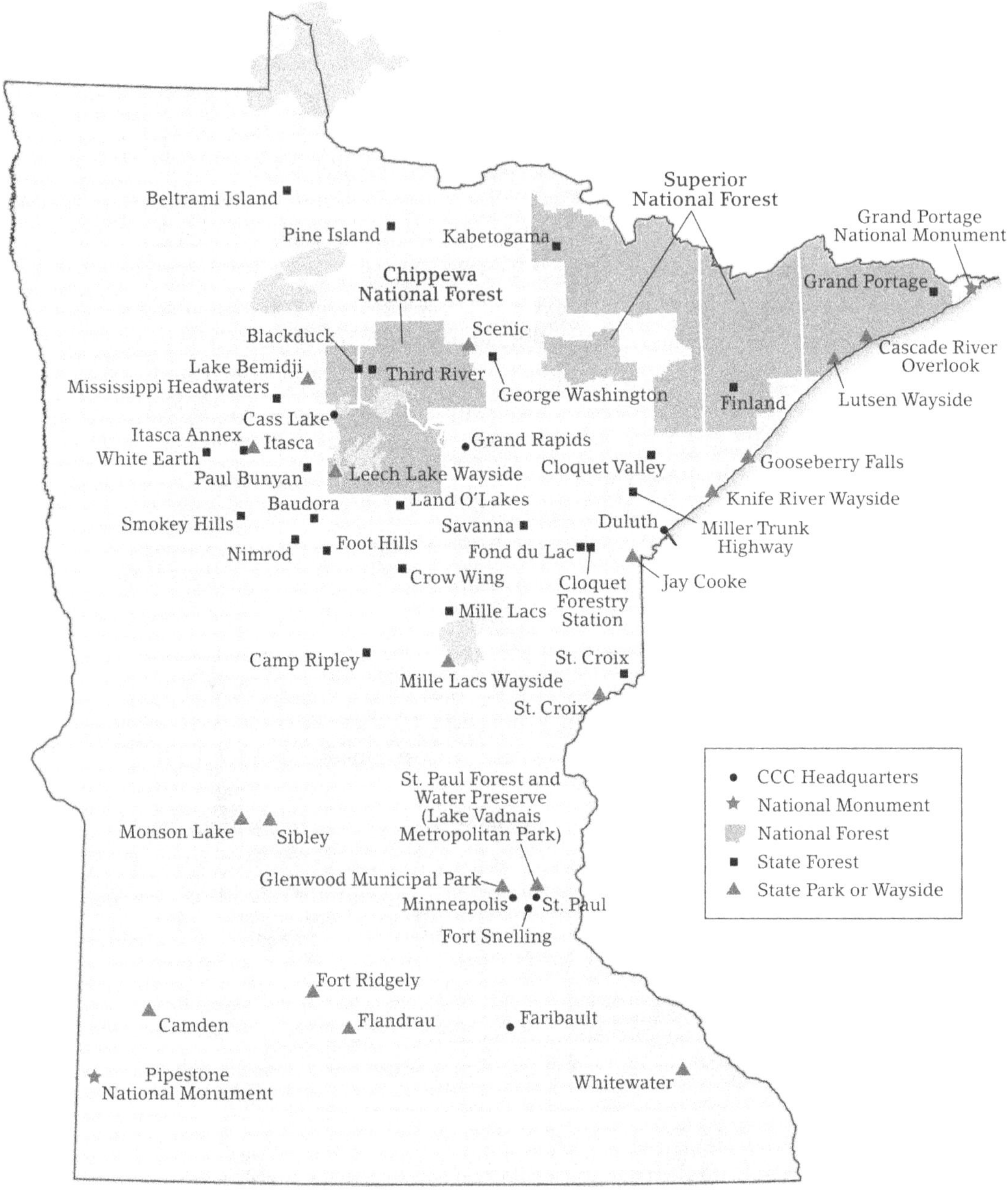
Superior National Forest
Grand Portage National Monument
Beltrami Island
Pine Island
Kabetogama
Chippewa National Forest
Grand Portage
Blackduck
Scenic
Cascade River Overlook
Lake Bemidji
Third River
Mississippi Headwaters
George Washington
Finland
Lutsen Wayside
Cass Lake
Itasca Annex
Itasca
Grand Rapids
White Earth
Paul Bunyan
Leech Lake Wayside
Cloquet Valley
Gooseberry Falls
Baudora
Land O'Lakes
Knife River Wayside
Smokey Hills
Savanna
Duluth
Miller Trunk Highway
Nimrod
Foot Hills
Fond du Lac
Crow Wing
Cloquet Forestry Station
Jay Cooke
Mille Lacs
Camp Ripley
St. Croix
Mille Lacs Wayside
St. Croix
St. Paul Forest and Water Preserve (Lake Vadnais Metropolitan Park)
Monson Lake
Sibley
Glenwood Municipal Park
Minneapolis
St. Paul
Fort Snelling
Fort Ridgely
Camden
Flandrau
Faribault
Pipestone National Monument
Whitewater
CCC Headquarters
National Monument
National Forest
State Forest
State Park or Wayside

CCC and CCC-ID Conservation Work Areas in Minnesota, 1933–42

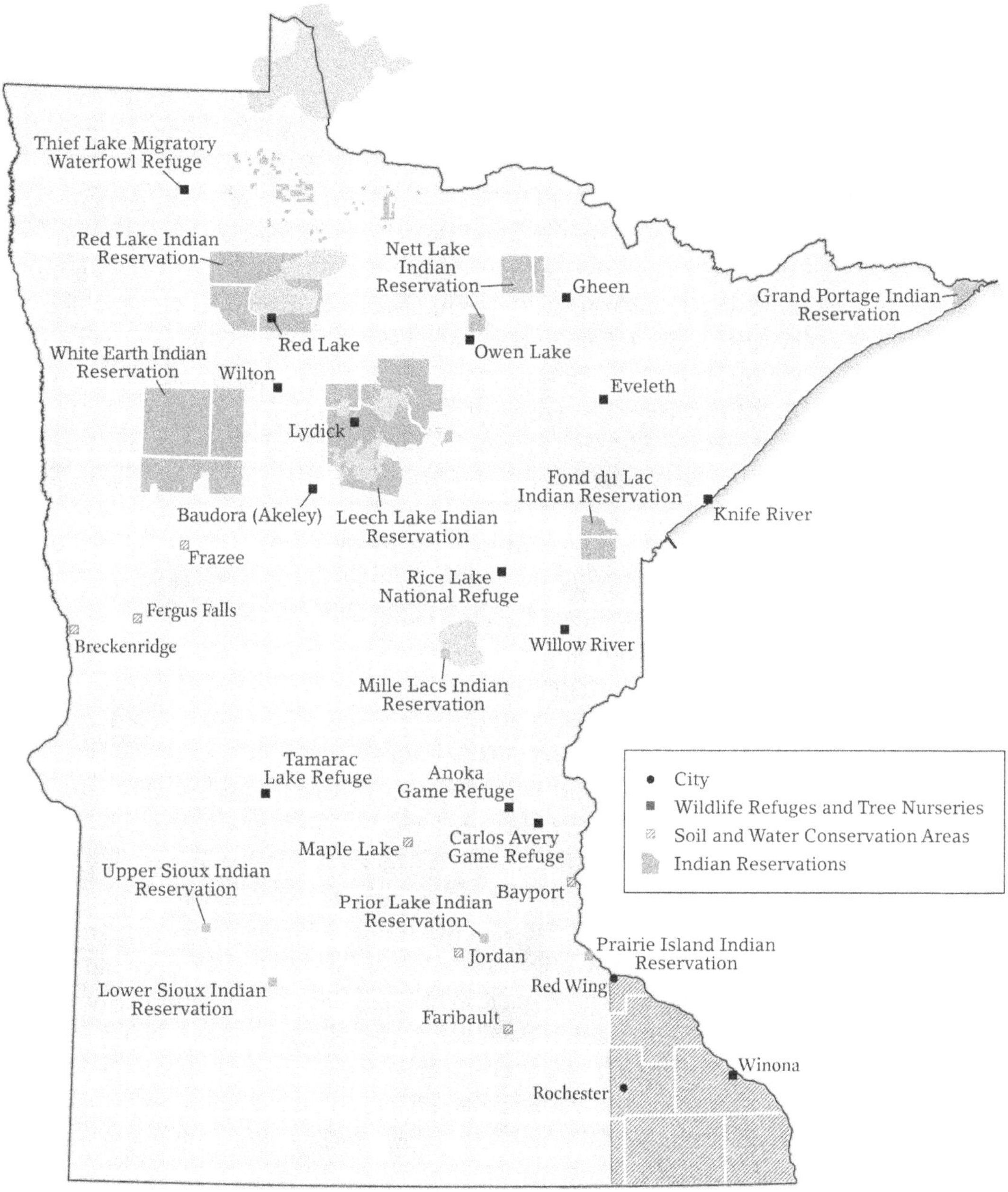

CCC and CCC-ID Conservation Work Areas in Minnesota, 1933–42

resources to carry out the work. Forests that had been preserved, mainly in the two national forests, weren't in much better shape. The state park system, which in some cases helped manage northern forestlands, was in its infancy. Both forests and parks needed more active management than the state could afford in prosperous times—and in 1933 times were hard.[11]

Conditions in southern Minnesota were much the same. Long an important contributor to the agriculture economy, this part of the state could be divided into three sections—the southwest, south central, and southeast. Throughout, farmers grew corn, oats, and soybeans and raised cattle and hogs. The terrain, however, differed considerably across the region. Southwestern Minnesota is flat, prairie country, while south-central Minnesota contains flat and rolling areas. The southeastern area, known as the Driftless Area because it was left untouched by the continental glaciers that covered much of the rest of the state, is characterized by a rugged topography of rolling hills and deep river valleys.[12]

By the early 1930s, only 73,000 of the 23 million acres of native grasslands remained in southern Minnesota. Stands of hardwoods—maple, basswood, oak, elm, beech, and willow—had been cut from the Big Woods, an area of trees that once covered most of Ramsey, Hennepin, Dakota, Scott, Carver, Rice, and LeSueur Counties in the south-central and southeastern parts of the state. The most common farming method, using straight rows, wasn't well suited to much of southern Minnesota, particularly the hilly Driftless Area. Using steep lands for pasture to support the expanding dairy industry created even more problems. As the dairy cooperative movement grew and more land was put to this use, cattle tore up topsoil, making it vulnerable to runoff. Water erosion—sheet, rill, and gully—was rampant, especially in southeastern Minnesota, causing huge topsoil losses. With every rainstorm or snowmelt, layers of soil washed away, widening the rills and gullies that snaked through fields and clogging lakes and streams. Estimated runoff was 3,000 to 4,000 cubic yards of topsoil per square mile per year, and, in many places, the foot of topsoil originally found on the land was reduced to less than a fraction of an inch. Eroded soil flowed into the Mississippi River in such large amounts that it threatened the river's new lock and dam system. The damage, reported the state's Commission of Conservation, was "as fully destructive of soil and water resources, fish, and other aquatic life, as fire is destructive of timber and game"—strong words in a state with Minnesota's history of devastating forest fires.[13]

By 1933, although some changes were still needed, with the development of the DOC and identification of conservation needs, the basic structure for conserving and protecting natural resources in Minnesota was in place. But the state lacked the ability to carry out needed work. It would take the CCC to provide the men, muscle, and money vital to meeting Minnesota's conservation needs.

6: PLANTING TREES AND FIGHTING FIRES

The ccc's impact on the environment was perhaps greatest in Minnesota's forests. Most camps in Minnesota were located on federal or state forestlands. ccc work programs focused not just on developing new state forests—thirteen were established in 1933 alone—but also on protecting existing ones. Enrollees planted trees, did forest and lake surveys, conserved marshland and hunting preserves, built administrative and other structures, and worked on fire prevention projects, including fighting forest fires. By the ccc's end, the program had developed and carried out major forest conservation projects in the Chippewa and Superior national forests and in twenty-one new and existing state forests in all parts of the state. The ccc's forest conservation work spread to Camp Ripley, Miller Trunk Highway, Itasca Annex, the Anoka Game Refuge, and Nimrod—where state forest camp enrollees completed work projects outside state forest areas.[1]

ccc work programs in the Chippewa and Superior national forests were supervised by the U.S. Forest Service (usfs) under the U.S. Department of Agriculture (usda). Minnesota belonged to the sixth of nine regional divisions, headquartered in Milwaukee. The state administrative headquarters for Superior National Forest were in Duluth; the Chippewa National Forest headquarters were in Cass Lake. Superior National Forest district offices, run by forest rangers, were located at Tofte, Two Harbors, Grand Marais, Isabella,

An unidentified enrollee from the Side Lake camp leans on a sign at George Washington State Forest, one of many state forests in which the ccc worked.

Aurora, Brittmount, Cook, and Ely. Many of these locations in Minnesota's Arrowhead region would host ccc camps. The same was true for Chippewa National Forest district office locations at Cass Lake, Walker, Remer, Bena, Cut Foot Sioux, Marcell, Blackduck, and Dora Lake.[2]

The Minnesota State Forest Service was established in 1911, but state forest (also called state forest preserve) administration was, at best, loosely managed for many years. The organization of the Department of Conservation in 1925 and its 1931 reorganization improved the situation. Grover Conzet, Minnesota's director of forestry, was guided by the "economic principle that all lands be put to their highest and most productive long time use for the permanent good of the greatest number of people." He called for the establishment of nine new state forests—Beltrami Island, Cloquet Valley, Finland, George Washington, Grand Portage, Kabetogama, Savanna, Third River, and White Earth—and suggested they be developed on cutover lands to encourage reforestation of these areas. The Minnesota legislature approved his plan and expanded it, adding Fond du Lac, Foot Hills, Land O'Lakes, and Pine Island. In 1933, Minnesota Laws Chapter 419 created these thirteen new state forests, defined the boundaries for each, and gave the state the authority to acquire privately held lands in their boundaries for forest management and development. Significantly, this legislation also provided Minnesota with the legal grounds to establish ccc camps in state forests.[3]

Rangers at both national and state forests determined work program needs and developed plans which they sent to state conservation officials for approval. Once authorized, rangers worked with ccc camp personnel to carry out plans, with the camp superintendent overseeing the work. J. C. "Buzz" Ryan, a forest superintendent at the Sullivan Lake state forest camp, described the process: "When you talk of the forest service, you're talking about the work agency of the cccs. The [enrollees] were turned over every day, and they were in [the] charge of the work agency until they came back at night and were turned back to the army. The [forest] superintendent's duties ended when they were turned back to the army, but he was responsible for them when they were out in the field." This same division of labor also existed in ccc camps in the Chippewa and Superior national forests.[4]

Forest and ccc camp personnel developed work priorities that included increasing the size and number of forests, improving game habitat, conducting lake surveys, and aiding in the development of long-term planning. Work projects were wide ranging. Certainly, enrollees found themselves involved in tree planting, improving forest stands, supporting tree nurseries, and collecting tree seeds. But they also built and improved forest structures such as bridges, buildings, and water supply systems. They strung thousands of miles of telephone lines. They helped with transportation improvements, such as building roads and fire trails, and with forest protection, such as reducing fire hazards and fighting forest fires. The ccc also stocked lakes with fish and engaged in emergency wildlife feeding. Other ccc activities included mapping (topographic and relief), reconnaissance work, and timber estimating and surveying. All met Minnesota conservation needs by developing, enlarging, and improving existing forests and putting bare, cutover, and tax-forfeit lands back into productive use through up-to-date forest resource management.

When the ccc began, federal and state forest leaders realized they had access to thousands of workers. At first, forest rangers and ccc camp work superintendents organized programs involving quick start-up and little training—projects that could keep many people busy. Roadside cleanup and disposing of slash—logging or conservation work residue—helped reduce hazards and prevent fires, so these were common early programs. Enrollee Luke Walker remembered the work: "Roadside clean-up was cleaning an area 100′ back on each side of the road or trail of all dead or dying timber standing or lying."[5]

By January 1934, officials were ready to initiate projects requiring more planning and start-up time. Such projects focused more on long-term conservation needs, including building and caring for forests—or "forest cultural work, such as releasing and weeding, planting and thinning," as one source put it. These standard forest conservation projects—the work for which the ccc is best known—were soon being given top priority.[6]

In 1935, in another example of long-term projects, state conservation officials used ccc labor to begin a broad-based statewide reconnaissance program for state forest lakes. Three years later, the state expanded this to include an inventory of areas outside, but adjoining, state forests. Under this program, ccc enrollees collected information on land uses, types of trees and other ground cover, wildlife, and the number of fish in the lakes. The information the men and boys of the CCC gathered in these work projects helped lay the groundwork for long-range forest planning and management in the state. William Webb, working as a game technician in state forest camps, wrote of his part of the reconnaissance process: "I've been assigned to seven camps within a radius of about 100 miles. The instructions were to take a game census on the sample areas which had to be picked in each of these camps during the month of April. . . . I took one (practically alone) on the 2,400 acre sample area of Camp S-81, Ray, Minn. . . . Monday I moved down to Camp S-52 at Cusson."[7]

Doing forestry work required coordination, and projects were well organized. To carry out the work, enrollees were split into platoons and squads or crews. Camp superintendents gave daily assignments to foremen who were responsible for enrollees on the job site. Work programs and projects were supervised by camp superintendents. Enrollees clearly remembered the line between camp and work project responsibilities. As Arthur Pryor, an enrollee in a forest camp, said: "In camp, the cleanup and stuff belonged to the army, but out in the field, that was the forest service." Clarence Johnson, an enrollee in another forest camp, remembered this, too: "I know we always remarked that when you're in camp, you're in the army, and when you're out in the woods, you're with the forestry."[8]

At times, work crew leaders were hardly older than the enrollees they supervised. Forrest Stillwell, an LEM at federal and state forest camps, was about the same age as the enrollees, but, he said, "[it was my job] to watch the men. We were divided into platoons. . . . We got all our instructions before we left camp in the morning. You tell them what to do, and that's the way it got done. We was all alone."[9]

Fred Bohrer and his crew pause after a winter workday at the Sullivan Lake state forest camp near Brimson.

Enrollees on job sites worked in many different conditions. They remembered going out in intense cold in the winter, although there were some controls in place. Ernest Anderson remembered his camp near Ray, Minnesota: "It was cold up there.... One morning it was sixty-nine below. The walls were popping more than usual. You know how a building pops. That morning it was really cranking. We started talking about how cold it must be out there. So somebody went out to look at the thermometer. They came back and told us sixty-nine below. We didn't do much work that day." According to Eino Lahti, "[In the winter] if the temperature dropped below thirty below, we didn't have to go out. Up to thirty below, you went out for all day. I guess they figured you had adequate clothing for that."[10]

William Webb wrote about early spring at the Cusson camp in northern Minnesota in 1935:

> *Greetings from the back woods. From winter to summer, from hell to heaven or something like that.... The snow is nearly gone on south facing slopes here, but the north slopes still have snow waist deep. Every little gully is like a river, and every little depression is full of water. Believe me that makes for hazardous going most any place in the woods. I walked 200 yards today with icy water gurgling around my knees, and then when I finally reached dry land I took my pants and boots off and let them dry for about half an hour.*[11]

Summer created other memories. Eino Lahti described this season as well: "In the summertime, in some of those areas, the mosquitoes were so bad that we wore our wool shirts and had head nets on to keep the mosquitoes away. And they would bite right through that stuff. We wore gloves, and when you took those off, I tell you, they were right there. That was rough." Forest supervisor Lorenz R. Lindstrom described one mosquito remedy: "We have a wonderful black liquid that we call fly dope that is about half tar that we smear all over our faces and hands that does a little bit toward keeping the bloody little black flies and mosquitoes away. It has quite a smell, too." In spite of sometimes adverse conditions, however, enrollees generally were proud of being able to withstand just about anything. Paul Wood summed up this sentiment: "We worked in all kinds of weather. We were young and healthy, and there was a pride in being able to do that."[12]

Tree planting, for which the ccc is best known today, was only a part—albeit a significant part—of forest camp work. It was and remains the symbol of the ccc. By planting trees, the ccc helped reclaim cutover land and introduced high-quality plantings, such as white and red pine, into existing forests. Enrollees also planted trees previously thought to be economically worthless, including jack pine, aspen, poplar, and other "scrub growth." By the time of the ccc, the wood products industry had made many advances, recognizing the usefulness of a wider range of trees. As conservation principles became better understood, the public came to see, more and more, the importance of all renewable resources—trees being among them. Thus, with a higher value being placed on trees, ccc enrollees planted all kinds of them.

Tree planting, part of most camp work programs, remains emblematic of the CCC. In Minnesota, enrollees planted almost 124 million trees. Notice the prepared furrows and boxes of seedlings at the Side Lake camp. A member of another forestry camp shows the result of this work, a newly planted tree on cutover land.

As part of conservation field training, enrollees were taught strict planting procedures. Raymond Noyes remembered those lessons almost fifty years later:

> *[Tree planting] was a procedure we had to follow very accurately. They had furrowed in the woods, and we would come along with a little box, and we'd have a tool where we'd make a little wedge in the soil, and we'd take the young seedling. We had to put it way down as far as we could and draw it back up. And where the branches start, there is a little knob, and that had to be level with the surface of the soil. The reason for dipping it down—the roots had to be downward. If they bent up, the tree would die. Then we took our foot and tamped it.*[13]

Enrollees sometimes worked in pairs, with one person making the hole and the second carrying the bag of trees and putting the seedling in and both tamping down the soil around it. Tree planting was not easy. Enrollees carried bags or boxes of seedlings on their shoulders and bent over to plant each tree. They described it as backbreaking work.[14]

The men and boys of the CCC planted millions of trees in Minnesota, often putting in thousands per day. Lorenz R. Lindstrom, a forest service supervisor, described one situation: "I've got a crew of the boys sorting trees . . . that will be planted tomorrow. We have about 100 men on planting now and they plant between 16,000 and 18,000 trees a day." Chester Erickson, a U.S. Forest Service superintendent, remembered how he got his teams to work: "Most of the planting crews was about a twenty-man crew, and we started a competition between whoever planted the most trees this week got a keg of beer. We'd try to get competition to get more trees planted."[15]

Big Lake camp officials near Cloquet recorded planting 304 acres of white pine, Norway pine, Scotch pine, and jack pine between the start-up of camp operations in 1933 and April 1, 1935. Between June 1935 and July 1, 1938, enrollees in the Larsmount camp planted 3,655,090 trees. These included 1,842,183 jack pine, 1,600,700 Norway pine, 169,163 white pine, and 42,974 white spruce. During the fall planting seasons, several crews averaged more than one thousand trees per planter per day. Similar results were reported by other forest camps.[16]

The demand for trees grew so large that existing tree nurseries were expanded and new ones created. Often run with CCC labor, these nurseries supplied millions of seedlings for planting. The Badoura, Lydick, Knife River, Eveleth, and Willow River nurseries were among those that supplied trees for the CCC to plant in federal and state forests. At Red Lake, the CCC-ID took over a small nursery that, by 1940, had produced four million trees for planting on the Red Lake and Consolidated Chippewa reservations.[17]

Tree planting led to another project for enrollees: gathering thousands of pounds of pinecones to supply seeds to grow new trees. After enrollees collected cones, they took them to nurseries where other enrollees opened the

Enrollees from the Spruce Lake national forest camp weed beds and rake paths in a white spruce transplant bed at the Knife River Nursery in 1940.

cones, extracted seeds, and planted them. When the resulting seedlings were large enough, enrollees trucked them to camps to be planted.[18]

The CCC didn't just plant trees; enrollees also worked to ensure the long-term health of forests. Even the newly planted trees received care. "[W]hen they planted the trees," Ernest Anderson recalled, "then the brush would grow around. . . . They'd send the crews out there to cut this brush down so the trees would get more light and no interference."[19]

Enrollees spent hundreds of thousands of hours on timber stand improvement, one of the most common conservation work projects. By thinning trees and clearing underbrush, the men and boys of the CCC helped maintain forests, encouraging healthy tree growth. Luke Walker described the work: "[We did] timber stand improvement. This was an action that had no real rule of thumb. You just went into a given area and removed some and left some—the object being removing where [it was] too thick to make good timber. The weak and crooked and the bent had to go." Paul Wood remembered, "We thinned the forest. In some cases where trees were starting to die, we could cut them down and bring them in." The goal was to leave behind forests with strong stands of trees, which would in turn create a vital, renewable resource.[20]

The CCC was also actively involved in disease control projects, another important element in maintaining healthy forests. One of the most common tree diseases in Minnesota during the CCC years was blister rust, a fungus that grows on white pine trees, usually killing them. Still a problem today, the fungus came to the United States from Europe around the turn of the twentieth

CCC-ID enrollees from the Nett Lake camp do slope planting to prevent topsoil from washing away. Notice the worker, upper right, preparing a hole, stakes marking seedling locations, and a box full of seedlings, one of which has just been planted by the man in the foreground.

century. Although trees in Europe generally were immune to it, the disease spread rapidly in this country and was first reported in Minnesota in 1916. The state enacted a blister rust control law in 1929, just one measure of the enormity of the problem. Forester Don Burcalow described what it took to get rid of blister rust:

> *I started work at Cass Lake in the Chippewa National Forest as a junior forester. My first job was when they gave me a crew of about forty men to start out on blister rust control work, which I had had one day's experience in at the Cloquet Forest Experiment Station. This is a job confined to white pine stands: . . . it was removing all of the gooseberry and currant bushes that you could find and pulling them up and hanging them up, because they were the ones that transferred the blister rust disease to the white pine. In other words, they were the alternate host. From Cass Lake, I was moved to several different camps within the Chippewa National Forest. . . . Whatever you got started on, you got stuck with. So, every place I went, I was the blister rust control man. My boss was a federal forest service employee who was in charge of the whole blister rust control program for Minnesota.*[21]

Blister rust control work was labor intensive but effective. As Lawrence Ritter, Sr., said, enrollees "could only pull the gooseberries and currants when

ccc workers did much to improve forest infrastructure, completing projects like this forestry road, built by enrollees from Big Lake camp near Roosevelt, ca. 1933.

the plants were leafed out. . . . They had to make sure they got all the bush, all the roots. If you pulled out a gooseberry bush and left some roots, it would grow back." The problem was not confined to state and federal forests: areas on several reservations also suffered from a blister rust invasion. Red Lake ccc-ID enrollees protected 12,311 acres of native white pine and 187 acres of planted white pine from blister rust damage.[22]

The ccc also ensured forest growth by reclaiming land, turning cutover farms back into the forested areas they had once been. The Clear River (also called the Norris) camp, built by the ccc in 1935 and now listed in the National Register of Historic Places, was the headquarters for a federal program known as the Beltrami Island Project. This project, one of two in Minnesota that were part of the Land Utilization Project authorized in 1937, came under the jurisdiction of the scs in 1938, but its work programs were overseen by the Department of Conservation. The two Minnesota projects—Beltrami Island and Pine Island—covered 1,540,000 acres in Beltrami, Roseau, Lake of the Woods, and Koochiching counties and were a pioneering experiment in relocation and land-use planning. Through the project, farmers on cutover lands were relocated and the land was reclaimed by the ccc, whose enrollees went to work "developing and managing forestry, wildlife and recreational resources."[23]

During the ccc era, forest service leaders placed a high priority on pre-

venting and fighting fires. The policy was influenced by destructive forest fires in the late nineteenth and early twentieth centuries and by the especially dry conditions of the 1930s. With both federal and state forestry leaders urging fire prevention, the men and boys of the CCC were naturally thrown into all aspects of this work. CCC-ID enrollees, for example, spent time stringing telephone lines (to ease communication in case of fire), clearing fire breaks, building truck and foot trails, building fire towers, and clearing dead and down timber—along with all the usual forest conservation work of planting trees and improving timber stands.

At forest camps, building fire trails was an important part of fire prevention work. Clarence Johnson described the process: "This one year, I was in charge of fire trails. I had a 75 Cat [Caterpillar] with a huge grader on it, and we had a bulldozer, and we had four trucks. We used to grade the road; then, wherever there was fill [areas where the road wasn't flat], we would use the trucks to haul dirt in there and make fills. A crew went ahead to chop the smaller trees down for the fire trails, and we made some pretty good roads." Harley Heegard, an enrollee who worked his way up to squad leader, remembered joining the road crew and driving a Caterpillar when he got to the camp: "They would build roads. The grader would roll rocks up on the road. I worked behind the grader throwing the rocks off the side of the road so that they didn't have the rocks on the road. I worked with them pretty near a year, and then I got a chance to work a little on the grader and also on the Cat. . . . Later on I went on steady on the Cat and on fire protection roads." Some sections of Minnesota's well-known trails were built by ccc enrollees for conservation and fire prevention access. Godfrey Rawlings remembered, "If you ever go up on the Gunflint Trail [which runs from Grand Marais to the Canadian border], I can say I was part of that."[24]

As part of their fire prevention work, enrollees strung and maintained thousands of miles of telephone wires and built and maintained fire towers. Fire towers were located on high ground whenever possible, standing taller than the trees around them, and were used to help spot forest fires. Building them was a job Claude Ingram called a "tough proposition." He remembered drilling and blasting into solid rock: "It was kind of a slow doggone job. It was all handwork." Although most have been removed, there are still a few ccc-built fire towers in northern Minnesota.[25]

ccc forest conservation work included preventing and fighting forest fires. This forest fire watchtower built by enrollees at the Cut Foot Sioux camp was one of almost 150 such towers the ccc erected in Minnesota.

Along with the ccc's emphasis on fire prevention came its commitment to fire fighting. The ccc-ID established forest fire training schools at the Consolidated Chippewa, Red Lake, and Pipestone agencies. By offering enrollees the necessary training for fighting forest fires, these schools provided an essential service to the state. They became part of the World War II defense effort after the ccc-ID ended.[26]

Nearly all enrollees knew they could be called upon to fight forest fires. During the fall fire season, regardless of anything else, fighting fires became everyone's job. Fully equipped trucks were ready to go at all times, passes to town were canceled, and enrollees were kept on standby, waiting for the call—often from an enrollee in a fire tower—that smoke had been sighted.

Enrollees vividly remember fire fighting as some of the hardest and most dangerous work they did. Depending on the size of the fire, enrollees from all forest camps in an area might be brought in. If more people were needed, they came in from camps across the state. When fighting forest fires, enrollees often stayed out for days at a time, supplied with food and water by runners. They dug firebreaks by hand and used hand pumps to spray water. Clarence Johnson remembered, "We used . . . the pump tank

During fire season, all Minnesota enrollees were on alert, ready to be transported to fight forest fires. It was hot and dangerous work, mostly done by hand. These enrollees are trying to keep ahead of the McFarlane Lake Fire in the Superior National Forest.

you put on your back. It was about a five-gallon pump can, had a hand pump on it. And, of course, the shovels for patrolling the fire lines."[27]

Raymond Noyes remembered the training he received:

Sometimes they would conduct school right out in the forest. I remember one was pertaining to fighting fires. And I learned from the old-timers, the foremen, many of whom were former loggers. There were a lot of old lumberjacks around, and many of them made very good foremen. I remember them telling us about conditions in fighting forest fires, how the best time to fight the fire would be early morning and late afternoon, at sunrise and sunset. The reason why, the wind commonly goes down at that time of the day. And, of course, the wind was our worst enemy in fighting fire.[28]

Ernest Anderson described fighting several big fires, including one in the Namakan-Crane Lake area of northern Minnesota:

[The fire] lasted over thirty days. We slept on the ground. They woke us up in the dark. We had our breakfast and took off for the job area. Stayed there until just before dark. Came back in, had our evening meal, and, of course, we was pretty tired. Soon as we got done with that, you were looking for a place to lay down for the night. And that was on the ground. No tents; on the ground. . . . In them days, it was all handwork. Shovel, grub hoe, mostly that, and an axe. [We would] clear a path—a "fire break," they called it—right down to the ground, so nothing could burn. But if a wind comes up, it was so dry, the spark would fly over and start in again.

Michael Sanchelli summed it up: "Believe me, nobody will ever know what it is to face an inferno until they actually get into it, with roaring flames above threatening to collapse on top of you and roaring flames on both sides wanting to engulf you, not to mention the searing heat."[29]

Many enrollees remember 1936 as the year of fires. With an extended period of low humidity, high temperatures, and extremely dry conditions, fires broke out frequently across northern Minnesota in July and August and again in October. Many enrollees spent a month or more fighting fires. The situation was severe enough to warrant a special section in the state Department of Conservation annual report that year.[30]

When the fall fire fighting season was over, enrollees in forest camps sometimes took on special projects. One type of work, evidence of which can still be seen throughout northern Minnesota, was constructing forest service buildings, adding to state and national forest infrastructure. CCC enrollees worked on water towers, warehouses, and latrines, among other assignments. Most CCC structures were small and utilitarian, but many, such as the Kabetogama and Marcell ranger stations, have proved durable and serviceable over the years. One better-known structure—the Minnesota Department of Natural Resources log building on the state fairgrounds—is visited by thousands of people each year. Another is the Chippewa National Forest headquarters in Cass Lake, built for $225,000 in 1935 and 1936 by CCC and WPA personnel.[31]

The Chippewa National Forest headquarters project—carried out with the help of LEMs such as Ike Boekenoogen, an expert in log building techniques—serves as an excellent example of CCC construction. It is made entirely, inside and out, from Minnesota forest products. The exterior is Scandinavian style notch-and-groove (chinkless) log construction. And many interior details, including the fifty-foot glacial stone fireplace designed by Nels Bergley, the wooden stairway, and the ironwork on the door hinges and fireplace, were made by hand. Chippewa National Forest personnel moved into the building on April 8, 1936, and continue to use it today. It was listed in the National Register of Historic Places in 1976, ten years before the standard national fifty-year age limit. Such projects help define the broad scope of work in the CCC's forest camps.[32]

During the CCC years, Minnesota's forests increased dramatically in number and size, with thirteen new state forests established in 1933 and another thirteen established two years later. Existing state forests and the Superior and Chippewa national forests also grew in the CCC era. Enrollees planted millions of trees in these new and expanded forests, giving rise to a popular nickname: "Roosevelt's Tree Army." Today, Walter Okstad, forest archeologist and historian at the Superior National Forest, says, "Whenever you see a stand of red pine about 10–12 inches in diameter, it is almost certain to have been planted by the CCC."[33]

Perhaps just as importantly, the hard-working men and boys of the CCC gave state forests a healthier infrastructure—in the shape of roads, buildings, fire towers, tree nurseries, and disease control programs—than existed before 1933. Forest service leaders still say the work of the CCC moved forest conservation and development in Minnesota twenty years ahead of where it would otherwise have been.

7: BUILDING UP PARKS

State and federal forests weren't the only public lands to benefit from ccc labor. Many enrollees also worked in Minnesota's state parks. Minnesota was one of the first states in the country to develop a park system, with the first state memorial site established at Camp Release near Montevideo in 1889. Itasca State Park, located at the headwaters of the Mississippi River, was established just two years later.

By 1925, the number of state parks had grown, but their management was uneven. Although in theory the Department of Forestry, the Game and Fish Commission, and the state auditor each administered some of the parks, in reality local advisory committees provided daily management. This situation began to change in 1925 when the Department of Conservation gained jurisdiction over state parks. It changed again in 1931 when the Department of Conservation was reorganized. With that reorganization, supervision of Minnesota's parks was consolidated under the Division of Forestry, led by Grover Conzet.[1]

When the ccc began its work, the National Park Service (NPS), under the U.S. Department of the Interior, oversaw work projects in state parks. Responding to the need for better in-state coordination, the park service appointed Harold W. Lathrop supervisor of ccc state park work in Minnesota in 1934 with a salary paid from federal funds. Almost immediately, state legislators began examining overall state park management and administrative needs. Their goal was to put state parks under the direction of someone just as highly trained in park management as the director of the state's Division of Forestry was in forest management. In 1935, the Minnesota legislature created the Division of State Parks within the Department of Conservation and appointed Lathrop as the first director of the system, which had by this time grown to thirty sites. Through the new office, Lathrop coordinated CCC work conserving existing parks and developing new ones, following NPS guidelines. The agency had several decades of development and management experience—based on the beliefs of John Muir—preserving and maintaining natural areas while making them available for public use. NPS personnel were in a position to make this knowledge available nationwide through the CCC.[2]

Work on Minnesota's state park system began quickly. On April 29, 1933, even before Lathrop's appointment, NPS officials contacted Minnesota conservation department personnel and asked them to begin work on architectural and landscape designs for the state's parks. At the Minnesota Central Design Office on the fifth floor of the Post Office and Federal Courts Building in St. Paul (now the Landmark Center), chief architect and Duluth native Edward W. Barber, architect V. C. Martin, landscape architect N. H. Averill, and engineer Oscar Newstrom began this task. In all, "about a dozen" architects and landscape architects, working with NPS regional office personnel, developed plans for Minnesota parks. They created design concepts, master plans, and site plans that emphasized an "appropriate relationship between the built environment and the natural landscape."[3]

Any plans developed at the Minnesota office in St. Paul had to first be approved by the NPS before CCC enrollees could start work. Conrad Wirth, son of Minneapolis park developer Theodore Wirth, was named by the NPS to oversee state park CCC work throughout the country. Developing a system of regional offices and inspectors, Wirth ensured that architects, landscape architects, park specialists, and engineers adhered to NPS guidelines and standards. Regional inspectors carried out these directives. In the camps, superintendents made sure projects were done according to the architect's plans. Bernard Penner, an LEM at the Gooseberry Falls State Park camp, remembered, "[The architect] and the engineer were in charge." Each superintendent was allowed up to ten foremen, at least two of whom had to have training in landscape architecture, to provide technical support. LEMS offered specialized guidance and training to enrollees, frequently while serving as crew foremen.[4]

CCC enrollees often arrived with little or no training or expertise, but they learned quickly on the job. Raymond Noyes noted, "[M]any of them were working for the first time in their lives. They had to learn the skills." Edward Schubert remembered, "It was strictly hands-on experience and learning."[5]

By June 1933, enrollees in Minnesota's first state park camps, following designs approved by the NPS regional office, began work in Scenic State Park

Enrollees in the veterans' camp at St. Croix State Park worked on a number of park projects. Here they are putting up a log building, probably in one of the group camp areas, ca. 1941.

in Itasca County, Jay Cooke State Park near Duluth, and Itasca State Park. Edward Barber remembered the situation: "you had to have a lot of work to have a CCC camp because these boys turned out a lot of work, you know." This work fit CCC goals and fulfilled national park conservation ideals by preserving and maintaining natural areas and making them available for public use. Enrollees got right to work: removing unneeded or undesirable structures, building new park structures, clearing lakes and ponds, improving beaches, landscaping the grounds, developing campgrounds, picnic grounds, overlooks, and parking areas, and restoring historic structures.[6]

Enrollees worked hard. Raymond Noyes remembered that, even with an ongoing emphasis on safety, there were "a lot of cut legs and feet" as he and others learned to use the tools. Like enrollees at other CCC camps, those at state park camps took pride in working all year round and in all conditions. Edward Schubert described one work assignment area: "There was poison ivy all over the place. Most of the fellows it didn't affect too much. We found out that if you got into poison ivy and started itching, we'd just take a little gasoline and rub it on our arms and leave it for five or ten minutes and then wash it off. Usually that was the end of it. . . . On some people the gasoline would react worse than the poison ivy, so beware!" Enrollee Weikko Seppo remembered, "[Some work] had to be done in the wintertime when it was all ice and everything was frozen. We never went out if it was more than ten degrees below zero."[7]

The boys and men of the CCC arrived at state parks that were always sce-

A work crew takes a break at the first of two CCC camps established at Whitewater State Park, ca. 1934.

nic but in some cases entirely undeveloped. "The area [of Whitewater State Park] was beautiful. But there was little else in the way of amenities to take care of people"—so said Frederick Johnson, recalling enrollees' arrival. Things didn't stay that way for long. Using designs from the state office, enrollees quarried limestone right in the park for buildings they constructed there.[8]

Much of the architecture in Minnesota's state parks was in the rustic style, in which buildings are designed to harmonize with nature while reflecting the individual site. Following NPS guidelines, architects fit buildings and structures into each park's natural setting and cultural context, incorporating native materials into their designs wherever possible. Edward Barber commented many years later: "we'd try to use native stone. We never imported stone for anything. . . . If a park didn't have stone, why, we didn't use stone." Designs by chief architect Barber and his staff of state architects are in twenty-two state parks, and CCC enrollees worked in twelve of those parks: Camden, Flandrau (formerly called Cottonwood River), Fort Ridgely, Gooseberry Falls, Itasca, Jay Cooke, Lake Bemidji, Monson Lake, St. Croix, Scenic, Sibley, and Whitewater. Work in the remaining ten parks was done by the WPA.[9]

"Our work, in modern terminology, was very labor intensive," one CCC enrollee remembered later. "Except for a fleet of dump trucks, the projects were completed with hand tools wielded by young men." Yet those young, largely untrained enrollees created buildings of lasting beauty. Some of the finest examples of CCC-built designs—all classified as rustic style architecture—include the refectory, concourse, caretaker's cabin, and entrance portals at Gooseberry Falls State Park; the River Inn at Jay Cooke State Park; the east contact station, Old Timer's Cabin, headquarters building, and Forest Inn at Itasca State Park; and the shelter building and bathhouse at Whitewater State Park. CCC craftsmanship is especially evident at Flandrau State Park near New Ulm; buildings there were made from local quartzite in a design that reflects the area's German heritage. The River Inn at Jay Cooke State Park, one of the largest CCC buildings in Minnesota, was made from local gab-

Enrollees in the second Gooseberry Falls State Park CCC camp built the water supply tower. The colors and patterns of the stonework throughout the park were carefully chosen by the LEM stonemasons.

bro, a dark rock quarried nearby. Jay Cooke State Park CCC enrollees also rebuilt the swinging suspension bridge over the St. Louis River in 1934–35 and reconstructed the historic Fond du Lac trading post, now no longer standing, in 1935. Reflecting the change in times and architectural styles, as well as pride in the work, Reuben Law, deputy director of parks, southern district, said later, "The [park] buildings that are being built [today] are entirely different in design than the buildings that we built in the CCC days. . . . [Y]ou can't afford to build [the CCC-built buildings] today, I suppose. . . . [But the new buildings] don't fit the landscape as well, either."[10]

The stonework at Gooseberry Falls State Park is some of the best known in the state. CCC enrollees built it all under the guidance of John Berini and Joe Cattaneo (also spelled Catanio), Italian American stonemasons from Duluth, and Axel Anderson, a Swede. This stonework features red, blue, brown, and black granite laid in artistic patterns. LEM Bernard Penner remembered finding the colors. According to Penner, the CCC quarried blue granite along the North Shore of Lake Superior near an area known as "A Bit of Norway," not far from East Beaver Bay. The dark rock was found in the same vicinity, and the red rock came from near the College of St. Scholastica in Duluth. Highlighting the attention to detail common in Minnesota's CCC state park structures, Penner described the importance of the colors: "Like that highway wall: that is all black rock. It didn't need any dressing up there. The buildings: you want more than just somber gray color. And that is where we hired a stonemason to come in. . . . He was a great man on laying out, making it look good. Artistic."[11]

Enrollees quarried the stone by hand, as Ray Glockner described: "I remember the first day at the quarry. Our crew pusher [leader] asked if any of us could drive a truck. About ten hands went up. He pointed to some wheelbarrows and said, 'There's your truck. Start loading them up with that stone and rock.'" Enrollee Raymond Noyes remembered the sense of pride he felt in helping build these structures: "[Some] boys could see the camps being more beneficial in the years to come, because a lot of the things that we had done were going to be on a permanent basis. Take Gooseberry State Park, with those rock constructed buildings. We could see where stuff like that would outlast us."[12]

CCC enrollees used log as well as stone construction. The newsletter of the World War I veterans' CCC camp at Sibley State Park, *Sibley Speaks,* described how Burt Morton, an LEM, selected trees for one of the buildings there:

> *The park was combed thoroughly for suitable dry white oak. The logs had to scale to a certain size. They had to be just so long and straight as a die. No large knots or dry rot would be considered. All in all it was quite a task to find material that would measure up to Mr. Morton's specifications. Many a day was spent in his company, tramping over the park in an attempt to find exactly what he wanted. Red oak, bur oak, and scarlet oak would not do. Nothing but the straightest, soundest, and finest of white oak.*

One of Minnesota's most well-known attractions, the dam topped by stepping-stones across the headwaters of the Mississippi River at Itasca State Park owes its existence to the men and boys of the CCC.

Some of the logs used in park projects were enormous. The Old Timer's Cabin at Itasca State Park, one of the first CCC-built state park structures, was constructed of logs so large just four of them made an entire wall.[13]

The same company of World War I veterans who did log construction at Sibley State Park also helped build the log and stone Forest Inn at Itasca State Park, the largest CCC-constructed park building in the state. Ole Evensen, a local woodsman, supervised the log work, while CCC blacksmith John Wiber made the metal fixtures. In 1935 Udert W. Hella, a regional inspector for the NPS, commented on the attention to detail paid by this crew of veterans doing stonemasonry work for the Forest Inn: "[They] had a continuous horizontal joint running almost the entire length of the wall. This had to be broken up, a job that 'only required six or eight hours.' . . . To make this stonework look rustic and random required a great deal of planning and skill."[14]

At Itasca, the enrollees also constructed one of the best-known tourist sites in the state. In addition to a pageant grounds at the park, they hauled 40,000 cubic yards of fill to create a forty-four-foot dam topped with stepping-stones across the headwaters of the Mississippi River.[15]

At Scenic State Park, described as a "gem" and "the most ideal" of any park in the state, the CCC developed an "ideal campground location" for tourists. In 1935, the park's log and stone shelter pavilion, designed by Barber and built by enrollees, was featured in the 1935 National Park Service publication

Park Structures and Facilities, which stated that the best park structure "would assuredly specify logs and log construction from Minnesota." The shelter contains rustic style furniture built by CCC enrollees under the direction of Ole Evensen, along with paintings by enrollee William Lewis.[16]

Fort Ridgely State Park represents an example of combined state park and historic site facilities. The original fort, built by the U.S. Army in 1853, is most closely associated with the history of the U.S.–Dakota War of 1862 (sometimes called the Sioux Uprising). At the park, the CCC not only put up new buildings using locally quarried Morton rainbow granite but also did an archaeological survey under the direction of the Minnesota Historical Society. This survey defined the locations of eight fort buildings no longer standing. CCC enrollees partially restored one original building, the fort commissary, to house a state-run museum and a meeting hall. Within all of Minnesota's state parks, the fort commissary is the only remaining historic reconstruction done by the CCC.[17]

St. Croix State Park is another example of an innovative program involving the CCC. The park grew out of an NPS program, headed by Conrad Wirth, designed to transform lands unsuited for agricultural or industrial use into recreational areas. Each Recreational Demonstration Area (RDA) was usually located within fifty miles of a major metropolitan area and was meant to allow underprivileged children to enjoy the outdoors. Following NPS guidelines, buildings and landscapes in RDAs were designed to fit closely with the locale's

National Park Service officials, impressed by CCC work at Scenic State Park, called it a "gem" constructed in an "ideal campground location for tourists." This park pavilion was built by the CCC, ca. 1940.

natural features and scale. Perhaps the most important structures in RDAS were the camp units, designed to accommodate up to twenty-four campers—boys, girls, or families. Each camp unit—RDAS typically contained up to four—had its own lodge and latrine and four to six sleeping cabins.[18]

The St. Croix RDA, developed on cutover lands acquired in 1934, was one of the largest in the country. CCC enrollees, along with WPA workers, built three camp units, encompassing about one hundred buildings in all. Each camp unit was named for its location—the St. John's Landing Group Camp, the Head of the Rapids Group Camp, and the Norway Point Group Camp—and was set apart from the other two and from the central administration area. Signs pointing to all locations were made from half-round pine logs with four-inch gouged letters, according to Andy Anderson, a CCC enrollee assigned to the camp sign shop.[19]

CCC enrollees built several structures at St. John's Landing Group Camp, the first camp unit completed. It opened in July 1936 to provide a "healthy outdoor experience" for ten- to fourteen-year-old girls from urban families on relief. After completion, the St. Croix RDA was transferred to the state, where it became part of Minnesota's state park system in 1943. Many of its RDA buildings are still in use today. St. Croix State Park, now one of the largest in the state park system, is listed in the National Register of Historic Places and was designated a national historic landmark in 1997, largely because of the historic value of its CCC buildings and structures.[20]

In a program closely related to CCC state park camps, enrollees also were assigned to highway wayside camps. The Minnesota Highway Department established the Roadside Development Division in 1932. At least one half of one percent of highway funds had to be spent on promoting safety, construction, economic maintenance, and beautification. The CCC helped make this work possible. They completed projects out of four camps, supervised jointly in Minnesota by the NPS and the Roadside Development Division. Enrollees at these camps helped design and build wayside rest stops on Mille Lacs and Leech Lake and in such areas as the North Shore of Lake Superior near Knife River and Lutsen. They also developed another North Shore site, the Cascade River overlook, with hiking trails, a footbridge, and a public area. The Cascade River overlook was one of the first projects to incorporate natural rock outcroppings into a scenic overlook and served as a demonstration project for this type of highway design.[21]

In 1938, spurred on by the work of the CCC and the partnership between the state and the NPS, the Minnesota Department of Conservation prepared its first long-range plan for state park development. The Park, Parkway, and Recreational Area Study grew out of the 1936 federal act of the same name. It defined policies and standards for using parks and recreational areas. The study also set forth the goal of developing a statewide, efficient, and economical park and recreation system—a park within thirty miles of every resident. It set the standard for ongoing state park development in Minnesota and helped serve as a guide for the ccc's work through the remaining years of the program's operation in the state.[22]

Much of the future growth envisioned in the 1938 study would occur on foundations laid by the ccc. According to Conrad Wirth, the ccc accomplished fifty years' worth of state park work in fewer than ten years. In 1942, as the ccc was nearing its end, Minnesota officials said the value of its improvements, using even the most conservative estimates, exceeded the "total value of lands purchased and improvements" in the state during the fifty-three years that Minnesota had had a state park system. Minnesota's ccc enrollees expanded existing parks and developed new ones, constructing 119 buildings and other structures in the process.[23]

The impact of the ccc is visible still in many of Minnesota's state parks. At Camden, Flandrau, Fort Ridgely, Gooseberry Falls, Itasca, Jay Cooke, Lake Bemidji, Monson Lake, St. Croix, Scenic, Sibley, and Whitewater state parks, evidence of ccc work abounds. Pass through the entrance portals at Flandrau State Park or touch the rough stone retaining walls at Gooseberry Falls State Park, and you will see the ccc's legacy up close. Stand in the shadow of the huge logs used to build the Old Timer's Cabin in Itasca State Park, then stride across the headwaters of the Mississippi River on the walkway that men and boys constructed years ago. In each place, you will experience the work of the ccc—a lasting contribution to Minnesota's state parks, a legacy in land and stone.[24]

8: PRESERVING SOIL, WATER, AND TRADITIONS

The men and boys of the ccc did much to conserve parks and forests in Minnesota. But their work protecting and preserving the state's soil, water, and traditions was just as important. Through soil conservation programs, ccc enrollees kept wind and water from carrying away the state's rich dirt. Enrollees also conducted drought relief programs and monitored wildlife that used the state's precious water resources. Finally, through several unique projects of the ccc-ID, enrollees preserved and celebrated important facets of the state's Native American cultures and traditions.

Work started first to protect the land itself, stemming the tide of erosion. Soil erosion was one of the most severe conservation problems in the United States in the ccc's early years. Photographs of huge clouds of topsoil blowing off fields are some of the most remembered and easily identified images of the Great Depression. They gave rise to the term *Dust Bowl;* the first of these great dust storms occurred on May 11, 1934. Although Minnesota was not one of the Dust Bowl states, it suffered from water and wind erosion, which led to serious topsoil losses. Approximately 46 percent of the state's total land area was affected by erosion, including the Minnesota River valley and much southern Minnesota farmland. Worst hit was the Driftless Area of southeastern Minnesota: Houston, Fillmore, Winona, Olmsted, Wabasha, and Goodhue counties. Other areas, such as Rice County, were also heavily affected.[1]

THE BEST SECURITY IS SOIL SECURITY

As farmland blew or flooded away, people began to understand the need for effective soil conservation. Editorial cartoons published by the U.S. Soil Conservation Service helped spread the message.

In April 1933, before any CCC soil erosion camps were established, work started on two model terracing projects in Houston and Winona counties. Both projects were designed to teach area farmers how to use soil conservation techniques. H. B. Roe, from the Institute of Agriculture at the University of Minnesota, directed the projects, working with extension agents for each county.[2]

The state's first soil erosion camps were set up later that spring. From those camps, CCC members went to work on flood and erosion control programs to stabilize farmland and encourage long-term productivity in southeastern counties. Work projects were overseen by the U.S. Forest Service, the Department of Agriculture at the University of Minnesota, the DOC Drainage and Water Division, and the Minnesota Highway Department. Enrollees in the Caledonia and Houston camps, for example, worked on erosion control on farms and along highways, attempting, in part, to slow runoff filling lakes Winona and Como with silt. Those in other camps established at that time—Red Wing, Wabasha, Winona, Preston, Chatfield, and Rochester—did similar work. These first soil erosion camps were temporary, and enrollees lived in tents. When autumn came, they closed and their enrollees were transferred elsewhere.[3]

Initially, all Minnesota's CCC soil erosion camps were temporary. But a visit from President Franklin D. Roosevelt to Rochester, Minnesota, on August 8, 1934—at which he received dozens of requests from area farmers for new soil conservation demonstration projects—helped spotlight the importance of soil erosion conservation work in the state.

When Roosevelt visited Rochester, his honor guard was made up of CCC enrollees from area soil conservation camps. Claude Darst described the day:

Roosevelt dedicated some things in Rochester. . . . They drilled us pretty hard. We rode in trucks [from the camps] with no canopy over the top, just benches. It was on the hottest day of the year. I was put right opposite where Roosevelt was with his convertible. I must have stood there for an hour in the sun, as close as you and I are now. He had a big smile for everybody. Terrific showman. He was the "man of the hour." When it was all over, we had to ride clear back to Houston in that hot sun. It's one of those days I am proud of. I was there for it.[4]

In 1935, just months after Roosevelt's visit, soil erosion came under the direction of the new Soil Conservation Service (SCS) and camps like the one Claude Darst served at became permanent. Throughout the administrative changes from the SES to the SCS, the CCC continued its work, guided by the soil conservation principles of national and state leaders. While the bulk of CCC soil conservation work in the state began after the Soil Conservation Service took over, in 1935 Minnesota already had three demonstration projects in place—at Beaver Creek, Deer and Bear creeks, and Gilmore Creek—all of which benefited from CCC labor.[5]

The Beaver Creek Project (34,530 acres) was located at the center of a large eroded area drained by Beaver Creek, a tributary of the Root River, itself a tributary of the Mississippi River. Prior to soil conservation work, the area had lost an average of 3.51 inches of topsoil on cultivated land. One hundred twenty-two farms participated in the project. The Deer-Bear Creek Project (about 50,000 acres) was drained by Deer and Bear creeks, both of which also are tributaries of the Root River. The Gilmore Creek Project was the smallest at 5,600 acres, covering the Gilmore Creek watershed, which drained into Lake Winona. Within two months, over half the farms in the Gilmore Creek area had signed up for the program. By 1938, all but one of the fifty-five farms in the watershed area were involved in it, making it the project with the highest participation rate in the state.[6]

Gilmore Creek was one of several demonstration projects in Minnesota that eventually garnered national attention. Describing the project, the Soil

Plowed furrows, the beginning of contour strip farming, at Gilmore Creek, a CCC soil conservation work project. Much of this kind of erosion abatement work may still be seen today throughout southeastern Minnesota.

Enrollees quarried limestone by hand to build dams and de-acidify soil, tasks typical of soil conservation work done by the ccc across southeastern Minnesota.

Conservation Service said in 1938, "Of the 176 Soil Conservation Service projects now demonstrating erosion control projects in 45 states and Puerto Rico, none is more famous, nor more spectacular, than the Gilmore Creek project in Winona, Minnesota." The report went on to describe how soil conservation work on the project had "healed a sick valley" through changes in crop systems, use of contour farming and terraces, grazing protection, and woodland planting.[7]

Support for demonstration projects was so strong that area farmers often worked with the soil conservation leaders to recruit more farmers to join. Participation was voluntary but entailed a five-year conservation agreement. That agreement guaranteed farmers an erosion control plan designed specifically to the needs of their land—along with ccc labor to carry it out. Work program leaders at the ccc camp developed the specifics of the plan, identifying what the landowner would do and what the ccc would do (typically cut fence posts, provide lime, furnish and plant trees, and so on). As John Buskowiak, a soil conservation camp enrollee, recalled, "We built miles and miles of fence for farmers to teach them about strip farming and contour farming."[8]

For all ccc projects designed to preserve and protect the land, the scs furnished manpower, planning help, equipment, and materials—seed, seedlings, lime, wire, fertilizer, and cement. Working in a radius of about eight to twenty miles from each camp, enrollees put in hours protecting stream and lake banks, building ditches and check dams, terracing, planting to stem sheet erosion, and quarrying limestone for erosion control projects. These projects were designed to help hold the land in place and absorb moisture, thereby sustaining levels of production while protecting the topsoil.[9]

Eldor Rahn remembered his work quarrying and crushing limestone to build erosion control dams and to de-acidify the soil: "We quarried the rock by hand. . . . It was hard work." Using the rock, the ccc built flumes to direct water flow, retaining dams in gullies, and walls along highways and roads. Then, enrollees graded, sodded, and seeded ditches and side slopes as needed. Victor Pope described building by hand these flumes, many of which are still in use today: "We done a lot of sod-rock flumes. Rock and sod laid in a big ditch with the banks sloped down, so they don't wash out any deeper. Done for soil erosion."[10]

Claude Darst remembered building dams to stop gullies from forming:

> *We worked on the dams. We built brush dams and dams built out of native stone. [Brush ravines were used] in a small ravine or pasture where the soil was washing down there. And so we would dig it out and pile brush in there. And we would keep all that dirt back that was washing away. Save that farmland from going to New Orleans. The big gullies, that was where we put the native stone [dams] in. We had to learn how to do that. It wasn't built with cement blocks or bricks. We had to shape the native stone. You didn't dare have it over a quarter of an inch off. I learned on the job. The work was done by the [enrollees] themselves. The native stone dams are hard to find now. They conserved all that soil. It's built all up now; you have a hard time even finding them. In other words, it's reclaimed land. It worked.*[11]

Limestone dams, such as this one built by enrollees in the Chatfield (Little Sahara) camp, were permanent conservation treatments for areas prone to water erosion. Over time, the dams became less visible, yet they continued to stop soil loss and prevent further damage.

Soil conservation work was not confined to southeastern Minnesota even in the first years. During the summer of 1934, the water supply for communities in the Red River Valley began to noticeably diminish, so three soil conservation camps were assigned to clean up about four hundred miles of the Red River from Fargo to Breckenridge, as well as the Otter Tail, Red Lake, and Clearwater rivers. At these drought/water conservation camps, men and boys were given the job of removing debris and sandbars and clearing the rivers of weeds, ensuring that affected communities would have water. Enrollees at Waterville, another camp assigned to work on water conservation projects, helped build dams in Le Sueur, Rice, Scott, and Waseca counties. These dams eventually held over 50,000 acre-feet of water.[12]

Soil conservation camps weren't the only ones actively protecting water resources. Enrollees in forest and state park camps also worked on special projects fighting drought. Many of the CCC years were exceptionally dry. Minnesota responded in 1934 by establishing six state forest camps and four state park camps to focus on drought relief in other parts of the state. CCC enrollees at these camps, along with enrollees at a soil conservation camp dedicated to drought relief, built dams to add to the average size of lakes. This in turn allowed extra water to seep into underground reservoirs and increase total supplies. E. V. Willard reported on the success of the program in 1936 when he told members of the Conservation Commission, "our plans for conserving waters by increasing storage facilities within natural lakes are setting the pace and are copied by states and the federal government wherever opportunities for water conservation of this class develops."[13]

The CCC in Minnesota also conducted Bureau of Biological Survey work, tracking how wildlife used the state's water resources. Biological survey camps were established to help conserve wildlife, particularly migratory waterfowl and big game animals. The camps were first run under the U.S. Department of the Interior and then the Bureau of Biological Survey of the U.S. Department of Agriculture. In 1939, the biological survey merged with the Bureau of Fisheries in the Department of Commerce to form the Fish and Wildlife Service (FWS), and the new department was put back under the direction of the Department of the Interior. Biological survey camps, also called migratory waterfowl camps, came under FWS direction in 1940.[14]

Enrollees in Bureau of Biological Survey/FWS camps improved migratory waterfowl habitat by building dams and dikes to control water, planting wildlife food and cover-producing vegetation, planting trees as windbreaks and for wildlife cover, providing stream and lake bank protection, and constructing feeding boxes, nesting islands, and wildlife shelters. They also built truck trails, bridges, lookout towers, fire lanes, and administrative buildings and strung telephone lines on the refuge sites. Minnesota's three biological survey camps were responsible for this work along the "natural flyway" of birds from Canada to the Gulf of Mexico in the Thief Lake, Tamarac Lake, and Rice Lake migratory waterfowl refuges.[15]

Enrollees install soil conservation treatments on hilly land along Hudson Road in Woodbury, 1937.

Bureau of Biological Survey/FWS camps used the resources of three CCC game food nurseries in Minnesota—at Gheen, Owen Lake, and Wilton. There, enrollees grew cedar, mountain ash, mountain maple, dogwood, grape, balsam, and high bush cranberry seedlings to provide windbreaks and wildlife cover and habitat. In 1938, CCC survey crews from Company 1722 on Bustie's Lake documented one of the largest wild celery beds in the Midwest, parts of which were collected and transplanted to other lakes to supply game birds with food.[16]

Getting the work done wasn't easy, and conditions at camps were not always perfect. Claude Darst described summers at his soil conservation camp: "The mosquitoes were so bad they finally gave us mosquito netting for our cots. The fish flies hit another time. They had to go out with big highway scrapers and get them out of there." Victor Pope remembered winters: "If it got real cold, I think we didn't go out that day. But then, some days we worked on Saturday to make up for it." John Buskowiak, who cut fence posts along the Whitewater River in southeastern Minnesota, recalled unwelcome visitors to the work site: "Those bluffs above the Whitewater were loaded with rattlesnakes. It was nothing to bring in ten or twelve snakes a day into camp."[17]

Enrollees—particularly in soil conservation camps—did whatever work was called for. John Buskowiak described the duties at his camp this way: "As

I remember the boys who worked in the field were divided into five different crews with a foreman for each crew. Some were on the surveying crew, some on the sod and rock flume crew, some were fence post cutting crew, some on the fencing crew." Jim Flaherty said, "I had various jobs. The ones that I stayed with the most were fence crew, sod laying crew for flumes, and, in the winter, permanent structures. . . . We would cut trees from the farmer's land and make the fence posts, and then the farmer would supply the barbed wire and staples, and we would put up three- and four-strand fences on his property." Victor Pope added, "We fenced a lot for farmers. We fenced in the trees; otherwise the cattle would get in and step them down when they were small. After the trees got bigger, they could let the cattle in there. We cut the fence posts right in the woods. We always used oakwood. We never peeled them. We just cut them the right length and then we planted them. We split them if they were too big. We used barbed wire." After his stint making fence posts, John Buskowiak learned to operate a Caterpillar tractor and other equipment: "Well I took the Caterpillar crew and after about two weeks I was digging cow ponds for farmers with the Cat and Tumble Bug and also building dikes around the hills in contour fashion to enable the farmers to cut down on erosion."[18]

When necessary, enrollees in soil conservation camps also fought forest fires. During fire seasons in the late summer and fall, convoys of trucks carried men from southern soil conservation service camps up north to federal and state forests. There, soil conservation service enrollees worked alongside ccc enrollees from camps throughout the state in difficult and often uncomfortable conditions, staying as long as a month when needed, before they were sent back to their own camps.[19]

As with enrollees in other types of ccc camps, they also planted trees. Victor Pope described the work:

> *We used to plant trees. Every spring, plant a lot of trees. We planted oaks and maple and walnut and pine. We never planted any willow. They weren't too hard to plant, but it was hard on the back. We planted them where the farmers wanted them. We dug a hole with a round rod and then filled it in again with a spade. We had a lot of small trees. Planted them three, four feet apart. Had the trees in gunnysacks. We carried them on our backs. They weren't too terribly heavy, but the worst job was bending over all the time.*[20]

Tree planting was an important part of soil conservation, helping protect vulnerable land and rebuilding lost hardwood forests. In 1937, enrollees planted almost 1.4 million trees in southeastern Minnesota, including 460,000 conifers, 790,000 hardwoods, and 145,000 shrubs, while collecting almost 20,000 pounds of hardwood seeds for future plantings. Tree planting supported a nursery in Winona, which started in 1935 and operated until 1954. In 1938, the nursery contained 18.5 million coniferous and deciduous trees, mostly raised from seed, ready for enrollees to plant. In 1992, Eldor Rahn described the renewable results of this work: "The boys planted them. They cut them last year."[21]

In Minnesota, soil conservation camps had an impact that went beyond the soil. In April 1937, responding to an initiative from President Roosevelt, the state passed the Soil Conservation District Law to ensure that new soil conservation techniques would be "implemented beyond the demonstration areas." The state's first Soil Conservation District (SCD), the Burns-Homer-Pleasant District, was organized on May 3, 1938. Today, Minnesota has ninety-one such districts, administered through the Board of Soil and Water Resources, the University of Minnesota Extension Service, the Department of Natural Resources, the Pollution Control Agency, the Department of Agriculture, and the Department of Health.[22]

As was the CCC, the CCC-ID was organized into regions for administrative purposes. Nationally, there were nine regions; Minnesota, Wisconsin, and South Dakota were in the Lake States region with headquarters in Minneapolis. The region was administered by J. H. Mitchell, district supervisor. William Heritage, working with Norman Scherer, was production coordinating officer.[23]

Enrollees in CCC-ID camps worked on projects that had significant impact on the conservation of reservation resources. George Morrison remembered this work at the Grand Portage camp. "I worked outside in the woods. Foresters were foremen and told us what to do. We spent every day pulling up small trees that were beginning to be diseased. Could have been white pine that got blister rust. We pulled them out of the ground so the disease wouldn't spread." As with all enrollees, Indian enrollees worked in every kind of weather. A February 1934 issue of *Indians at Work* described winter conditions at Nett Lake: "In spite of bursting thermometers, blinding snows and a few hours of daylight, the Chippewa Indian Emergency Conservation Workers carry on—snowed in, to be sure, but not under."[24]

In addition to standard conservation projects, enrollees at several Minnesota CCC-ID camps worked on programs directly related to Native culture and heritage. Enrollees on the Nett Lake Reservation built a stop-log dam in 1936 to regulate water levels for wild rice production, bringing the reservation into a "new era in which water management became an integral part of wild rice management." Rice Lake camp unit enrollees on the White Earth Reservation cleared five wild rice campsites of about ten acres each, furnished them with sanitary facilities and docks, and dredged six-foot canals to make unloading full canoes easier. At one campsite, under sixteen inches of sand, crews uncovered two rice roasting pits containing broken bits of pottery. Officials at the Minnesota Historical Society, informed of the find, said the pits probably dated to the seventeenth century, when the Dakota, or Sioux, occupied the area. The Rice Lake project was singled out by the commissioner of Indian Affairs as "unique" in the whole CCC-ID system and worthy of "praises in highest terms."[25]

The CCC-ID was involved not just in standard conservation work projects but also in projects tied to native tradition and culture. One example is this visitor contact station at Pipestone National Monument, built by the CCC-ID and shown in a photograph from about 1950.

A CCC-ID crew rests at the end of the first day's work on the North West Company Fur Post site. CCC-ID enrollees would eventually complete the reconstruction of several major buildings at the post, a historic fur trade site at Grand Portage on the North Shore of Lake Superior.

When the Pipestone National Monument was established in 1937 as part of the National Park Service to protect quarries sacred to many Native American groups, the site already had picnic tables and a shelter built by the CCC-ID. In 1939, an educational program on maple sugar production was held at the Nay-tah-waush and Beaulieu (Consolidated Chippewa) sites. Through it, program leaders taught sugar bush improvement and modern maple sugar production.

Of all the Minnesota CCC-ID projects, perhaps the most well known is the reconstruction of the North West Company Fur Post, a historic fur trade site at Grand Portage on the North Shore of Lake Superior. Grand Portage ("the great carrying place") was part of an age-old route connecting Lake Superior with inland waterways used first by Indians and later also by fur traders. Between 1778 and 1802, a large fur trading organization, the North West Company, built a summer rendezvous and supply center there, on the shores of Lake Superior. In 1933, CCC-ID enrollees started work by clearing nine miles of the old Grand Portage trail to lessen fire danger in the area. Little additional work was done for several years until the superintendent of the Consolidated Chippewa Agency and the Minnesota Historical Society formed plans to reconstruct the old fur post stockade, at which Indians had conducted business with fur traders. Conceived jointly by the Chippewa and the

After assisting with archaeological studies at the Grand Portage site, CCC-ID enrollees reconstructed the wooden stockade and the Great Hall. Here, a crew finishes up roof trusses in winter 1938–39.

historical society, the purpose of the project was to research and restore the historic site.[26]

The project began in 1936 with archeological work. Under the direction of Ralph D. Brown, a crew of CCC-ID enrollees located the original stockade. Eventually, this work yielded three pickets from the original stockade, providing workers with an exact pattern and wood type (white cedar) for reconstruction. George Morrison, an enrollee in the CCC-ID camp at Grand Portage, remembered the attention paid to detail. Adhering to the original style of construction, he and other enrollees fashioned wooden pegs rather than nails to hold the structure together. He said, "I remember making the pegs that went into the holes to hold the logs together. We whittled dowels down, then put points on them like a nail. The local blacksmith made the metal hinges for the doors and things."[27]

Although funds were always a concern, the CCC-ID and others involved in the project decided to maintain a high level of accuracy even if it involved extra cost. After finding the original fence posts, William Heritage reported to the commissioner of Indian Affairs on October 1, 1936, that it was possible to "reconstruct the stockade in such a manner as to be an almost exact replica of the original stockade" but that "a large part of the material now prepared will not be acceptable to the [Minnesota Historical] Society because of its large size and it will be necessary to cut a large amount of additional timber as only about half of that on hand will be acceptable to the Historical Society." In spite of the time and cost involved, CCC-ID enrollees cut new pickets and began work on the post stockade. That year, they also built a monument at the fort for $263.37 and spent an additional $56.55 to build a small monument at the site of old Fort Charlotte on the western end of the Grand Portage trail.[28]

Due to lack of funding, construction on the project stopped for a time after completion of the stockade, not resuming until 1938. Meanwhile, CCC-ID enrollees, working under the direction of Minnesota Historical Society archaeologists, uncovered the full perimeters of the stockade, the stone foundation of the great hall (the business and social center of the stockade), a well containing a bucket and samples of "Spanish brown" paint used on the buildings, the possible remains of thirteen other buildings and structures, and hundreds of artifacts including trade goods, pipes, hinges, and nails. When new funds were finally released in October 1938, enrollees began work rebuilding the great hall on its original stone foundation. They also completed the stockade, putting the palisades in the original trenches and the gate in its original location. Participants in a WPA handicraft project prepared exhibits for the great hall. With this, the project was complete.[29]

The Grand Portage project was much more expensive than originally anticipated. Although in danger of being canceled several times by CCC director Robert Fechner, it evolved into one of the most important CCC work projects in Minnesota. The CCC-ID–built Great Hall, which burned in 1969, was reconstructed on the same site by the National Park Service, and the archeological work defining the site helped lay the groundwork for continued preservation of what is now the Grand Portage National Monument. In 1940, John Collier described the impact of not just the Grand Portage reconstruction but of all the many and varied CCC-ID projects this way: "There is no part of Indian country, there are few functions of Indian life, where it has not made an indispensable contribution."[30]

In their work rebuilding historic structures, fencing farmland to fight erosion, battling severe drought, and preserving habitat for animals, the men and boys of the CCC and CCC-ID left behind a legacy for generations of Minnesotans to enjoy. But while they could see the impact of their work on the land, water, and traditions of the state, many enrollees felt an equally impressive change within themselves. "My days in the C.C.C.'s cannot be expressed in words," one soil conservation enrollee recalled. "You have to live in the mind of an 18 year old boy. I must say that it taught me the respect of authority, of individual responsibility, how to work and get along with others. My days in the C's developed me into a man."[31]

9: THE CCC'S IMPRINT ON MINNESOTA

The ccc's impact was great, and even in its day the program was popular. Despite political difficulties that surrounded many other New Deal "alphabet" programs, the ccc received support both from the general population and from conservation administrators. A poll of the general public taken by the American Institute of Public Opinion in April 1936 reported that 82 percent of respondents favored the ccc. The poll also asked the opinion of enrollees, 97.87 percent of whom said they favored the program. While falling just short of unanimous, poll results indicated overwhelming national support for the ccc among those benefiting most from it.[1]

Yet in spite of its popularity, the ccc remained a temporary program. The first of two efforts to make it permanent began in 1936. The program was then at the height of its popularity, and it was an election year. FDR mentioned the ccc often during the campaign. The push to permanency seemed strong, but some of President Roosevelt's own advisors favored continuing the ccc on a temporary basis. The army, for its part, was not anxious to become part of an ongoing program.

In his annual budget message for 1937, Roosevelt suggested extending funding for the ccc (scheduled to end that year) and making the program permanent. He made the request again on April 5, asking for a permanent enrollment of 300,000 young men and veterans in the CCC, as well as 10,000 Indians in the CCC-ID. FDR also requested 5,000 enrollees in U.S. territories. But while nearly everyone liked the CCC, a majority of members of Congress, not ready to follow the president's lead, supported extending the program only on a temporary basis. Congress approved a bill which Roosevelt signed into law in June 1937, extending the program for three years as an independent agency.[2]

As the United States began to emerge from the Great Depression and the economy strengthened, fewer men and boys enrolled in the CCC. From a high point in 1935 of approximately 18,500 enrollees, by July 1937 enrollment in Minnesota declined to about 8,700, of which 6,775 hailed from the state. Calvin Drews described a sense of heightened experience as enrollees prepared to leave his camp: "During the last month I have made more contacts and received more experiences which will help me in later life than I thought possible in such a short time." Allen Mapes summed up post-CCC opportunities for enrollees: "There was any number learned a trade of their choice, from cooks and bakers and mechanics, carpenters, bookkeepers, any—just about anything you wanted you could go to school for. And it was good schools. . . . There was a lot of boys come out of there with educations that they could go to a job and earn a living the rest of their lives."[3]

A CCC enrollee strings telephone wire in August 1940. This work was done in forests to aid communications and was especially intended to help fight forest fires.

In 1939, the issue of making the CCC permanent came up one last time. But in spite of President Roosevelt's continued support, Congress again voted for a temporary extension. On August 8, 1939, the president signed a bill authorizing funding for the CCC until July 1, 1943, and changing the program's status. With this bill, the CCC was no longer independent but instead was part of the newly formed Federal Security Agency (FSA), along with several other agencies overseeing health, education, and social programs.[4]

Enrollment numbers in the Minnesota CCC changed little during much of the late 1930s. But as the economy continued to strengthen into the early 1940s, those numbers dropped. Those who did enroll found it easier to leave the program as the nation geared up for war and more jobs became available. Many found work in defense industries. In northern Minnesota, enrollees left camps to work in iron mines, which were expanding again because of the National

Defense Program. In Congress, support for the program was weakening. A request to extend the CCC on July 2, 1942, was not successful, and Congress ordered the program's complete liquidation by June 30, 1943. In Minnesota, the end of the camps and active work programs came earlier, in 1942, when the last camps in the state closed.[5]

During its years of active operation, the CCC averaged fifty-one camps per year in Minnesota, although at the program's peak in 1935 the state had 104 camps. Minnesota ranked ninth in the country in 1935 for the number of camps operating in a state. In 1941 and 1942, however, the number of CCC camps in the state and nationwide decreased rapidly. Those that remained open operated almost consistently at low company strength or as side camps. During the final years, enrollment in many camps was half or less than half of the full two hundred–person company strength. Most camps also were showing their age, some needing "complete rehabilitation and reconstruction." Many were short of commanding officers.[6]

In 1942, reports on the Gunflint camp, one of the last operating forest camps in Minnesota, showed there had been four changes in command in four months. By this time the United States was at war, and the current commander expected to be called to active duty at any time. As conditions at the Gunflint camp declined and company strength decreased, there were, for the first time, reports of safety and fire hazards, unsanitary conditions, and poor policing of camp buildings. Conditions were similar at other Minnesota camps in the last years of the CCC. Enrollment in the state fell to almost nothing as the last camps closed in preparation for the CCC's final shutdown. All camps in Minnesota closed permanently by the summer of 1942.[7]

By this time, most of the regular and reserve army personnel who had staffed CCC camps were being called to active duty. Nick Radovich remembered a "great" commanding officer who was called up and later killed at Wake Island. The fears of some in the CCC—that, as Michael Sanchelli put it, "If war starts they have to go first!"—were unfounded. Yet when the United States did enter World War II, many current and former enrollees chose to join the armed forces.[8]

While some saw the end of the CCC as a natural consequence of an improving economy and a coming war, others fought to keep the program going. When word arrived that CCC-ID funding also would end in 1943, Minnesota reservation superintendents protested. Although jobs were opening up in defense work and many Native Americans also were enrolling in the armed forces, requests to continue the CCC-ID flowed in. The Pipestone Sioux Agency superintendent wrote, "We cannot too strongly urge the necessity of a continuation of the CCC-ID program." In Minnesota, the CCC-ID so successfully emphasized leadership training that the percentage of white supervisors dropped from 70 percent in 1933 to 30 percent in 1937. Overall, the CCC-ID was a strong factor in the ability of many Indian families to withstand the Great Depression.[9]

Ojibwe Indians use traditional methods to gather wild rice in 1938. Work on a rice camp on the White Earth Reservation, done in cooperation with E. J. Carlson, Indian Service forest supervisor, was singled out as an exemplary project worthy of the highest praise by national CCC-ID leaders.

Tied as it was to the CCC, however, the CCC-ID ended on July 10, 1943. Afterward, Bureau of Indian Affairs commissioner John Collier said, "The ending of the CCC was a heavy, heavy blow to Indian Service, to all Indians, and to social policy in the United States. It is just that: a heavy and undeserved blow." Noting that the program started "from scratch," with no precedents, another government official sang its praises. Conrad Wirth in a 1943 report stated that the CCC-ID contributed directly to the rebuilding of reservations and reservation resources. It improved the economic lives of the people, giving work where work was needed. And by helping thousands of enrollees become skilled workers, Wirth noted that the program "revitalized Indian life." Several of the most important projects included work at Grand Portage National Monument, blister rust control on the Red Lake Reservation, and developing forest fire training schools.[10]

The value of the CCC-ID and CCC was already clearly apparent to some during the 1930s and 1940s. Others realized its benefits only after the CCC era had come to an end. This revolutionary program of putting needy young men to work on conservation projects lasted only about ten years, yet its importance to those who served in it and to conservation has not always been adequately recognized. As one enrollee put it years later, "In short, [the CCC] served the cause for which the corps was created: the conservation of the country and its resources." Within the state, CCC enrollees translated the conservation philosophies of experts into action and tangible accomplishments. Only with the readily available labor of the "boys" of the CCC could Minnesota's forests, parks, and farmlands have been conserved and protected as they were during the program's active years. But the program's impact on conservation in the state continues even today. Because the CCC worked within local administrative structures—in state and federal forests, state parks, and soil conservation districts—it helped to solidify these structures for the future. The CCC lifespan was brief, yet it shaped the way in which Minnesotans continue to care for natural resources.[11]

The state Department of Conservation (now the state Department of Natural Resources), for example, had been reorganized prior to the formation of the CCC. But enrollees helped give the department legitimacy, putting hours of hard labor into all areas administered by the DOC: forestry, state parks, game and fish, drainage and water, and lands and minerals. Don Burcalow, a retired forester who began his career in the CCC, described the program's impact on the DOC: "They increased their staff and number of employees because of the nature and variety of conservation work that was done statewide. They certainly didn't have the organization [before the CCC] that they were able to build up during and after these emergency conservation work programs." The same was true in other state agencies. The U.S. Department of Agriculture's Soil Conservation Service (SCS) was organized early in the CCC era, in 1935, and Minnesota enrollees put ideas and theories into practice, reducing erosion and saving "farmland from going to New Orleans."[12]

Through their efforts, enrollees helped to make the work and responsibilities of the DOC and the SCS clear to the public. Simply by putting labor, materials, and planning into conservation in key areas, the CCC helped Minnesotans realize their commitment to preserving and protecting natural resources. The state's Soil and Water Conservation Districts continue this legacy today. Just as significantly, the CCC's work set the pattern for ongoing natural resource management in the state.

As with any large program, there were initial concerns about the CCC in Minnesota, most notably when the state took control of tax delinquent and abandoned forestlands. There was no precedent for developing such a large work program in the state, and procedures were not always smooth. Yet, state forest rangers in 1934—when the CCC had been in operation for only about eighteen months—wrote that forestry work in the state had already advanced eight to ten years.[13]

Minnesota's forests still benefit from the work of CCC enrollees. By 1943, when CCC funding ended nationally, both of the state's national forests were larger than when the program started. The Chippewa National Forest expanded to 1,313,000 acres and the Superior National Forest to 3,725,000 acres (including lands held in state trust and allotments to Native Americans), with much of this new forestland formerly classified as cutover or tax forfeit.[14]

The impact of the CCC is perhaps most visible in stands of trees. Walter Okstad of the Superior National Forest notes that "whenever you see a stand of red pine about 10–12 inches in diameter, it is almost certain to have been planted by the CCC."

State forests benefited, too. Enrollees worked in twenty-one of them—Beltrami Island, Blackduck, Cloquet Valley, Crow Wing, Finland, Fond du Lac (including the university experimental station), Foot Hills (including Badoura State Forest), George Washington, Grand Portage, Kabetogama, Land O'Lakes, Mille Lacs, Mississippi Headwaters, Paul Bunyan, Pine Island, St. Croix, Savanna, Smokey Hills, Third River, and White Earth—and did additional forest conservation work at Camp Ripley, Miller Trunk Highway, Itasca Annex, Anoka Game Refuge, and Nimrod. Enrollees in the fifty-one federal forest camps and forty-four state forest camps developed the first comprehensive forest inventory in the state (covering 3,729,500 acres), performed fish surveys or counts on 336 lakes, stocked lakes with over 275 million fish, and built hundreds of dams as part of water conservation work.[15]

The CCC was best known for its work with trees: in Minnesota, enrollees planted 123,607,000 of them, including white pine, red pine, Norway pine, Scotch pine, and jack pine. Of these trees, 24,786,000 were planted in state forests and adjoining land. Enrollees collected thousands of bushels of pinecones for seeds, provided over 267,000 days of work in the state's tree and game food nurseries, and did 113,000 days of work fighting diseases that threatened forest health.[16]

Fire fighting and fire prevention are also important parts of the CCC legacy. In Minnesota, enrollees spent 283,000 man-days fighting forest fires and over 225,000 more on fire suppression and prevention, such as fire tower duty. They built 149 fire lookout towers and support buildings and 795 other buildings and structures. Along with stringing 3,338 miles of telephone lines, the men and boys of the CCC built 4,500 miles of new roads, including those used for fire fighting, and did roadside maintenance on another 23,000 miles. In all, they provided 3.5 million days of labor for the U.S. Forest Service and for forest-related work through the Minnesota DOC. Forester J. C. "Buzz" Ryan described the results: "The CCC program was, without a doubt, the most beneficial [forest and conservation] program of the 'Roosevelt New Deal.'"[17]

The CCC also played a major role in building and developing Minnesota's state park system. A total of twenty-two CCC camps were established in twelve state parks for varying periods of time, and several parks (Itasca, Whitewater,

Gooseberry Falls, and Jay Cooke among them) had more than one camp. The camp at Scenic State Park was one of the first established in a Minnesota state park, along with those at Jay Cooke and Itasca state parks. Itasca's second camp, for World War I veterans, was the last CCC state park camp to close in the United States, on July 15, 1942. The second camp at Gooseberry Falls State Park, established on July 24, 1934, was the longest operating CCC state park camp in Minnesota, having served the state for more than seven years when it closed in 1941.

Between 1935 and 1942, Minnesota's state park system grew from thirty to forty-seven units. Park attendance tripled, topping one million for the first time in the state's history toward the end of the CCC era. The design of buildings and landscapes at each park was no longer haphazardly developed. Chief architect Barber and his staff, along with the skill and hard work of CCC enrollees and others, created instead a cohesive set of buildings and structures, each design specific to its site. With the CCC providing much of the labor, Minnesota's parks took on the distinctive look they now have.

Minnesota's active and ongoing soil conservation program had its beginning during the CCC years. In all, enrollees worked on more than 160,000 acres of land. The efforts of CCC enrollees in Minnesota's nineteen soil conservation service camps may still be seen today. Instead of rectangular fields, straight

Contour farming helped reclaim significant amounts of Minnesota farmland. Much of the soil conservation work of the CCC is still visible today on farms throughout the southeastern parts of the state. This photograph is from Winona County, ca. 1950s.

Through the work of the CCC-ID, trees were planted over many acres of Indian land in Minnesota. William Heritage, Minnesota CCC-ID commissioner, examines Norway pines at Ponemah Point on the Red Lake Indian Reservation in August 1938.

rows, and pastures on land not suitable for cultivation, there are now curved rows of contour farming matched to topography, terraces, and woodlots on steep slopes. The land is free of gullies and other marks of erosion and has clean streams and silt-free lakes. A study of one farmer, whose land was examined twelve years after conservation work was completed, found that crop yields increased, feed production improved, and livestock production expanded. The farmer's costs for participating were comparatively low, and his income rose regularly, along with the value of his land. As he said then, "Soil conservation pays on my farm." Herbert Flueck, a pioneer in Minnesota soil conservation, talked about the value of CCC soil conservation work more than thirty years after the program ended, saying, "It served as a demonstration for many, many people, and it was great for taxpayers to come and see what can be done in erosion control." The ongoing work of local soil conservation associations and districts, which collaborate with the Soil Conservation Service, is part of the CCC's continuing legacy in the state today.[18]

The work of the CCC-ID also left an enduring legacy. Ranging from standard conservation projects such as reforestation, road and trail building, fire tower construction, and blister rust control to projects that focused specifically on reservation needs, its impact may still be seen. At Pipestone, it was CCC-ID enrollees who began the task of clearing and maintaining the quarry area before it was listed as a national monument in 1937. The Red Lake Chippewa ran a large tree nursery and were involved in maple syrup production. The Consolidated Chippewa at White Earth drew national attention with their work clearing and developing the Rice Lake ricing site, while those at Grand Portage did the extensive work on what later became the Grand Portage National Monument. Several Minnesota reservations ran successful fire fighting schools.

Robert Fechner, in an understated comment written in 1934, said the work of the CCC-ID "compared favorably with the work of the CCC in every respect." Underscoring its importance, he added, "My feeling is that the money spent under this program to help Indians to help themselves has been worth every dollar put into it."[19]

And what of enrollees and others in the CCC? One historian concluded, "They did more, of course, than reclaim and develop natural resources. They reclaimed and developed themselves. They came from large cities and from small towns. . . . Their muscles hardened, their bodies filled out, their self-respect returned. They learned trades; more important, they learned about America, and they learned about other Americans." Minnesota enrollee Frederick Johnson echoed these words when he reflected on his work at Whitewater State Park:

> *I believe that its intangible effect on the youth of the depression generation is harder to evaluate than the visible results of their work. One can only speculate what would have happened to thousands of young men who without the CCC would have spent their early productive years in enforced idleness. The corps was not a handout; it was a fair exchange. At a time when it was desperately needed, we were offered the opportunity to work for the preservation and improvement of America, and while the pay was not high by today's standards, the greater reward came in the elevation of the human condition. The CCC member felt good about himself and what he was doing. In those difficult days, that was enough.*[20]

In Minnesota, conservation leaders could see this aspect of the program's impact even in its early days. A conservation report from 1936 stated, "The CCC unquestionably has proven its worth not only as a force to revitalize and stimulate public concern about conservation of the natural resources of the nation but has offered gainful employment and healthy mental and physical training to the youth of this state and nation during a time when other means of employment and occupation have been beyond reach."[21]

In terms of numbers, during its years of operation in the state the CCC spent $85 million and received an estimated immediate value of $664 in conservation work done by each of the 77,224 men who served in Minnesota's camps—more than $51 million. Between 1933 and 1942, the CCC sent $17 million in dependent payments to Minnesotans at $25 per month per family. The CCC-ID served 2,536 Native American families in Minnesota with expenditures of $1.7 million to the Consolidated Chippewa, $1.16 million to the Red Lake Chippewa, and $165,000 to the Sioux Agency at Pipestone.[22]

Although the payments sent home to individual families may not sound like much in today's dollars, Harvey Richart described the impact on his

Enrollees left camps proud of the conservation work they did.
Here men and boys from the Halfway Camp board a train
that will take them home at the end of their enrollment periods.

family this way: "My dad died when I was fifteen, and he hadn't worked for a couple of years before that. This left the family in pretty dire straits. I went into the CCs when I was eighteen. That twenty-five dollars that went home every month just made the difference to my mother and the five kids still at home." Michael Sanchelli's mother made the monthly payments stretch as well: "[T]he cash my mother [got she] could work miracles with, she would buy some stuff from the Good Will store."[23]

After their time in the CCC and CCC-ID, enrollees, officers, and employees moved on and grew up. Many, including most of the people quoted in this book, fought in World War II and then came home to Minnesota's businesses, factories, and farms. Some went on to college. Martin J. McCarty became a student and coach of the baseball team at Hamline College (now University) in St. Paul. Thor Bergstrahl won a scholarship to study physics at Carleton College in Northfield. George Morrison won a scholarship to the Minneapolis School of Art (now the Minneapolis College of Art and Design). Bergstrahl graduated Phi Beta Kappa from Carleton and was awarded a fellowship to continue his studies in physics. He became a radiation researcher at the Massachusetts Institute of Technology and the Naval Research Center in Washington, DC. Morrison, an enrollee at the CCC-ID camp at Grand Portage, won his school's most prestigious prize, the Vanderlip Traveling Scholarship, and became a nationally known abstract painter, sculptor, and teacher.[24]

Norman Borlaug interrupted his studies at the University of Minnesota to work with the U.S. Forest Service on and off from 1935 to 1938. As he later said, he did this "to make a little more money . . . working in forestry programs under the emergency . . . Civilian Conservation Corps." Assigned to work in Idaho and Massachusetts forests, Borlaug was greatly impressed by the CCC enrollees he worked with: "The men working in these programs were in dire need of food and job opportunities. I saw young men, seventeen or eighteen years old, arrive at the Civilian Conservation Corps camps hungry and malnourished. At the camps they were able to recover . . . health and self-confidence. I saw how food changed them." Borlaug later credited this experience with helping him develop life values that led to research toward eradicating hunger throughout the world, for which he was awarded the Nobel Peace Prize in 1970.[25]

Many who worked in the CCC learned a trade. Eino Lahti became a cartographer after "pestering [his] superiors" in the camp to teach him. He worked on maps and photographs in the CCC, preparing many of his camp's work records. Then, "I got myself up to a good profession," working for the U.S. Geological Survey in Washington, DC. Other enrollees became machine operators, road builders, landscape workers, radio operators, bookkeepers, or cooks in restaurants or held a variety of jobs at Minnesota companies including Hormel, radio station WDGY, Red Wing Pottery, and Northwest Airlines among

Although the CCC's impact can easily be seen in trees, buildings, parks, and farmland across the state, it also made a difference in the lives of the enrollees, like the members of this work crew at the Cut Foot Sioux camp. "I know a lot of guys that went in there that gained fifteen and twenty pounds after six months. . . . " Mike Vuksech recalled. "They went in pretty weak looking, and in six months they looked rugged and tan and strong and healthy."

many others. Some stayed in the military, making it a career. John Blatnik, a camp educational coordinator, became a member of the U.S. Congress, representing the Iron Range districts of northern Minnesota for many years.[26]

In spite of varied backgrounds and varied achievements in life, the men interviewed for Minnesota's oral history projects invariably remembered their ccc work with pride. Many also movingly described the program's enduring effects in personal terms. This, too, is part of the ccc legacy in Minnesota. Claude Darst said, "I watched a lot of people that had been in trouble [before going] in the CC camp. They got their life straightened around in there. They found they could do something." Frank Chernivec, an enrollee in forest conservation camps, said, "[the enrollees] matured. Next thing you know they were young men, and they were responsible, and they got work done because they knew how to work." Sergeant P. J. Halloran said, "The cccs gave me discipline. It gave me a work ethic. It gave me knowledge how to deal with people on a large basis that I had never experienced before."[27]

Halloran and many others recalled close friendships made in the ccc. These, for him, were the "best memories," along with the recollection of "being overwhelmed by the beauty of the country that was there." Godfrey Rawlings echoed this sentiment when he said, "I had never been in the woods, seen such beauty." And William J. Fraser, a mechanic employed by the ccc, remembered how excited enrollees were when they saw the northern lights for the first time.[28]

An enrollee operates a Caterpillar tractor at a Minnesota ccc camp in 1940. While many enrollees lacked specific training, Frank Chernivec remarked that "they were young men, and they were responsible, and ... they knew how to work."

CCC alumni gather to dedicate the Minnesota Civilian Conservation Corps History Center at the Ironworld Discovery Center in Chisholm, June 6, 1993.

"It was a good program," recalled George Morrison. "It helped out younger Indian boys like myself. We were taken care of with board and room and minimum wage." Mike Vuksech, an enrollee in several forest camps, said, "I knew a lot of guys that went in [to the CCC] that gained fifteen to twenty pounds after six months. They went in pretty weak looking, and in six months they looked rugged and tan and strong and healthy." The lifelong impact was described by Raymond Noyes when he said, "It came along as a wonderful blessing. . . . It gave us a new lease on life." Guy Osborn, a Missouri enrollee who served in a Minnesota forest camp, summed it up best when he said, "It was good, just a good deal."[29]

APPENDIX I: MINNESOTA CCC AND CCC-ID CAMPS

The listing below contains detailed information about Minnesota's CCC and CCC-ID camps. Where more than one camp bears the same name, an effort has been made to put the camps in chronological order. Camps known by more than one name have alternate names listed in parentheses. Where more than one company served at a particular camp, the company numbers have been placed in chronological order, although reporting varied from source to source, so dates may not be exact. To aid in locating camps, the nearest post office and the county in which the post office is located have been included. It is important to note, however, that camps were not always located in the same county as the nearest post office. Each camp was given a letter-number designation, and these too are listed below. SP-1, for example, was the letter-number designation for Itasca State Park camp, the first state park camp established in Minnesota. The letters in these designations are

Army	U.S. Army
BF	Migratory Bird Refuge
BS	Bureau of Biological Survey
D	Private Land, Soil Conservation Service
DPE	Drainage Private Land Erosion
DS	Drought State Forest
DSP	Drought State Park
F	National Forest
FWS	Fish and Wildlife Service
NP	National Park
P	Private Forest
PE	Private Erosion
S	State Forest
SCS	Soil Conservation Service
SP	State Park

ANGORA

CAMP NUMBER: F-29
Post Office: Cook/Virginia (St. Louis County)
Known Company Number: 725
Camp Dates: 1933–34

Notes: Company 725 built Angora, as well as Cusson (S-52) and Vermilion (S-94). Angora operated from November 1933 to May 1934. Its assigned work area was in the Superior National Forest. The newspapers of Company 725 were the *Northern Hi-Lights* and *Northern Hi-Lites.*

BADOURA

CAMP NUMBER: S-144
Post Office: Akeley (Hubbard County)
Known Company Number: 2708
Dates: 1939–41

Notes: The camp opened between October 5 and 10, 1939, and operated through the winter of 1941. One of the last six state forest camps to operate during the winter of 1941, its assigned work area was Foot Hills State Forest and Badoura State Forest and Nursery. The newspaper of Company 2708 was the *Badoura Banner.*

BAPTISM

CAMP NUMBER: F-54
Post Office: Ely (St. Louis County)
Known Company Number: 3703
Dates: 1935–41

Notes: The camp opened on September 3, 1935, and closed in the spring of 1941. Company 3703 transferred to the camp on October 26, 1935. The Baptism camp's assigned work area was in the Superior National Forest. The newspaper of Company 3703 was the *Baptism Blade.*

BAYPORT

CAMP NUMBER: SCS-17
Post Office: Bayport (Washington County)
Known Company Number: V-1774
Dates: 1939–42

Notes: A company of World War I veterans (V-1774) opened the camp, located on the present site of the Bayport Golf Course, on May 8, 1939. The camp operated until the spring or summer of 1942, serving as a demonstration project in the Bayport area. Shortly before closing, officials described it as an "outstanding camp showing . . . evident pride." Bayport was the last Soil Conservation Service camp in Minnesota to close. The newspapers of Company V-1774 were the *Veterans Voice* and *Vets Voice.* During World War II, the site was used as a glider training school.

BENA

CAMP NUMBER: F-13
Post Office: Bena (Cass County)
Known Company Number: 702
Camp Dates: 1933–42

Notes: Company 702 was organized at Fort Snelling on April 28, 1933. It opened Bena between May 9 and May 11, 1933, and operated the camp until being disbanded on May 28, 1942. Bena was one of two federal forest camps, with Gunflint 1 (F-5) near Grand Marais, to operate continuously throughout the duration of the ccc in Minnesota. It was also, along with Gunflint 1 and Gegoka (F-2) at Ely, one of the last three federal forest camps to operate in the state. The Bena camp's assigned work area was in the Chippewa National Forest. The newspaper of Company 702 was the *Chippewa Pioneer.* The facility was used to house German prisoners of war from 1943 to 1945.

BIG FALLS

CAMP NUMBER: S-143
Post Office: Big Falls (Koochiching County)
Known Company Number: 4751
Dates: 1938–42

Notes: Big Falls camp opened between August 10 and August 11, 1938. Along with Deer Lake (S-95), it was one of the last two state forest ccc camps to operate in Minnesota. Big Falls closed in the spring of 1942. Its assigned work area was Pine Island State Forest. The newspapers of Company 4751 were the *Pine Island Press, the Pelican Press,* and *Jusumpin.*

BIG LAKE

CAMP NUMBER: F-28
Post Office: Cass Lake (Cass County)
Known Company Number: 720
Camp Dates: 1933–35

Notes: Company 720 was organized at Fort Snelling on May 27, 1933. The company first served at Clear River (S-56) near Roosevelt and Warroad before opening Big Lake (F-28) between November 2 and 4, 1933. Company 720 transferred to Larsmount (S-98) in Wilton Lake in 1935, and Big Lake closed permanently at that time. The assigned work area for Big Lake was in the Chippewa National Forest.

BIG LAKE

CAMP NUMBER: S-79
Post Office: Cloquet (Carlton County)
Known Company Number: 1760
Dates: 1933–37

Notes: Company 1760 was organized in Kansas on May 25, 1933, and opened Big Lake (S-79) on June 28, 1933. Enrollees had completed all buildings in the camp by October 1, 1933. The camp closed on May 29, 1937. The camp's assigned work area was Fond du Lac State Forest and the university experimental station. The camp newspaper was the *Big Lake Breeze.*

BIG RICE LAKE (BRITTMOUNT)

COMPANY NUMBER: F-30
Post Office:Virginia (St. Louis County)
Known Company Number: 715
Camp Dates: 1933–38

Notes: Company 715 was organized on May 23, 1933, and opened Big Rice Lake on October 24, 1933. The camp, with an assigned work area in the Superior National Forest, closed in January 1938. The newspapers of Company 715 were the *Tiger* and the *Whispering Pine.*

BIG SANDY LAKE (SAVANNAH)

CAMP NUMBER: S-61
Post Office: McGregor (Aitkin County)
Known Company Number: 1724
Dates: 1933

Notes: Company 1724 was organized at Fort Snelling on June 22, 1933. It was known as the "Rambling 24th" for the number of moves it made during the first several enrollment periods. The company opened Big Sandy Lake between June 23 and 28, 1933, and operated the camp until it closed on November 7, 1933. The camp's assigned work area was Savannah State Forest.

BLACKDUCK

CAMP NUMBER: S-99
Post Office: Hines (Beltrami County)
Known Company Number: 4703
Dates: 1935–36

Notes: Blackduck was established on September 9, 1935, and operated until April 29, 1936. Its assigned work area was Blackduck State Forest. The camp newspaper was the *Maple Leaf.*

BRECKENRIDGE

CAMP NUMBER: DPE-139
Post Office: Breckenridge (Wilkin County)
Known Company Number: 2703
Camp Dates: 1934

Notes: Company 2703 opened the camp on July 30, 1934. Breckenridge was one of the first three camps, along with Frazee (DPE-137) and Fergus Falls (DPE-138), to provide water conservation work in the state, preserving the water supply for communities in the Red River Valley. The three camps worked on the Red, Otter Tail, Red Lake, and Clearwater rivers. The newspaper of Company 2703 was the *Timber Wolf's Howl.*

BUCKBOARD

CAMP NUMBERS: DS-141, S-141
Post Office: Bagley (Clearwater County)
Known Company Number: 2705
Dates: 1934–39

Notes: Camp Buckboard opened on October 26, 1934, as a drought relief camp. Its work program expanded to all aspects of forest cultural work, and it operated until October 5, 1939. Its assigned work area was White Earth State Forest. The camp newspaper was the *Buckboard Whip.*

BURNS LAKE

CAMP NUMBER: F-23
Post Office: Cass Lake (Cass County)
Known Company Number: 1765
Camp Dates: 1933–37

Notes: Company 1765 was organized in Kansas on May 31, 1933, and opened Burns Lake on June 28, 1933. During its years of operation, the camp had an assigned work area in the Chippewa National Forest. It closed in 1937. The newspaper of Company 1765 was the *Jayhawk.*

CABIN CITY

CAMP NUMBERS: DPE-13, S-83
Post Office: Big Falls (Koochiching County)
Known Company Numbers: 1716, 2701
Dates: 1933–34, 1934–36

Notes: Company 1716 opened the camp on June 25, 1933, building the twenty-two cabin-style barracks, each accommodating eight men, that gave the camp its name. Cabin City closed on April 19, 1934, when Company 1716 transferred to Lewiston (SCS-11). The camp was reestablished by Company 2701 on August 1, 1934, and operated until January 14, 1936. Its assigned work area was Pine Island State Forest. Company 1716's newspaper, the *Tamarack,* was picked as the best ccc newspaper in the Seventh Corps area in the spring of 1934. The newspaper of Company 2701 was the *Cabin City Crier.* The company also published the *1716 Tamarack.*

CALEDONIA

CAMP NUMBERS: PE-88, SCS-2
Post Office: Caledonia (Houston County)
Known Company Numbers: 723, 1720
Dates: 1933, 1934, 1935–42

Notes: Caledonia operated as a private erosion tent camp during the summers of 1933 and 1934. Company 723 was organized on May 29, 1933, and served first at Vermilion Dam (S-55) before moving to Caledonia on April 21, 1934. Company 1720, originally stationed at Gooseberry Falls State Park (SP-5), replaced Company 723 at Caledonia on June 4, 1935, when the first Gooseberry camp closed. Caledonia became a year-round Soil Conservation Service camp in the summer of 1935 and operated until 1942. The camp was assigned to the Beaver Creek Project. When it closed, Caledonia along with Lanesboro (SCS-7) was the longest-running Soil Conservation Service camp in Minnesota. Company 723's newspaper was the *Caledonia Record.* The newspaper of Company 1720 was the *Flash.*

CAMDEN STATE PARK

CAMP NUMBERS: DSP-3, SP-11
Post Office: Lynd (Lyon County)
Known Company Number: V-2713
Dates: 1934–36

Notes: Camden State Park camp opened on August 10, 1934, and closed in October 1936. A company of World War I veterans arrived in 1935 and were said to have the most outstanding entertainment activities of any camp. Admission to dances they held every week was by invitation only. Camden, initially designated a drought camp, later became a state park camp. The newspapers of Company V-2713 were the *Camp Call* and the *Vet's Call* (various spellings).

CAMP RIPLEY

CAMP NUMBERS: DS-64, S-64
Post Office: Little Falls (Morrison County)
Known Company Numbers: 1723, 2707
Dates: 1933–34, 1934

Notes: The camp operated from June 26, 1933, to April 28, 1934, when Company 1723 was transferred to Whitewater State Park (SP-4, DSP-4). Before Company 1723's transfer, Camp Ripley became the only ccc camp in Minnesota to be struck by a tornado. The camp was reestablished by Company 2707 on August 1, 1934, and operated until October 26, 1934. Its assigned work area was Camp Ripley Military Reservation. The newspaper of Company 1723 was the *Pine Knoll Echo.*

CARIBOU

CAMP NUMBER: F-11
Post Office: Lutsen (Cook County)
Known Company Number: 703
Camp Dates: 1933–34, 1934–35

Notes: The camp was established on May 13, 1933, and operated for one year. It was reestablished in October 1934 and operated for six months before closing permanently. The Caribou camp's assigned work area was in the Superior National Forest. Company 703 had several African American members when first formed. The company's newspaper was the *Caribou Ripsaw.*

CASCADE (DEVIL'S TRACK LAKE)

CAMP NUMBER: F-4
Post Office: Grand Marais (Cook County)
Known Company Numbers: 714, 2707
Camp Dates: 1933–34, 1934–37

Notes: Company 714 operated the camp from June 15, 1933, through the fall of 1934. Company 2707 operated the camp from October 27, 1934, through 1937. The camp's assigned work area was in the Superior National Forest. The newspaper of Company 714 was the *Lone Wolf,* while Company 2707 published *Devil's Track Ripples.*

CHATFIELD (LITTLE SAHARA)

CAMP NUMBERS: PE-92, SCS-14
Post Office: Chatfield (Fillmore County)
Known Company Numbers: 706, 2704
Dates: 1933, 1934, 1935–38

Notes: Chatfield operated as a private erosion tent camp during the summers of 1933 and 1934 and as a year-round Soil Conservation Service camp from 1935 to 1938. Its assigned work area was the Deer-Bear Creek Project area. Company 706, organized at Fort Snelling and originally sent to California, transferred to Chatfield on April 26, 1934, staying for the summer. Company 2704 opened Chatfield as a year-round camp sometime between October 15, 1935, and January 16, 1936. Company 2704 served at Chatfield until the camp closed in the spring of 1938. The newspapers of Company 706 were the *706 Spotlite* and the *Spotlite,* while that of Company 2704 was the *Score of 2704.*

CLEAR RIVER (BELTRAMI ISLAND, NORRIS)

CAMP NUMBER: S-56
Post Office: Warroad (Roseau County)
Known Company Numbers: 720, 3721
Dates: 1933, 1935–36

Notes: Company 720 operated the camp from June 13 until November 6, 1933. As a Warroad camp, twenty African American enrollees may have been assigned to it from July to November 1933. The camp was reestablished on June 11, 1935, and operated by Company 3721 until January 13, 1936. Its assigned work area was Beltrami Island State Forest. The camp, also known as Norris or Beltrami Island, served as headquarters for the federal relief program known as the Beltrami Island Project, a pioneering experiment in relocation and land-use planning on formerly forested land, which took place from 1936 to 1942. The camp site has been the headquarters for the Red Lake Wildlife Management Area of the Department of Natural Resources since the late 1930s. Fourteen original remaining ccc buildings were listed in the National Register of Historic Places in 1994.

COLD SPRINGS

CAMP NUMBER: F-9
Post Office: Ely (St. Louis County)
Known Company Number: 713
Camp Dates: 1933–36

Notes: Company 713 was organized at Fort Snelling on May 23, 1933, and opened Cold Springs on June 4, 1933. The camp closed in 1936. Its assigned work area was in the Superior National Forest. The newspapers of Company 713 were the *Big Bluff* and the *Echo Trail Echoes*.

COTTONWOOD RIVER STATE PARK (FLANDRAU)

CAMP NUMBER: SP-14
Post Office: New Ulm (Brown County)
Known Company Numbers: V-3722, 2714
Dates: 1935–42

Notes: Company V-3722 opened the camp between June 13 and 17, 1935. Company 2714 operated the camp from 1936 until its closing on January 15, 1942. Cottonwood River was one of the last state park camps in Minnesota to close. The newspaper of Company 2714 was the *Cottonwood ccc News*.

CROSS RIVER

CAMP NUMBER: F-43
Post Office: Grand Marais (Cook County)
Known Company Numbers: 4742, 3705
Camp Dates: 1935–37

Notes: The camp opened in the summer of 1935 and operated until May 1937. Its assigned work area was in the Superior National Forest. Company 3705 was sent to the camp on January 1, 1936. The newspaper of Company 3705 was the *Cross River Taps*.

CUSSON

CAMP NUMBER: S-52
Post Office: Orr (St. Louis County)
Known Company Number: 725
Dates: 1933–41

Notes: Company 725 was organized at Fort Snelling on June 2, 1933, and opened Cusson between June 16 and 17, 1933. Company 725 also built two other camps, Angora (F-29) and Vermilion (S-94). This camp was located in Cusson, a company town platted by the Virginia and Rainy Lake Lumber Company in 1909 and operated as their headquarters until 1929, after which it was sold in its entirety to Nick Ofstad. Initially, buildings for the camp were used under a lease agreement. Enrollees built four additional shop buildings. Company 725 operated the camp until it closed on October 30, 1941. Shortly before closing, officials described Cusson as an "outstanding ccc camp . . . rated by Army inspectors as the best camp in the Minnesota ccc district during the past year." Its assigned work area was Kabetogama State Forest. Enrollees also worked at the game food nursery at Gheen and, from 1935 to 1938, built the Orr roadside parking area, designed by landscape architect Arthur R. Nichols, under the direction of a stonemason from International Falls. The newspapers of Company 725 were the *Northern Hi-Lights* and *Northern Hi-Lites*. The four remaining ccc shop buildings were listed in the National Register of Historic Places on March 2, 1989.

CUT FOOT SIOUX

CAMP NUMBER: F-14
Post Office: Deer River (Itasca County)
Known Company Numbers: 707, 2704
Camp Dates: 1933–41

Notes: Company 707 was organized at Fort Snelling on May 3, 1933, opening the camp between May 25 and 26, 1933. Company 2704 came to the camp on June 11, 1935. Cut Foot Sioux operated until November 1941. Its assigned work area was in the Chippewa National Forest. Company 707 was quarantined for measles in June 1934. The company had a championship baseball team while at the camp, beating all the ccc camp teams it played, as well as the Deer River city team, a Kansas City team, and the championship Native American team. Company 707's newspapers were the *Brush Banter, Tomahawk,* and *Pee Wee Press*. Company 2704 published the *Score of 2704*. Camp buildings housed German prisoners of war from 1943 to 1945.

DAY LAKE

CAMP NUMBER: F-34
Post Office: Grand Rapids (Itasca County)
Known Company Numbers: 786, 1724
Camp Dates: 1933–41

Notes: Company 786, an African American company with enrollees from Kansas, Missouri, Nebraska, Arkansas, and Iowa, was formed in the summer of 1933. It was transferred from Culver to Day Lake in mid-December 1933 and then back to Kansas on May 1, 1934, where it was assigned to a soil conservation camp. Company 1724 was formed at Fort Snelling on June 22, 1933. It was transferred from Mack (F-32) to the Day Lake camp on May 2, 1934. The camp closed in 1941. Its assigned work area was in the Chippewa National Forest. Company 1724's newspaper was the *Day Lake Tattler.* The facility was used as a German prisoner of war camp from 1943 to 1945.

DEER LAKE

Camp Number: S-95
Post Office: Effie (Itasca County)
Known Company Numbers: 766, 1763, 3711, 1722
Dates: 1933–42

Notes: Company 766 opened the camp on October 24, 1933. Company 1763 probably was assigned to the camp ca. 1934–35. Company 3711 moved to the camp between June 10 and 11, 1935, and operated it until 1936. Company 1722 occupied the camp from January 14, 1936, through 1942. This camp, along with Big Falls (S-143), was one of the last two state forest camps to close in Minnesota. It was also, along with Owen Lake (S-54), the longest-running state forest camp in Minnesota. Deer Lake's assigned work area was George Washington State Forest. Company 1722's newspaper was the *Deer Lake Echo,* while the newspaper of Company 1763 was the *Woodpecker*.

DUNNIGAN (DUNNIGAN LAKE)

CAMP NUMBER: F-16
Post Office: Ely (St. Louis County)
Known Company Numbers: 3743, 1720
Camp Dates: 1933–34, 1934–35

Notes: The camp was established on June 20, 1933, and operated for one year. Reestablished in October 1934, it operated for one year, closing permanently in October 1935. The Dunnigan camp's assigned work area was in the Superior National Forest. The newspaper of Company 1720 was the *Flash*.

ELBOW LAKE

CAMP NUMBER: S-58
Post Office: Arago or Waubun
(Mahnomen County)
Known Company Numbers: 785, 710
Dates: 1933, 1934–35

Notes: Company 785 was organized in May 1933 in Kansas. It served at Elbow Lake from June 6, 1933, until its transfer to Sand Lake (F-26) on November 1, 1933. Company 710 was organized in May 1933. Sent first to Fenske Lake (F-7), the company was transferred to Elbow Lake to reopen it on April 28, 1934. The camp operated until October 24, 1935. Its assigned work area was White Earth State Forest. The newspapers of Company 710 were the *Peat Smoke News Flash, the Peat Smoke,* and the *Peat Smoke Weekly*.

ENGINEER COMPANY (ENGINEER'S CAMP)

CAMP NUMBER: F-21
Post Office: Bena (Cass County)
Known Company Numbers: 1742, 3714
Camp Dates: 1933–34, 1935–36

Notes: Also called Engineer's Camp, the camp was opened on June 25, 1933, by Company 1742. These enrollees from Missouri, Kansas, and Minnesota were supplemented by members of Company 702 from Bena (F-13) for a time. The Engineer Company camp closed in June 1934 but was reopened by Company 3714 on June 1, 1935, before closing permanently in 1936. The camp's assigned work area was in the Chippewa National Forest.

FENSKE LAKE (SPRING CREEK, SPRING LAKE)

CAMP NUMBER: F-7
Post Office: Ely (St. Louis County)
Known Company Numbers: 710, 3707
Camp Dates: 1933–34, 1935–36

Notes: Company 710 originally occupied the camp on May 30, 1933, and while there was chosen "Outstanding Company in the Western Subdistrict." Company 710 was transferred to Elbow Lake (S-58), and Fenske Lake was closed on April 28, 1934. The camp was reestablished on June 11, 1935, and operated by Company 3707 for one year before closing permanently. Its assigned work area was in the Superior National Forest. Some buildings may have survived and been used by a girls' camp in the Ely area during the 1960s. Company 3707's newspaper was the *Spring Creek Crier,* while the newspapers of Company 710 were the *Peat Smoke, the Peat Smoke News Flash,* and the *Peat Smoke Weekly.*

FERGUS FALLS (UNDERWOOD)

CAMP NUMBERS: PE-137, SCS-21
Post Office: Fergus Falls (Ottertail County)
Known Company Numbers: 2705, 713
Dates: 1934, 1941–42

Notes: Company 2705 was sent to the camp, also known as Underwood, on August 1, 1934, but did not stay long. The camp opened again on June 30, 1941, and operated until late winter or early spring 1942. It was the last Soil Conservation Service camp to open in Minnesota and, with camp S-145 at Kelliher, was one of the last CCC camps to open in the state. The newspaper of Company 2705 was the *Wall Lake Seer,* while Company 713 published the *Big Bluff* and the *Echo Trail Echoes.*

FERGUS FALLS

CAMP NUMBER: DPE-138
Post Office: Fergus Falls (Ottertail County)
Known Company Number: 2701
Camp Dates: 1934

Notes: Company 2701 opened this camp on August 1, 1934. The camp was one of the first three, along with Breckenridge (DPE-139) and Frazee (DPE-137), to provide water conservation work in the state, preserving the water supply for communities in the Red River Valley. The three camps worked on the Red, Otter Tail, Red Lake, and Clearwater rivers. Company 2701 published the *Dora Lake Ripples.*

FERNBERG

CAMP NUMBER: F-44
Post Office: Ely, Virginia (St. Louis County)
Known Company Number: 3702
Camp Dates: 1935–36

Notes: Fernberg was listed as a "new camp" in the summer of 1935. It took its name from the nearby Fernberg Ranger Station. Its assigned work area was in the Superior National Forest. In 1936, eight men at the camp died during a typhoid epidemic. The newspaper of Company 3702 was the *Sturgeon River Star.*

FILLMORE (SPRING VALLEY)

CAMP NUMBER: SCS-1
Post Office: Spring Valley (Fillmore County)
Known Company Number: 706
Dates: 1935–36

Notes: The camp opened in the summer of 1935 and operated until October 1936, when Company 706 was moved to Lanesboro (SCS-7). Enrollees at Fillmore were assigned to the Deer-Bear Creek Project. The company newspapers were the *Spotlite* and the *706 Spotlite.*

FINLAND STATION

CAMP NUMBERS: P-63, S-63
Post Office: Finland (Lake County)
Known Company Number: 721
Dates: 1933–36

Notes: Company 721 was organized at Fort Snelling on May 28, 1933, and opened Finland Station between June 13 and 14, 1933. The camp operated as a private forest camp (P-63) until May 1934, when its work area was absorbed into Finland State Forest. It operated as a state forest camp (S-63) until closing on January 14, 1936. The newspaper of Company 721 was the *Northern Light Beacon.*

FOOT HILLS

CAMP NUMBER: S-66
Post Office: Pine River (Cass County)
Known Company Numbers: 1784, 1797
Dates: 1933

Notes: Company 1784 was organized in Kansas on May 25, 1933, opening Foot Hills between June 26 and 28, 1933, as a summer tent camp. Company 1784 became Company 1797 during that summer and was transferred to Inger (F-27) on November 3, 1933. Foot Hills closed permanently at that time. The camp's assigned work area was Foot Hills State Forest and Badoura State Forest and Nursery.

FORT RIDGELY MEMORIAL STATE PARK

CAMP NUMBERS: DSP-4, SP-12
Post Office: Fairfax (Renville County)
Known Company Numbers: 2712, V-2713
Dates: 1934–35, 1936–38

Notes: Company 2712 opened the camp on July 31, 1934, but the camp was closed in October 1935, when the state's quota was unexpectedly reduced. Company V-2713 reestablished the camp on October 24, 1936, and occupied it until it closed in the spring of 1938. Designated as a drought camp, it operated through the state park program. It was the only state park camp in Minnesota to restore a historic building as part of its work plan. Enrollees participated in an archeological excavation that identified the locations of eight original fort buildings and helped restore the 1853 commissary building at the fort. The newspapers of Company V-2713 were the *Camp Call* and the *Vet's Call* (various spellings).

FORT SNELLING

CAMP NUMBER: ARMY-1
Post Office: Fort Snelling (Dakota County)
Known Company Names and Numbers: Supply Company, Headquarters Company, V-2714
Camp Dates: 1933–37

Notes: Organized on April 29, 1933, the first company at the Fort Snelling CCC camp was called Supply Company. The name was changed to Headquarters Company early in 1934. Company strength at that time was between two and three hundred men. Company V-2714 was listed at Fort Snelling from June to October 1935. The fort ceased serving as a CCC enrollee processing center in September 1937. The camp newspaper was the *New Model*.

FRAZEE

CAMP NUMBER: DPE-137
Post Office: Frazee (Becker County)
Known Company Number: none
Camp Dates: 1934

Notes: This camp was one of the first three, along with Breckenridge (DPE-139) and Fergus Falls (DPE-138), to provide water conservation work in the state, preserving the water supply for communities in the Red River Valley. The three camps worked on the Red, Otter Tail, Red Lake, and Clearwater rivers.

GEGOKA (ISABELLA)

CAMP NUMBER: F-2
Post Office: Ely (St. Louis County)
Known Company Numbers: 701, 704
Camp Dates: 1933–37, 1938–42

Notes: Company 701 was the first CCC company organized in the Seventh U.S. Army Corps area, on April 5, 1933. It occupied Gegoka from the time the camp opened, between May 7 and 8, 1933. Gegoka was closed from May 1937 to October 1938. After reopening Gegoka, Company 704 operated the camp until May 1942. The company had several African American members when it was first formed. Gegoka's assigned work area was in the Superior National Forest. It was one of the last three federal forest camps in Minnesota to close, along with Gunflint 1 (F-5) in Grand Marais and Bena (F-13) in Bena. Company 701's newspapers were the *Leader, Pioneer News*, and *Portage River Ripples*. Company 704's newspapers were the *Gegoka Newsette* and the *Birch Lake Newsette*.

GLENWOOD MUNICIPAL PARK

CAMP NUMBER: SP-8
Post Office: Minneapolis (Hennepin County)
Known Company Numbers: 787, 2767
Dates: 1935–38

Notes: The camp was occupied from the summer of 1935 through the spring of 1938. The newspaper of Company 787 was the *Glenwood Gazette*. Company 2767 published the *Glenwood Newsetter*.

GOOD HARBOR (CASCADE)

CAMP NUMBER: F-20
Post Office: Grand Marais (Cook County)
Known Company Numbers: 1741, 3702
Camp Dates: 1933–36

Notes: Company 1741 first occupied the camp between June 25 and 26, 1933. Company 3702 was transferred to the camp in 1935. Company 1741 at Good Harbor was selected as the outstanding CCC company in the Seventh Corps area at the end of the second enrollment period, in June 1934. In July 1936, CCC director Robert

Fechner visited the camp on his way to Isle Royale National Park. The Good Harbor camp had an assigned work area in the Superior National Forest and closed in October 1936. The newspaper of Company 3702 was the *Sturgeon River Star.*

GOOSEBERRY FALLS STATE PARK

CAMP NUMBER: SP-5
Post Office: Two Harbors (Lake County)
Known Company Number: 1720
Dates: 1934

Notes: Company 1720 operated the camp from May 3 to September 30, 1934, when the company moved to Caledonia (SCS-2). This was the first of two CCC camps to operate in Gooseberry Falls State Park. The newspaper of Company 1720 was the *Flash*.

GOOSEBERRY FALLS STATE PARK

CAMP NUMBERS: DSP-2, SP-10
Post Office: Two Harbors (Lake County)
Known Company Number: 2710
Dates: 1934–41

Notes: This second CCC camp at Gooseberry Falls State Park opened on July 24, 1934, and closed in January or February 1941. Originally designated as a drought camp, it operated through the state park program. The camp was first located in tents near the park entrance. When the park's first CCC camp (SP-5) closed, enrollees from SP-10 moved into its facility. The newspapers of Company 2710 were the *Gooseberry Times* and the *Gitchi Gummi Undertow*.

GRAND PORTAGE (MINERAL CENTER)

CAMP NUMBER: S-68
Post Office: Grand Portage (Cook County)
Known Company Number: none
Dates: 1936–42

Notes: Construction on this CCC-ID camp began on April 14, 1936. As with Nett Lake, the first CCC-ID camp, Grand Portage was designed to serve enrollees from Minnesota Consolidated Chippewa reservations. The camp had eleven buildings. Its best-known work project was the archaeological excavation of the North West Company Fur Post site and the reconstruction of the stockade and great hall. The camp baseball team won the North Shore League championship silver cup trophy and the superb sportsmanship trophy in 1937. The Grand Portage site, including the fur depots at Grand Portage and Fort Charlotte along with the nine-mile Grand Portage trail, was designated a national monument in 1958 and listed in the National Register of Historic Places in 1966.

GRAND RAPIDS

CAMP NUMBER: UNKNOWN
Post Office: Grand Rapids (Itasca County)
Known Company Name: none
Dates: 1937–42

Notes: In August 1937, an article in the *Grand Rapids Herald Review* noted the CCC forest headquarters was scheduled to move from Fort Snelling to the community. Grand Rapids remained the headquarters from September of that year until CCC funding ended, with the camp open perhaps as late as 1943. Operating originally from a regional supply depot at a temporary site in the 4-H building on the county fairgrounds, the camp was built at Sixteenth Avenue and Third Street Northwest on the Mississippi River. This currently is the location of the *Mississippi Melodie Showboat,* a summer tourist attraction dating from 1956. A maintenance building from the CCC camp houses equipment for community organizations. The camp headquarters building stood until about 2004.

GUNFLINT 1

CAMP NUMBER: F-5
Post Office: Grand Marais (Cook County)
Known Company Numbers: 712, 2707
Camp Dates: 1933–42

Notes: Company 712 was organized at Fort Snelling on May 17, 1933, and opened Gunflint 1 on June 4, 1933. Company 2707 transferred to Gunflint 1 after Cascade (F-4) closed. The Gunflint 1 camp had an assigned work area in the Superior National Forest. Along with Bena (F-13), this was one of two federal forest camps to operate continuously throughout the duration of the CCC in Minnesota. It closed in May 1942, one of the last three federal forest camps to operate in the state, with Bena and Gegoka (F-2). The bell from this camp hangs in the memorial bell tower at the Cook County Historical Society in Grand Marais in honor of M. J.

Humphrey, a local resident who was a minister and photographer in the camps. The newspaper of Company 712 was the *Gunflint Trailer*. The nearby Grover Conzet Camp, a WPA camp, had a newsletter called the *Gunflint Trail*.

GUNFLINT LAKE

CAMP NUMBER: S-67
Post Office: Grand Marais (Cook County)
Known Company Number: 1785
Dates: 1933–34

Notes: The camp operated from July 19, 1933, to April 20, 1934. Its assigned work area was Grand Portage State Forest.

HALFWAY

CAMP NUMBER: F-1
Post Office: Ely (St. Louis County)
Known Company Number: 704
Camp Dates: 1933–38

Notes: Company 704 was organized at Fort Snelling on April 26, 1933, and opened the Halfway camp on May 18, 1933. The camp's assigned work area was in the Superior National Forest. Company 704, which had several African American members when first formed, operated Halfway through May 1938. The newspaper of Company 704 was the *Birch Lake Newsette*.

HOUSTON (HOKAH)

CAMP NUMBERS: PE-89, SCS-4
Post Office: Houston (Houston County)
Known Company Numbers: 738, 714, 3712, 3710
Dates: 1933, 1934, 1935, 1936–37

Notes: Company 738 was at Houston during the summer of 1933. Company 714 was sent to the camp on April 26, 1934, serving throughout that summer. Company 3712 arrived at the camp on June 18, 1935, again serving throughout the summer. Company 3710 was the last company assigned to Houston, staying from January 6, 1936, until the summer of 1937. The camp was a private erosion tent camp during the summers of 1933 and 1934 and a year-round Soil Conservation Service camp beginning in the summer of 1935. It was assigned to the Gilmore Creek Project. The newspaper of Company 3710 was *Root River Echoes,* while the newspaper of Company 714 was the *Lone Wolf*.

HOVLAND

CAMP NUMBER: S-62
Post Office: Grand Marais (Cook County)
Known Company Number: 722
Dates: 1933–37

Notes: Company 722 was organized at Fort Snelling on May 30, 1933, and opened Hovland on June 13, 1933. The camp closed on April 9, 1937. Its assigned work area was Grand Portage State Forest. The company had several African American members when first formed. The newspaper of Company 722 was *Camp Chips*.

INGER

CAMP NUMBER: F-27
Post Office: Deer River (Itasca County)
Known Company Numbers: 1797, 4709
Camp Dates: 1933–36

Notes: A company of Kansas and Missouri enrollees opened the camp on August 16, 1933. Company 1797 was organized on May 25, 1933, and moved to the camp on November 2, 1933. The company was quarantined in the camp for three weeks in April 1934 because of a measles epidemic. Company 4709 was transferred to Inger in 1935. The company was then transferred to Wirt (F-37) in May 1936, at which time the camp closed. Its assigned work area was in the Chippewa National Forest. The newspaper of Company 4709 was *Tres Lacs*.

ISABELLA (DUNNIGAN)

CAMP NUMBER: F-17
Post Office: Ely (St. Louis County)
Known Company Number: 1721
Camp Dates: 1933–35

Notes: Also called Dunnigan, but not to be confused with F-16, the Isabella camp was established on June 20, 1933. It operated as a "mixed" camp, with twelve African American enrollees in October 1934 and eight African Americans in July 1935. The camp was listed as reestablished in October 1936, but it did not reopen. Its assigned work area was in the Superior National Forest. The newsletters of Company 1721 were the *Jumpin Frog* and the *Isabella Trail Blazer*. An enrollee from Company 1721, Bernard Fitzpatrick of St. Paul, enlisted in the army after serving at Isabella and survived the Bataan Death March during World War II.

ITASCA STATE PARK

CAMP NUMBER: SP-1
Post Office: Lake Itasca (Hubbard County?)
Known Company Numbers: 1764, 3701
Dates: 1933–37

Notes: Company 1764, from Fort Riley, Kansas, opened the camp between June 28 and 29, 1933. Company 3701 occupied the camp from June 14, 1935, until the camp closed in 1937. This was the first of two CCC camps in Itasca State Park. The newspaper of Company 3701 was *Northern Notes*.

ITASCA STATE PARK

CAMP NUMBER: SP-19
Post Office: Lake Itasca (Clearwater County)
Known Company Number: V-1785
Dates: 1937–42

Notes: This second CCC camp in Itasca State Park opened in 1937 and operated until July 15, 1942. It was designated as a veterans camp in 1938 after the arrival of Company V-1785, whose members served at Scenic State Park (SP-3) and Sibley State Park (SP-7) before transferring to Itasca. At its closing, it was the last state park camp operating in the United States. The camp was located on the present site of the Pine Ridge Campground, where a plaque commemorating the June 6, 1936, visit of CCC director Robert Fechner may be seen. In 1942 officials wrote, "As usual, this camp is found to be very satisfactory. A veteran company with the men having a great deal of personal pride in their camp." The newspapers for Company V-1785 were the *Three Bears Camp,* the *Old Hobnail, Ye Olde Hobnail,* and *Sibley Speaks*.

ITASCA STATE PARK ANNEX

CAMP NUMBER: S-70
Post Office: Douglas Lodge (Itasca County)
Known Company Numbers: 788, 1723
Dates: 1933–34, 1934–35

Notes: Company 788 opened the camp on June 24, 1933, and operated it until April 10, 1934. The camp was reestablished on October 13, 1934, by Company 1723 and operated until November 5, 1935. Its assigned work area included Itasca State Park and surrounding state forest areas. The newspaper of Company 1723 was the *Pine Knoll Echo*.

JAY COOKE STATE PARK

CAMP NUMBER: SP-2
Post Office: Thomson (Carlton County)
Known Company Numbers: 1712, 2710, 2773, 3703
Dates: 1933–35

Notes: Company 1712 opened this camp, the first of two to operate in Jay Cooke State Park, between June 22 and 26, 1933. Company 2710 transferred to the camp on July 22, 1934, followed by Company 2773 on October 23, 1934. Company 3703 occupied the camp from June through October 1935. At that time, the camp was unexpectedly closed. Enrollees at this camp worked on a variety of projects, including building the John Jacob Astor fur trade post replica at Fond du Lac in far western Duluth. The newspaper of Company 1712 was the *Jay Cooke Arrowhead,* while the newspaper of Company 3703 was the *Jay Cooke Echo*.

JAY COOKE STATE PARK

CAMP NUMBER: SP-21
Post Office: Thomson (Carlton County)
Known Company Number: 2711
Dates: 1939–42

Notes: This second camp in Jay Cooke State Park opened on July 7, 1939, and operated until March 25, 1942. It was one of the last state park camps to close in Minnesota. The camp newspaper was the *Ogantz Trail*.

JORDAN

CAMP NUMBER: SCS-19
Post Office: Jordan (Scott County)
Known Company Number: 2770
Dates: 1940–42

Notes: The camp opened on May 12, 1940, and operated until late winter or early spring 1942. Its buildings were moved in from Red Wing (SCS-9) when that camp closed in the spring of 1940.

KABETOGAMA LAKE

CAMP NUMBER: S-81
Post Office: Ray (Koochiching County)
Known Company Number: 724
Dates: 1933–37

Notes: The Kabetogama Lake camp opened on June 17, 1933, and closed on September 30, 1937. The camp's design was unique in that all main buildings were connected by underground tunnels, so that enrollees did not have to go outside to move from building to building. The camp's assigned work area was Kabetogama State Forest. Company 724's newspaper was the *North Star*.

LAKE CITY (PEPIN)

CAMP NUMBERS: PE-86, SCS-16
Post Office: Lake City, Wabasha (Wabasha County)
Known Company Numbers: 1750, 785, 737, 713
Dates: 1933, 1934, 1935–41

Notes: Company 1750 opened the Lake City camp on June 18, 1933, near Wabasha, on the Mississippi River. Company 785 moved to the camp between April 22 and 23, 1934. That company had also served at Elbow Lake (S-58) and Sand Lake (F-26), before moving to Lake City. Company 737 occupied the camp from 1935 to 1936, and Company 713 arrived on January 16, 1936, staying until the camp closed in the spring of 1941. Lake City operated as a private erosion tent camp during the summers of 1933 and 1934 before opening as a year-round Soil Conservation Service camp in the summer of 1935. Its assigned work area was initially the Gilmore Creek Project, changing to the Prairie Creek Demonstration Project (Faribault) in 1937. In 1938 officials described the camp as having an "excellent camp area, well kept, and a well-commanded company." The newspapers of Company 713 were the *Big Bluff, Echo Trail Echoes, Lake Pepin Breezes, Pepin Breezes, Pepin Newsletter*, and *Pepinette*.

LAKESHORE WAYSIDE PARK

CAMP NUMBER: SP-18
Post Office: Knife River (Lake County)
Known Company Numbers: 1751, 2753
Dates: 1935–37

Notes: Company 2753 opened the camp on September 27, 1935. Company 1751 transferred to the Lakeshore Wayside Park camp on April 29, 1936, and operated the camp through 1937. Sponsored by the Minnesota Department of Highways, the Lakeshore Wayside Park camp was a state park camp with a work program that fell under the technical supervision of the National Park Service. Enrollees built several waysides, including one made of native stone south of Two Harbors. Enrollees also built the Knife River Historical Marker on old Highway 61. When the camp closed unexpectedly, enrollees helped complete several work projects in Jay Cooke State Park, including the picnic shelter at Oldenburg Point. The newspaper of Company 2753 was the *Dakota Wayside Camper,* while the newspaper of Company 1751 was the *Lakeshore Camp News*.

LAND O'LAKES

CAMP NUMBER: S-97
Post Office: Outing (Cass County)
Known Company Numbers: 4750, 4707, 2703
Dates: 1935–41, 1941–42

Notes: Company 4750 opened the camp on September 10, 1935. It was followed by Company 4707 on April 29, 1936. A foreman and three enrollees from Company 4707 spent four days moving ccc forest administration materials to the new location in Grand Rapids in September of that year. Company 4707 operated Land O'Lakes until it closed on August 15, 1941. Company 2703 reestablished the camp on October 21, 1941, and operated it until its closing on January 10, 1942. The camp's assigned work area was Land O'Lakes State Forest. The newspapers of Company 4707 were the *Kansas Outburst* and the *Sylvan Echo*. Company 2703 published the *Timber Wolf's Howl*.

LANESBORO (PRESTON)

CAMP NUMBERS: PE-91, SCS-7
Post Office: Preston, Lanesboro (Fillmore County)
Known Company Numbers: 751, 4713, 2771, 706
Dates: 1933, 1934, 1935–42

Notes: Preston was a private erosion tent camp operating only during the summer of 1933. It was located on the county fairgrounds in Preston. A group of about fifty African American enrollees from Iowa were attached to the camp for a month (June 29–July 20, 1933) before being transferred to forest camps. Company 751—organized at Fort Crook, Nebraska, and serving first in Berkeley, California—opened the camp after it was transferred to Lanesboro on April 27, 1934. Enrollees were described as a "pretty boisterous bunch" by the men in a company that followed. Lanesboro opened as a year-round Soil Conservation Service camp in the summer of 1935, with Company 4713 occupying the camp from June 19, 1935, to 1937. Company 2771 served at the camp in 1936. Company 706 arrived on April 13, 1937, and stayed until the camp closed on March 15, 1942. The camp's assigned work area was initially the Deer-Bear Creek Project (Dussche Creek watershed), changing in 1937 to the Prairie Creek Demonstration Project (Faribault). At the time of its closing, Lanesboro, along with Caledonia (SCS-2), was the longest-running Soil Conservation Service camp in Minnesota. After the camp was shut down, its prefabricated buildings were dismantled and shipped to Alaska to house workers building the Al-Can Highway. The newspaper of Company 2771 was *Dusschee Creek Ripples* (also called the *Duchee Creek Ripples*), while the newspapers of Company 706 were the *706 Spotlite* and the *Spotlite*.

LARSMOUNT

CAMP NUMBER: S-98
Post Office: Wilton (Beltrami County)
Known Company Numbers: 4729, 720
Dates: 1935–41

Notes: Company 4729 opened the camp on June 24, 1935. Company 720 moved to the camp from Big Lake (F-28) on April 29, 1936. The camp closed on November 11, 1941. Its assigned work areas were Mississippi Headwaters State Forest and Buena Vista State Forest. Enrollees also worked at the game food nursery in Wilton. The newspaper of Company 4729 was the *Dakota Eagle,* while the newspaper of Company 720 was the *Pine Needle Press.*

LEECH LAKE WAYSIDE PARK

CAMP NUMBER: SP-16
Post Office: Walker (Cass County)
Known Company Number: 4707
Dates: 1935–36

Notes: The camp opened in about 1935 and operated until Company 4707 was sent to Walker (F-48) in the spring of 1936. Sponsored by the Minnesota Department of Highways, the camp was a state park camp working under the technical supervision of the National Park Service. Enrollees are believed to have built a stone overlook on the south shore of Leech Lake near Whipholt. The newspapers of Company 4707 were the *Kansas Outburst* and the *Sylvan Echo.*

LEWISTON

CAMP NUMBERS: PE-87, SCS-11
Post Office: Lewiston (Winona County)
Known Company Numbers: 1716, 723
Dates: 1933, 1934, 1935–41

Notes: Company 1716, organized in Kansas in June 1933, went first to Cabin City (S-83) before opening Lewiston between April 24 and 25, 1933. The camp was a private erosion tent camp during the summers of 1933 and 1934; it opened as a year-round Soil Conservation Service camp in the summer of 1935. Company 723 occupied the camp from May 2, 1935, until it closed on August 15, 1941. The camp was initially assigned to the Gilmore Creek Project before being transferred to the Prairie Creek Demonstration Project (Faribault) in 1937. The newspapers of Company 1716 were the *1716 Tamarack* and the *Tamarack.* The newspapers of Company 723 were the *723 Broken Mirror, Broken Mirror,* and *723 Weekly Mirror.*

LITTLE BEAR LAKE (GEORGE WASHINGTON AT THISTLEDEW)

CAMP NUMBER: S-71
Post Office: Perch Lake (Carlton County)
Known Company Number: 1758
Dates: 1933

Notes: The camp, also known as George Washington at Thistledew, operated from June 22, 1933, to October 24, 1933. Its assigned work area was George Washington State Forest.

LONG LAKE

CAMP NUMBER: S-69
Post Office: Park Rapids (Hubbard County)
Known Company Number: 1787/1762
Dates: 1933

Notes: Company 1787/1762 occupied the camp from June 28, 1933, until its transfer to Squaw Lake (F-36) in November. The camp operated from July 1, 1933, to November 4, 1933. Its assigned work area was White Earth State Forest.

LONGVILLE

CAMP NUMBERS: S-100, F-47
Post Office: Longville (Cass County)
Known Company Number: 2704
Camp Dates: 1935–37

Notes: Established on October 28, 1935, as S-100, this camp never actually operated as a state forest camp; its work area was absorbed into the Chippewa National Forest before the camp could begin operation. Company 2704 was transferred to Longville on January 15, 1936, and operated the camp as a national forest camp until it closed in 1937. The newspaper of Company 2704 was the *Score of 2704*.

LOVELIS LAKE

CAMP NUMBERS: S-57, DS-142
Post Office: Park Rapids, Arago (Hubbard County)
Known Company Numbers: 784, 2703, 3719
Dates: 1933–41

Notes: Company 784 was organized at Fort Riley, Kansas, on May 6, 1933, and opened Lovelis Lake between June 16 and 21, 1933. Company 2703 moved to the camp on November 2, 1934, and Company 3719 arrived on October 26, 1935. The camp closed on October 28, 1941. Its assigned work area was Itasca State Park and White Earth State Forest. Longtime superintendent George "Haywire" Wilson was remembered fondly despite his habit of ignoring bureaucratic directives of all types. The newspaper of Company 2703 was the *Timber Wolf's Howl*.

LUNA LAKE

CAMP NUMBER: F-25
Post Office: Chisholm (St. Louis County)
Known Company Numbers: V-1775, 3702
Camp Dates: 1933–35, 1936–41

Notes: Company V-1775, composed of World War I veterans, was organized at Fort Snelling in June 1933 and opened Luna Lake on July 15, 1933. Company V-1775 occupied Luna Lake until being transferred to Partridge River (F-52) in October 1935. Company 3702 moved to the camp on January 1, 1936. The camp closed in November 1941. Its assigned work area was in the Superior National Forest. The newspaper of Company V-1775 was the *Sturgeon River Ripples*, while the newspapers of Company 3702 were the *Sturgeon River Star* and the *Voice of Minn-Mo-Dak*.

LYDICK NURSERY

CAMP NUMBER: F-42
Post Office: Cass Lake (Cass County)
Known Company Number: 3720
Camp Dates: 1935

Notes: Lydick Nursery opened as a tent camp during the summer of 1935. Construction started on a permanent camp but was never completed. The camp operated for less than a full six-month enrollment period. Its assigned work area was in the Chippewa National Forest.

MACK

CAMP NUMBER: F-32
Post Office: Mack (Itasca County)
Known Company Number: 1724
Camp Dates: 1933–34, 1934–37

Notes: Company 1724 formed at Fort Snelling on June 22, 1933, and transferred from Big Sandy Lake (S-61) in October 1933 to open the camp at Mack. When Company 1724 transferred on May 1, 1934, to Day Lake (F-34), the Mack camp was closed. The camp was reestablished in October 1934 by a North Dakota company and operated until 1937.

MAPLE LAKE

CAMP NUMBER: SCS-20
Post Office: Maple Lake (Wright County)
Known Company Number: 3710
Dates: 1940–42

Notes: The camp opened on June 21, 1940, and operated until winter or early spring 1942. The camp newspaper was the *Maple Ache*.

MILLE LACS LAKE HIGHWAY WAYSIDE

CAMP NUMBER: SP-15
Post Office: Garrison (Crow Wing County)
Known Company Numbers: 3716, 3738, 2711, V-2713
Dates: 1935–40

Notes: Company 3716 opened the camp on June 12, 1935. Company 3738 arrived on September 6, 1935. Company 2711 occupied the camp from 1939 until its closing in the spring of 1940. At that time, enrollees transferred to the St. Croix RDA camp (SP-6). Sponsored by the Minnesota Department of Highways, the camp was under the technical supervision of the National Park Service. Enrollees built a concourse and overlook at Garrison, a shelter and picnic facilities, the Kenney Lake Overlook, and three stone-faced highway bridges. They also relocated Highway 169 to keep a picnic shelter on the lake side of the road. Officials called it the "largest and most extensive of the highway ccc camps." The newspapers of Company V-2713 were the *Camp Call* and the *Vet's Call* (various spellings). The newspapers of Company 2711 were the *Challenge, New Challenge,* and *Scetch-o-graphs*.

MILLE LACS (VINELAND)

CAMP NUMBERS: DS-135, S-135
Post Office: Onamia (Mille Lacs County)
Known Company Number: 2711
Dates: 1934–35

Notes: Opened between August 24 and 27, 1934, as a drought relief camp, Mille Lacs's work program gradually expanded to forest cultural work. The camp operated until October 25, 1935. Its assigned work area was Mille Lacs State Forest. The newspapers of Company 2711 were the *Challenge, New Challenge,* and *Scetch-o-graphs*.

MILLER TRUNK HIGHWAY

CAMP NUMBER: S-77
Post Office: Culver (St. Louis County)
Known Company Number: 786
Dates: 1933–34

Notes: The camp operated from September 18, 1933, to January 9, 1934, with enrollees doing truck-trail construction and roadside cleanup. Company 786 was an African American company made up of men from Kansas, Missouri, Nebraska, Iowa, and Arkansas. They were transferred to the Day Lake camp (F-34) on December 13, 1933. The camp's assigned work area was Cloquet Valley State Forest.

MINERAL CENTER

CAMP NUMBER: S-68
Post Office: Grand Portage (Cook County)
Known Company Number: 1734
Dates: 1933

Notes: The camp opened between June 27 and 29, 1933, closing on November 11, 1933. Its assigned work area was Grand Portage State Forest.

NETT LAKE

CCC-ID CAMP NUMBER: 3 IN DISTRICT 1
Post Office: Bois Fort, Gheen (Koochiching, St. Louis counties)
Known Company Number: none
Dates: 1933–42

Notes: The first ccc-ID camp in Minnesota, with a company organized on June 27, 1933, opened at Nett Lake on July 16, 1933, to serve the Consolidated Chippewa reservations. The camp operated in its original location until 1941, when, needing extensive repairs, it was moved. The new Nett Lake camp, its post office in Gheen, opened on February 12, 1941, and closed in 1942. In 1936, officials called the original Nett Lake camp "very striking" because of its brick chimneys and painted buildings.

NIMROD

CAMP NUMBERS: DS-136, S-136
Post Office: Sebeka (Wadena County)
Known Company Number: 3704
Dates: 1934–35

Notes: Opened on August 22, 1934, as a drought relief camp, Nimrod later saw its work program expanded to include the Badoura Nursery. The camp operated through October 25, 1935.

NISSWA

CAMP NUMBER: S-76
Post Office: Merrifield (Crow Wing County)
Known Company Number: 4751
Dates: 1935–38

Notes: The camp opened between September 15 and 17, 1935, and operated until August 10, 1938. Its assigned work area was Crow Wing State Forest. The newspapers of Company 4751 were the *Pine Island Press,* the *Pelican Press,* and *Jusumpin*.

NORTHERN LIGHT

CAMP NUMBER: F-6
Post Office: Grand Marais (Cook County)
Known Company Numbers: 709, 721
Camp Dates: 1933–37

Notes: Company 709, organized at Fort Snelling on May 9, 1933, opened Northern Light between June 1 and 2, 1933. During the first enrollment period in the summer of 1933, the camp had nine African Americans among its members.

Company 721 was assigned to the camp in 1936. The camp closed in May 1937 "to raise average company strength" in other camps in the state. The assigned work area for the Northern Light camp was in the Superior National Forest. The newspaper of Company 709 was *Northernlight Rays,* while that of Company 721 was the *Northern Light Beacon.*

OWEN LAKE

CAMP NUMBER: S-54
Post Office: Coleraine (Itasca County)
Known Company Number: 718
Dates: 1933–42

Notes: Company 718, organized at Fort Snelling on May 26, 1933, opened the camp on June 10, 1933. Owen Lake was one of only six remaining state forest CCC camps in November 1941. It closed early in 1942. The camp's assigned work area was George Washington State Forest, but enrollees also worked at the Owen Lake game food nursery. The newspapers of Company 718 were *Northern Breezes* and the *Owen Lake Sun.*

PARK AVENUE

CAMP NUMBER: S-84
Post Office: Big Falls (Koochiching County)
Known Company Numbers: 1714, 1763
Dates: 1933–34

Notes: The camp operated from June 10, 1933, to January 10, 1934, on land owned by the Minnesota and Ontario Paper Company. Its assigned work area was Pine Island State Forest. The newspaper of Company 1714 was the *1714 Goldbricker*. The newspaper of Company 1763 was the *Woodpecker*.

PARTRIDGE RIVER

CAMP NUMBERS: F-52, P-52
Post Office: Allen Junction (St. Louis County)
Known Company Numbers: V-1775, 2767, 703
Dates: 1935–42

Notes: Company V-1775 opened the camp on October 20, 1935. Company 2767 moved to the camp on December 20, 1937, and operated it until the camp's closure in January 1942. The newspapers of Company V-1775 were the *Partridge River Cartridge* and *Sturgeon River Ripples.* Company 2767 published the *Partridge Newsletter,* while Company 703 published *Partridge River Ripsaw*.

PAUL BUNYAN

CAMP NUMBERS: DS-134, S-134
Post Office: Nevis (Hubbard County)
Known Company Number: 2708
Dates: 1934–39

Notes: Opened on August 1, 1934, as a drought relief camp, Paul Bunyan later saw its work program expanded to forest cultural work. The camp operated until October 5, 1939. Its assigned work area was Paul Bunyan State Forest and Anoka Game Refuge. Prior to service at Paul Bunyan, Company 2708 worked in the Carlos Avery Game Refuge near Wyoming, Minnesota. Company 2708's newspaper was the *Blue Ox*.

PIKE LAKE (PIKE BAY)

CAMP NUMBER: F-12
Post Office: Cass Lake (Cass County)
Known Company Numbers: 705, 3717, 3720
Camp Dates: 1933–41

Notes: Company 705, organized at Fort Snelling on April 28, 1933, opened Pike Lake on May 18, 1933. The camp operated until November 1941. Its assigned work area was in the Chippewa National Forest. The newspapers for Company 705 were the *Pike Bay Newsletter, Pike Bay Press,* and *Pike Bay Scandals*. Company 3717's newspaper was the *Beantown Bugle*.

PINE ISLAND RANGER STATION

CAMP NUMBER: S-82
Post Office: Big Falls (Koochiching County)
Known Company Numbers: 1714, 4751
Dates: 1933

Notes: The camp opened between June 25 and 28, 1933, and operated until October 24, 1933, on land leased from White Cedar Lumber Company. Its assigned work area was Pine Island State Forest. Company 1714 published the *1714 Goldbricker.* The newspapers of Company 4751 were the *Pine Island Press,* the *Pelican Press,* and *Jusumpin*.

PIPESTONE

CCC-ID CAMP NUMBER: UNKNOWN
Post Office: Pipestone (Pipestone County)
Known Company Number: none
Dates: ca. 1934–36

Notes: This CCC-ID camp served the Minnesota Sioux Agency and operated from about 1934 until about 1936. Working with R.W. Hellwig, a forester and landscaper, enrollees helped clear the Pipestone quarry area in 1934. They later built picnic tables and a shelter, which were completed in time for the area's 1937 designation as a national monument.

PLAINVIEW

CAMP NUMBERS: PE-96, SCS-13
Post Office: Plainview (Wabasha County)
Known Company Number: 2709
Dates: 1934, 1935–41

Notes: The camp operated as a private erosion tent camp during the summer of 1934, opening as a year-round Soil Conservation Service camp on October 29, 1935. The camp closed in the fall of 1941. Enrollees worked first at the Deer-Bear Creek Project area and later, beginning in 1937, at the Prairie Creek Demonstration Project (Faribault). Camp newspapers were variously titled the *2709 Loudspeaker, 2709 Reports, Loudspeaker, Loudspeaker of 2709,* and the *Voice of Plainview*.

PONEMAH

CCC-ID CAMP NUMBER: CAMP 1, UNIT 1
Post Office: Red Lake (Beltrami County)
Known Company Number: none
Dates: 1933–42

Notes: Ponemah was opened by October 1, 1933, in time for news of the camp to make the first issue of the Bureau of Indian Affairs publication *Indians at Work*. Located in an old logging camp, Ponemah housed about ninety men. In 1934, enrollees completed new buildings, new foundations for existing buildings, and the construction of banks around foundations lined with white-painted rocks. Its enrollees, from the Red Lake Indian Reservation, worked on conservation projects including blister rust control, road and truck-trail construction, lookout tower construction, and reforestation—running a nursery and planting trees on cutover lands. By 1934, the nursery already had 30,000 Norway and white pine seedlings ready for planting. Red Lake enrollees also mapped 80,000 acres of Red Lake forest reserve.

POPLAR LAKE

CAMP NUMBER: F-41
Post Office: Grand Marais (Cook County)
Known Company Numbers: V-1785, 3709
Camp Dates: 1934–36

Notes: The camp opened in October 1934, closing in 1936. Company V-1785, organized at Fort Snelling in June 1933, was one of the first three companies of veterans in Minnesota. After its organization, the company was sent to Poplar Lake, where enrollees built a barracks that became known as the "Veterans Hand Made Home" because company members cut the trees, sawed the lumber, prepared the original plans, and did all the construction work. Company 3709 was sent to the camp on June 11, 1935. Poplar Lake's assigned work area was in the Superior National Forest. The newspapers for Company V-1785 were the *Three Bears Camp,* the *Old Hobnail, Ye Olde Hobnail,* and *Sibley Speaks*. Company 3709 published the *Happy Hollow Noos*.

PORTAGE RIVER

CAMP NUMBER: F-8
Post Office: Ely (St. Louis County)
Known Company Number: 711
Camp Dates: 1933–41

Notes: Company 711, organized at Fort Snelling on May 18, 1933, opened Portage River on May 30, 1933. The camp operated until September 1941. There were several African Americans in the company when it was first formed. Portage River's assigned work area was in the Superior National Forest. Company 711's newspapers were the *Portage River Ripples* and the *Jack Pine Journal*.

RABIDEAU

CAMP NUMBER: F-50
Post Office: Blackduck (Beltrami County)
Known Company Numbers: 3749, 708
Camp Dates: 1935–41

Notes: Company 3749 opened the camp on September 5, 1935. Company 708, formed at Fort Snelling on May 5, 1933, transferred from Winnibigoshish (F-15) to Rabideau on January 5, 1936. Camp construction featured slate from old pool tables to create walkways by the education building. The camp closed in 1941. Its assigned work area was in the Chippewa National Forest. The newspapers of Company 708 were *Timber Notes* and *Pine Knots*. Although some sources indicate the Rabideau facility was used as a German prisoner of war camp, it was not. The University of Illinois has used the site for a summer school camp. The camp is one of the few remaining intact ccc camps in the United States. Placed in the National Register of Historic Places in 1976, it was designated a national historic landmark on February 17, 2006.

RED WING, HAY CREEK

CAMP NUMBERS: PE-85, SCS-9
Post Office: Red Wing (Goodhue County)
Known Company Numbers: 1752, V-1785, 4714, 2770, 3717
Dates: 1933, 1934, 1935–40

Notes: Company 1752 opened the camp on June 20, 1933, staying there through the summer. Company V-1785, one of the first three companies of veterans organized in Minnesota, went first to Poplar Lake (F-41), before being transferred to Red Wing on April 24, 1934, also remaining for the summer. Company 4714 occupied the camp from July 25, 1935, to 1937, and Company 2770 was stationed there from October 7, 1937, to 1940. In 1933 and 1934, Red Wing operated only in the summers as a private erosion tent camp. It opened as a year-round Soil Conservation Service camp in the summer of 1935. The camp was first located on the Izaak Walton Lodge property at the base of Mount La Grange before moving to its permanent site at Hay Creek. Enrollees initially worked on the Gilmore Creek Project but in 1937 transferred to the Prairie Creek Demonstration Project (Faribault). When the camp was disbanded in 1940, the buildings were moved to Jordan (SCS-19). The newspapers of Company V-1785 were the *Three Bears Camp*, the *Old Hobnail*, *Ye Olde Hobnail*, and *Sibley Speaks*. Company 4714's newspaper was the *ccc Seer*, while those of Company 2770 were the *Whistler*, *Dakota Duster*, and the *Red Wing Duster*. Company 3717 published the *Beantown Bugle*.

REMER

CAMP NUMBER: F-46
Post Office: Remer (Cass County)
Known Company Numbers: 4740, 1762, 764
Camp Dates: 1935–42

Notes: Company 4740 opened the camp on September 5, 1935. Company 1762 formed at Fort Riley, Kansas, on May 22, 1933, and transferred from Squaw Lake (F-36) to Remer in November 1935. Company 764 replaced 1762 on October 7, 1937, and operated Remer until its closing in April 1942. The camp's assigned work area was in the Chippewa National Forest. The newspaper of Company 1762 was the *Remer Camp News*, while Company 764 published the *Rambler*. The Remer camp facility later became the first German prisoner of war camp established in the Chippewa National Forest, operating from 1943 to 1945.

RICE LAKE

CAMP NUMBERS: BS-3, FWS-3
Post Office: East Lake (Aitkin County)
Known Company Number: 2705
Camp Dates: 1939–41

Notes: The camp was established on October 5, 1939, by the Bureau of Biological Services and supported work on the Rice Lake National Wildlife Refuge until the summer of 1940. The U.S. Fish and Wildlife Service operated Rice Lake from the summer of 1940 until the camp's closing in September 1941. The newspaper of Company 2705 was the *Rice Lake Quacker*.

ROCHESTER

Camp Numbers: PE-93, SCS-12
Post Office: Rochester (Olmsted County)
Known Company Numbers: 1757, V-1774
Dates: 1933, 1934, 1935–39

Notes: Company 1757 opened the camp on June 24, 1933, occupying it through the summer. Company V-1774, the first veterans' unit organized in Minnesota, was formed at Fort Snelling on June 25, 1933. It moved to Rochester for the summer on April 21, 1934, having previously served at Sand Lake (F-24). Rochester operated as a private erosion tent camp during the summers of 1933 and 1934. Company V-1774 opened Rochester as a year-round Soil Conservation

Service camp on May 12, 1935, and operated it until its closing in the spring of 1939. Enrollees worked at the Deer-Bear Creek Project before being transferred in 1937 to the Prairie Creek Demonstration Project (Faribault). The camp was a subdistrict headquarters and was described by officials in 1938 as an "unusually fine camp." The newspapers of Company V-1774 were the *Veteran's Voice* (various spellings) and *Vet's Voice*.

ROLLINGSTONE

CAMP NUMBER: SCS-15
Post Office: Rollingstone (Winona County)
Known Company Number: none
Dates: 1935

Notes: The camp was listed as a new Soil Conservation Service camp in the summer of 1935 but was never established, even though some preliminary work was done. It was removed from the camp inventory in August 1935.

ST. CROIX

CAMP NUMBERS: DP-140, DS-140, S-140
Post Office: Sandstone (Pine County)
Known Company Number: 2706
Dates: 1934–36

Notes: Company 2706 from North Dakota opened the camp on August 29, 1934, to address drought relief. The camp's work program later expanded to include all aspects of forest cultural work. Its assigned work area was St. Croix State Forest. After the CCC camp closed in 1936, the facility was turned over to the WPA as housing for workers on the St. Croix RDA (SP-6). The newspaper of Company 2706 was the *St. Croix Leader*.

ST. CROIX RECREATIONAL DEMONSTRATION AREA (YELLOWBANKS CAMP)

CAMP NUMBER: SP-6
Post Office: Hinckley (Pine County)
Known Company Number: 3715
Dates: 1934–37

Notes: Company 3715 occupied the camp from October 6, 1934, through the camp's closing on December 15, 1937. The camp was built on the site of an Indian village in an area known as Yellowbanks. Enrollees worked on park buildings, including the St. Croix Lodge, as part of the Recreational Development Area (RDA). St. Croix was one of the largest and most well-known RDAs in the country. This camp was one of two CCC camps, along with NP-1 (see below), to operate in the RDA. Close inspection of several full company photographs shows a trick common among enrollees—standing first at one end of the group photo and then moving ahead of the photographer's rolling camera to appear again at the other end of the picture. Company 3715 published the *Yellow Banks Holler*.

ST. CROIX RECREATIONAL DEMONSTRATION AREA (FLEMING)

CAMP NUMBER: NP-1
Post Office: Hinckley (Pine County)
Known Company Number: V-2713
Dates: 1940–42

Notes: The camp was opened on May 17, 1940, by a company of World War I veterans transferred from the Mille Lacs Highway Wayside (SP-15) project. This was the second CCC camp at the St. Croix RDA (SP-6). Enrollees worked on various projects including completing the Head of the Lakes Group Camp area. In 1941, officials described the camp as having "exceptionally fine exterior development" and a "very satisfactory relationship with the surrounding locality." The camp closed on May 22, 1942. The All Seasons Trail Center was developed on the site in about 1975. The newspapers of Company V-2713 were the *Camp Call* and the *Vet's Call* (various spellings).

ST. PAUL FOREST AND WATER PRESERVE (LAKE VADNAIS METROPOLITAN PARK)

CAMP NUMBER: SP-17
Post Office: St. Paul (Ramsey County)
Known Company Numbers: 2727, 4727
Dates: 1935–37

Notes: The camp was established on August 15, 1935, and operated until 1937. In 1937, Company 4727 erected at Lake Phalen in St. Paul a marker made of native stone and rock gathered from CCC camps in all of the then forty-eight United States and from the departments of Labor, War, Agriculture, and Interior, along with a cornerstone from the floor of the White House. The marker, which is still standing, was dedicated to young men across the country who had died while protecting the nation's natural resources. The newspaper of Company 4727 was the *Bear Facts*.

SAND LAKE

CAMP NUMBER: F-24
Post Office: Britt, Virginia (St. Louis County)
Known Company Number: V-1774
Camp Dates: 1933–34

Notes: Company V-1774, the first veterans' unit formed in Minnesota, was organized on June 25, 1933, at Fort Snelling. The company was sent to Sand Lake on July 15, 1933, where it served for one year before being transferred to Rochester (SCS-12) on April 21, 1934. Sand Lake (F-24) closed at that time. Its assigned work area was in the Superior National Forest.

SAND LAKE (CUT FOOT SIOUX 2)

CAMP NUMBER: F-26
Post Office: Deer River (Itasca County)
Known Company Numbers: 785, 3717, 4707
Camp Dates: 1933–34, 1934–36

Notes: Kansas Company 785 came from Elbow Lake (S-58) on November 1, 1933, to open the camp. The company transferred to Lake City (PE-86) on May 31, 1934, and Sand Lake (F-26) closed at that time. The camp was reestablished in October 1934 by Company 3717. Company 4707 from Missouri moved to the camp in the summer of 1935, operating the camp until 1936, when the company was sent to Walker (F-48). The camp closed permanently at that time. Its assigned work area was in the Chippewa National Forest. In the summer of 1936, a diphtheria epidemic broke out, and the camp was quarantined for a time. The newspaper of Company 3717 was the *Beantown Bugle*, while Company 4707 published the *Kansas Outburst* and the *Sylvan Echo*.

SAWBILL

CAMP NUMBER: F-10
Post Office: Tofte (Cook County)
Known Company Number: 716
Camp Dates: 1933–41

Notes: The camp opened between June 7 and 9, 1933, and operated until September 30, 1941. Company 716 had the highest rating in the East Superior Subdistrict based on work accomplished during the second enrollment period (October 1933–June 1934). Its assigned work area was in the Superior National Forest. The camp newspapers were the *Sawbill Sez-All, New Sawbill, Sawbill Journal, Sawbill Senator, Sawbill Trails End, Sawbill Smokeater*, and *Trails End*.

SCENIC STATE PARK

CAMP NUMBER: SP-3
Post Office: Big Fork, Coleraine (Itasca County)
Known Company Numbers: 1722, V-2713, V-1785
Dates: 1933–36

Notes: Kansas Company 1722 opened the Scenic State Park camp on June 21, 1933. Company V-2713 transferred to the camp on August 10, 1934. The camp closed in January 1936 when its remaining enrollees transferred to Deer Lake (S-95). Scenic was the first state park camp to begin operations in Minnesota. The newspapers of Company V-2713 were the *Camp Call* and the *Vet's Call* (various spellings). Company V-1785 published the *Three Bears Camp*, the *Old Hobnail, Ye Olde Hobnail*, and *Sibley Speaks*.

SCHLEY

CAMP NUMBER: F-22
Post Office: Schley (Cass County)
Known Company Numbers: 787, 4708, 765
Camp Dates: 1933–37

Notes: Company 787, organized in Fort Riley, Kansas, opened Schley between June 14 and 15, 1933. Company 4708 occupied the camp on September 1, 1935. The camp closed in May 1937. Its assigned work area was in the Chippewa National Forest. Company 765's newspaper was the *Nodak Rambler*, while Company 4708 published *Schley Tales*.

SEAGULL

CAMP NUMBERS: F-55, P-55
Post Office: Grand Marais (Cook County)
Known Company Number: 3709
Dates: 1935–39

Notes: The camp opened on October 30, 1935, and operated until the spring of 1939. Seagull was the most isolated camp in Minnesota, located at the end of the Gunflint Trail, fifty-three miles from Grand Marais, the nearest town, and 138 miles from the nearest rail point at Two Harbors. Its assigned work area was in the Superior National Forest. Camp newspapers were the *Seagull Times, Seagull Weekly Times,* and the *Seagullite.*

SIBLEY STATE PARK

CAMP NUMBER: SP-7
Post Office: New London (Kandiyohi County)
Known Company Number: V-1785
Dates: 1935–38

Notes: The camp opened on May 2, 1935, in a spring snowstorm and operated until the summer of 1938 when Company V-1785 transferred to Itasca State Park (SP-19). Enrollees constructed park buildings from waste rock taken from the Cold Spring and Rockville stone quarries. The newspapers for Company V-1785 were the *Three Bears Camp,* the *Old Hobnail, Ye Olde Hobnail,* and *Sibley Speaks.*

SIDE LAKE

CAMP NUMBER: S-53
Post Office: Side Lake (St. Louis County)
Known Company Number: 717
Dates: 1933–41

Notes: Company 717, organized at Fort Snelling on May 24, 1933, opened the camp between June 10 and 12, 1933. Side Lake was probably the only CCC camp in Minnesota to have blacktopped streets. Captain William Wipf, Infantry Reserve and commanding officer of Side Lake, struck a deal with a local blacktop contractor. In exchange for old army clothes "and stuff like that," the contractor blacktopped all streets and driveways in the camp. The company basketball team won the state CCC tournament two years in a row, publishing *Basketball Review, 1937–38,* in honor of the accomplishment. In 1939, four men from the camp were selected for the CCC All-American baseball team. Only one other camp in the country, located in the state of Virginia, had four players chosen for the team. In 1935, Side Lake was named the best camp in Minnesota and the second best in the Seventh Corps area. In 1940, it was still considered an "excellent all-around camp" and a "superior organization" by the Minnesota CCC District. Side Lake's assigned work area was George Washington State Forest. The camp closed on August 15, 1941, when Company 717 moved to Montana to work on defense projects. Camp buildings either were torn down at that time or moved to S-145 near Kelliher. Camp newspapers were the *(717) Once Over, Company Once-Over, Washington Post,* and *Side Lake Star.*

SMOKEY HILLS

CAMP NUMBERS: DS-142, S-142
Post Office: Osage (Becker County)
Known Company Number: 2703
Dates: 1934–35

Notes: Opened on November 1, 1934, to provide drought relief, the camp later saw its work program expanded to all aspects of forest cultural work. It operated until October 28, 1935, with an assigned work area of Smokey Hills State Forest. Company 2703's newspaper was the *Timber Wolf's Howl.*

SPRUCE CREEK HIGHWAY WAYSIDE (CASCADE RIVER WAYSIDE)

CAMP NUMBERS: SP-13, DSP-5
Post Office: Lutsen (Cook County)
Known Company Number: 2702
Dates: 1934–36

Notes: Also known as Cascade River Wayside, the Spruce Creek Highway Wayside camp opened on July 24, 1934, and operated through October 1936. Sponsored by the Minnesota Department of Highways, it was under the technical supervision of the National Park Service. The camp's work projects included building foot trails, a highway concourse, and the Cascade River overlook. This overlook was one of the first of its kind in the country and served as a demonstration project on how to incorporate rock outcroppings into wayside development.

SPRUCE LAKE

CAMP NUMBERS: F-53, P-53
Post Office: Two Harbors (Lake County)
Known Company Numbers: 752, 3707
Dates: 1935–42

Notes: Company 752 opened the camp on June 1, 1935. Company 3707 moved to the camp on April 29, 1936, and operated Spruce Lake through its closing early in 1942. The camp's assigned work area was in the Superior National Forest. Enrollees also worked at the Knife River Nursery. The newspaper of Company 3707 was the *Spruce Lake Splash.*

SQUAW LAKE

CAMP NUMBER: F-36
Post Office: Squaw Lake (Itasca County)
Known Company Numbers: 1787/1762
Camp Dates: 1933–35

Notes: Kansas Company 1787/1762 was organized on May 27, 1933, and served first at Long Lake (S-69), before opening Squaw Lake between November 10 and 11, 1933. The company occupied the Squaw Lake camp until being transferred to Remer (F-46) in November 1935. Squaw Lake closed at that time. In 1934, officials said the camp resembled "a high class summer resort." They further described a barracks floor "white enough to eat from, graveled walks bordered by stone, artistic and rustic benches in quadrangle, tennis courts, [and a] very homey recreational hall with comfortable reading room." The camp's assigned work area was in the Chippewa National Forest. The company's newspaper was the *Brush Happy*.

STOKES

CAMP NUMBER: F-35
Post Office: Grand Rapids (Itasca County)
Known Company Numbers: 1714, 4716
Camp Dates: 1933–37

Notes: The camp opened on June 25, 1933. Company 1714 was organized at Fort Leavenworth, Kansas, on June 3, 1933, transferring to Pine Island Ranger Station (S-82) and then to Park Avenue (S-84). On January 10, 1934, Company 1714 was sent to Stokes, operating the camp for one and one-half years. Company 4716 occupied the camp from July 15, 1935, until its closing in May 1937. The Stokes camp had an assigned work area in the Chippewa National Forest. The newspaper of Company 1714 was the *1714 Goldbricker,* while that of Company 4716 was the *Stokes Jayhawker*.

SULLIVAN LAKE (CAMP CHARLES)

CAMP NUMBER: S-51
Post Office: Brimson (St. Louis County)
Known Company Number: 719
Dates: 1933–41

Notes: Also known as Camp Charles, the Sullivan Lake camp was opened between June 10 and 12, 1933, by Company 719, which was organized at Fort Snelling on May 16 of that year. The company operated the camp until October 30, 1941, working in Cloquet Valley State Forest. J. C. "Buzz" Ryan was the camp forester. He later published several articles and booklets about his years in the CCC. The camp newspaper was the *Sullivanite*.

TAMARAC LAKE REFUGE

CAMP NUMBERS: BF-2, BS-2, FWS-2
Post Office: Rochert (Becker County)
Known Company Number: 4709
Camp Dates: 1937–41

Notes: The Tamarac Lake Refuge camp was established between June 15 and 18, 1937, as a migratory bird refuge camp and operated as such until the fall of 1939. From the fall of 1939 to the summer of 1940, the camp was operated by the Bureau of Biological Services, and enrollees worked at the Tamarac National Wildlife Refuge. Finally, from the summer of 1940 until its closing on July 30, 1941, the camp was operated by the U.S. Fish and Wildlife Service. Officials in 1937 described Company 4709 as "well commanded" and a "fine group of enrollees." The newspaper of Company 4709 was the *Tres Lacs*.

TEMPERANCE RIVER (CAMP TEMPERANCE)

CAMP NUMBER: F-19
Post Office: Tofte (Cook County)
Known Company Numbers: 1728, 2705, 3705
Camp Dates: 1933–34, 1934–36

Notes: Also known as Camp Temperance, this camp was occupied by African American Company 1728 from June 26, 1933, until June 1934, when the company was reassigned to a soil conservation camp in Missouri. The camp was closed from June 1934 to October 1934. Temperance River was reestablished and in the spring of 1935 was given an expanded program, with an assigned work area in the Superior National Forest. Company 2705 moved into the camp on June 11, 1935. The camp closed permanently in 1936. Company 3705's newspaper was the *Temperance Valley Echo*.

THIEF LAKE MIGRATORY WATERFOWL REFUGE (MUD LAKE MIGRATORY WATERFOWL REFUGE)

CAMP NUMBERS: BF-1, BS-1, FWS-1
Post Office: Middle River (Marshall County)
Known Company Numbers: 710, 3719
Camp Dates: 1935–42

Notes: Thief Lake operated as a migratory bird refuge camp from October 25, 1935, until the fall of 1939. Enrollees worked to restore the lake level for the benefit of breeding waterfowl and upland game. From the fall of 1939 to the summer of 1940, the camp was operated by the Bureau of Biological Services, and enrollees worked in the Thief Lake Wildlife Area. From the summer of 1939 until its closing in May 1942, the camp was operated by the U.S. Fish and Wildlife Service—during which time it was called the Mud Lake Migratory Waterfowl Refuge. The camp was one of the last CCC camps to remain in operation in Minnesota. The newspapers of Company 710 were the *Peat Smoke, Peat Smoke News Flash,* and *Peat Smoke Weekly*.

THIRD RIVER

CAMP NUMBER: S-59
Post Office: Alvwood (Itasca County)
Known Company Number: 1761
Dates: 1933–35

Notes: Kansas Company 1761 opened the camp on June 28, 1933. Third River operated as a state forest camp, with a work area of Third River State Forest, until September 9, 1935. At that time, its work area was absorbed into the Chippewa National Forest and it was reestablished as Thirteen Mile (F-45), which operated until 1936.

THIRTEEN MILE

CAMP NUMBER: F-45
Post Office: Alvwood (Itasca County)
Known Company Number: 1761
Camp Dates: 1933–36

Notes: The camp was first established by Kansas Company 1761 on June 28, 1933, as Third River (S-59), with an assigned work area of Third River State Forest. It became a federal forest camp, under the name Thirteen Mile, on September 9, 1935, when its work area was absorbed into the Chippewa National Forest. The camp closed in 1936.

VERMILION

CAMP NUMBER: S-94
Post Office: Orr (St. Louis County)
Known Company Numbers: 725, 723, 3710
Dates: 1933–34, 1934–35, 1935–36

Notes: Company 725 opened the camp on November 1, 1933, and operated it until April 10, 1934. The camp was reestablished on October 31, 1934, and operated until May 1, 1935. Vermilion was reestablished again between June 11 and 12, 1935, and operated until January 15, 1936. The camp's assigned work area was Kabetogama State Forest. The newspapers of Company 723 were the *Weekly Mirror* and the *Broken Mirror*, while Company 725 published the *Northern Hi-Lights* and *Northern Hi-Lites*. Company 3710's newspaper was *Vermilion River Echoes*.

VERMILION DAM

CAMP NUMBER: S-55
Post Office: Faunce, Beltrami Island (Lake of the Woods County)
Known Company Number: 723
Dates: 1933

Notes: Company 723 was organized on May 29, 1933, and opened the camp between June 13 and 15, 1933. The company closed the camp on October 24, 1933, and was later transferred to Caledonia (PE-88). Vermilion Dam's assigned work area was Beltrami Island State Forest. The newspapers of Company 723 were the *Weekly Mirror* and the *Broken Mirror*.

VERMILION DAM

CAMP NUMBERS F-56, P-56
Post Office: Tower (St. Louis County)
Known Company Number: 3708
Dates: 1935–37

Notes: Company 3708 opened the camp between October 30 and 31, 1935, and operated it until May 1937. The camp's assigned work area was in the Superior National Forest. Company 3708's newspaper was the *Leader*.

WAGNER LAKE (DORA LAKE)

CAMP NUMBER: F-51
Post Office: Northome (Koochiching County)
Known Company Numbers: 2701, 4728
Dates: 1935–37

Notes: A company of North Dakota CCC enrollees built the Wagner Lake camp while living in a nearby tent camp during the summer of 1935. Company 2701 transferred to the camp on November 1, 1935. The camp closed in 1937. Its assigned work area was in the Chippewa National Forest. Company 2701's newspaper was *Dora Lake Ripples,* while the newspaper of Company 4728 was the *Call of the Wild.*

WALKER

CAMP NUMBERS: S-101, F-48
Post Office: Walker (Cass County)
Known Company Numbers: 1723, 4707, 3709
Camp Dates: 1935–41

Notes: Walker was originally established as a state forest camp but never operated as one because its work area was immediately absorbed into the Chippewa National Forest. Company 1723 opened Walker as a national forest camp on October 29, 1935. Kansas Company 4707 was at the camp until its transfer to Land O' Lakes (S-97) in 1936. Company 3709 occupied the camp from July 16, 1939, until it closed in 1941. Company 1723's newspaper was the *Pine Knoll Echo.* Company 4707 published the *Kansas Outburst* and the *Sylvan Echo,* while Company 3709 published the *Walkerite.*

WANLESS

CAMP NUMBER: F-3
Post Office: Schroeder (Cook County)
Known Company Numbers: 703, 715
Camp Dates: 1933–35

Notes: The camp opened on May 15, 1933. It operated during the summers of 1933, 1934, and 1935 and closed in October 1935. In July 1933, thirty-one African American enrollees from Lanesboro (PE-91) were transferred to the camp to serve out their enrollment periods. Its assigned work area was in the Superior National Forest. The newspaper of Company 703 was the *Wanless Ripsaw,* while Company 715 published the *Tiger* and the *Whispering Pine.*

WATERVILLE

CAMP NUMBER: SCS-10
Post Office: Waterville (Le Sueur County)
Known Company Numbers: 4715, 3710
Dates: 1935–40

Notes: Kansas Company 4715 opened the camp on October 26, 1935. Company 3710 occupied Waterville from October 4, 1937, until the camp's closing in the spring of 1940. The camp's first assigned work area was the Deer-Bear Creek Project, but this changed in 1936, when enrollees began work on the Prairie Creek Demonstration Project (Faribault). A side camp was built at New Prague. The newspaper of both Company 4715 and Company 3710 was the *Lakeside Review.*

WHITEWATER STATE PARK

CAMP NUMBERS: SP-4, DSP-4
Post Office: St. Charles (Winona County)
Known Company Numbers: 1723, 2709
Dates: 1934

Notes: Company 1723—first stationed at Camp Ripley (S-64) on June 21, 1933—opened the Whitewater State Park camp (SP-4) on April 28, 1934. Enrollees were quarantined for a month with measles and mumps in May 1934. Company 2709 moved to the camp on September 28, 1934. This was the first of two state park camps to operate in Whitewater State Park. The newspaper of Company 1723 was the *Pine Knoll Echo.*

WHITEWATER STATE PARK

CAMP NUMBERS: DSP-1, SP-9
Post Office: St. Charles (Winona County)
Known Company Number: 2709
Dates: 1934–35

Notes: This second state park camp at Whitewater opened on July 1, 1934, and operated until it was unexpectedly closed in October 1935. Originally designated a drought camp, it operated through the state park program. During World War II, the buildings housed a German prisoner of war camp. The site was used as a youth camp until completely destroyed by a tornado in 1953. Company 2709's newspapers were variously titled the *2709 Loudspeaker, 2709 Reports, Loudspeaker, Loudspeaker of 2709,* and the *Voice of Plainview.*

WINNIBIGOSHISH

CAMP NUMBER: F-15
Post Office: Bena (Cass County)
Known Company Numbers: 708, 702
Camp Dates: 1933–36, 1937

Notes: Company 708, organized at Fort Snelling on May 5, 1933, opened Winnibigoshish between May 26 and 28, 1933. The company occupied the camp until its transfer to Rabideau (F-50) on January 5, 1936. The camp closed at the time of the transfer but reopened briefly during the summer of 1937, when it was occupied by Company 702. It closed permanently in July 1937. The Winnibigoshish camp had an assigned work area in the Chippewa National Forest. Company 708 was quarantined for scarlet fever in June 1934. Company 708 published *Pine Knots* and *Timber Notes,* while the newspaper of Company 702 was the *Chippewa Pioneer.*

WINNIBIGOSHISH/NORRIS

CAMP NUMBER: S-60
Post Office: Beltrami Island, Warroad (Roseau County)
Known Company Number: 786
Dates: 1933

Notes: The camp operated from July 19 to September 18, 1933. Its assigned work area was Beltrami Island State Forest. As a Warroad camp, twenty African American enrollees from the Lanesboro (PE-91) camp may have been assigned to it from July to September 1933.

WINONA (FLOYD B. OLSON)

CAMP NUMBERS: PE-87, SCS-18
Post Office: Winona (Winona County)
Known Company Numbers: 783, 714
Dates: 1933, 1939–42

Notes: Known as the Floyd B. Olson camp when it operated as a tent camp, the Winona camp was opened by Company 783 as a private soil erosion camp on June 19, 1933. It was reestablished as a Soil Conservation Service camp on November 1, 1939, and operated until the winter or early spring of 1942. Its assigned work area was the Gilmore Creek Demonstration Project. The newspaper of company 714 was the *Lone Wolf.*

WIRT

CAMP NUMBER: F-37
Post Office: Wirt (Itasca County)
Known Company Numbers: 3770, 4709
Camp Dates: 1935–37

Notes: Missouri Company 3770 opened the camp in August 1935. Company 4709 transferred from Inger (F-27) in May 1936 and operated the camp until its transfer to Tamarac Lake Refuge (BF-2) in 1937. The camp closed with this transfer. The Wirt camp's assigned work area was in the Chippewa National Forest. The CCC facility was later used by Iowa State University for an engineering school camp. The newspaper of Company 4709 was the *Tres Lacs.*

WIRT (BOY RIVER)

CAMP NUMBERS: S-102, F-49
Post Office: Boy River (Cass County)
Known Company Number: none
Camp Dates: 1935–37

Notes: The camp was originally designated as S-102 but never operated as a state forest camp because its work area was immediately absorbed into the Chippewa National Forest. It opened as a national forest camp in 1935 and operated until 1937.

ZUMBROTA

CAMP NUMBER: SCS-3
Post Office: Zumbrota (Goodhue County)
Known Company Number: 714
Dates: 1935–39

Notes: The camp opened on June 4, 1935, and operated until the fall of 1939. Enrollees worked on the Deer-Bear Creek Project before being transferred to the Prairie Creek Demonstration Project (Faribault) in 1937. The newspaper of Company 714 was the *Lone Wolf.*

CAMPS LACKING ADEQUATE INFORMATION

CCC CAMPS

ST. LOUIS COUNTY (F-57)

Notes: While the camp was scheduled to open in August 1935, there is no evidence it was ever built or that a company was assigned to it.

SNOWBANK (S-80)

Notes: No additional information.

PE-90

Post Office: Caledonia (Houston County)
Known Company Number: 1751
Dates: 1933

Notes: The camp opened on June 19, 1933, and operated during the summer of 1933. The newspaper of Company 1751 was the *Lakeshore Camp News.*

PE-136

Post Office: Sebeka (Wadena County)
Known Company Number: 2704
Dates: 1934

Notes: The camp was located in the vicinity of Sebeka and Nimrod. Company 2704 opened it on August 23, 1934. The newspaper of Company 2704 was the *Score of 2704*.

S-96

Post Office: Wilton (Beltrami County)
Known Company Number: 3718

S-145

Post Office: Kelliher (Beltrami County)
Known Company Number: 720
Dates: 1941–42

Notes: The camp was established on November 12, 1941, and operated until the winter or early spring of 1942.

CCC-ID CAMPS

MOBILE CCC-ID CAMPS

CASS LAKE RESERVATION

FOND DU LAC RESERVATION

LAKE VERMILION RESERVATION

WHITE EARTH RESERVATION

MOBILE AND PERMANENT CCC-ID CAMPS: RED LAKE RESERVATION

CAMP 4

RED LAKE (MOBILE)

MOBILE CCC-ID CAMPS: LOWER SIOUX AGENCY RESERVATION

EGGLESTON

GRANITE FALLS

MORTON

SHAKOPEE

SOURCES FOR APPENDIX I

BOOKS

Alleger, C. N., comp. *Civilian Conservation Corps, Minnesota District: That the Work of Young America May Be Recorded.* Rapid City, SD: Johnston and Bordewyk, Inc., 1934.

Benson, David R. *Stories in Log and Stone: The Legacy of the New Deal in Minnesota State Parks.* St. Paul: Minnesota Department of Natural Resources, Division of Parks and Recreation, 2002.

Nelson, Edward P., and Barbara Sommer. *It Was A Good Deal: The Civilian Conservation Corps in Northeastern Minnesota.* Duluth, MN: St. Louis County Historical Society, 1987.

Rudeen, Marlys, comp. *The Civilian Conservation Corps Camp Newspapers: A Guide.* Chicago: Center for Research Libraries, 1991.

Ruhland, Vic. *Through These Eyes: The First Seventy Years of Soil and Water Conservation in Minnesota.* [St. Paul]: Minnesota State Office, USDA, Natural Resources Conservation Service, 2005.

ARCHIVAL RECORDS

Camp Inspection Reports, ECW/CCC Camps in Minnesota, Periods 1– . Records of the Civilian Conservation Corps. General Records. Record Group 35. National Archives, Washington, DC.

Camp Newspaper Files, CCC Collection. Iron Range Research Center, Chisholm, MN.

CCC camp papers [microform]. Microfiche Call Number 1078; Microfilm Call Number 2051. Minnesota Historical Society, St. Paul, MN.

CCC Collections. Carlton County Historical Society, Cloquet, MN.

"CCC Days—1933–39," unpublished manuscript. Itasca County Historical Society, Grand Rapids, MN.

Correspondence Files, 1933–42. Records of the Bureau of Indian Affairs, Consolidated Chippewa Agency. Record Group 75. National Archives—Central Plains Region, Kansas City, MO.

Correspondence Files, 1933–42. Records of the Bureau of Indian Affairs, Pipestone Indian School. Record Group 75. National Archives—Central Plains Region, Kansas City, MO.

Correspondence Files, 1933–42. Records of the Bureau of Indian Affairs, Red Lake Agency. Record Group 75. National Archives—Central Plains Region, Kansas City, MO.

"Job Proposal for C.C.C.—Moving Central Office from St. Paul to Grand Rapids, Minn." Project No. ICW-7. Camp No. S-97. Mar 8, 1938. Department of Conservation Records. Minnesota Historical Society, St. Paul, MN.

Negative 1694-A, photographic collection. Minnesota Historical Society, St. Paul, MN.

Rosters and Directories of ECW/CCC Camps by Period, compiled by the U.S. Forest Service. Records of the Civilian Conservation Corps. General Records. Record Group 35. National Archives, Washington, DC.

PAMPHLETS AND REPORTS

Anderson, Rolf T., et al. "Minnesota State Park CCC/WPA/Rustic Style Historic Resources." National Register Multiple Property Documentation Form. 1989. Minnesota State Historic Preservation Office, Minnesota Historical Society, St. Paul, MN.

"Federal Relief Construction in Minnesota, 1933–41." National Register of Historic Places Continuation Sheet. 1993. Minnesota State Historic Preservation Office, Minnesota Historical Society, St. Paul, MN.

Matson, Keith W. "The Civilian Conservation Corps on the Chippewa National Forest, 1933–1942." 1985. Rev. ed., Washington, DC: U.S. Department of Agriculture, Forest Service. 2002. Document on file at Supervisor's Office, Cass Lake, MN.

Minnesota Department of Conservation. Annual and Biennial Reports. 1933–42.

Okstad, Walter. "Cultural Resources Inventory." U.S. Forest Service. Superior National Forest.

"Rabideau Civilian Conservation Corps (ccc) Camp." National Historic Landmark Nomination. 2003. Minnesota State Historic Preservation Office, Minnesota Historical Society, St. Paul, MN.

"St. Croix Recreational Demonstration Area, St. Croix State Park." National Historic Landmark Nomination Form. 1997. Minnesota State Historic Preservation Office, Minnesota Historical Society, St. Paul, MN.

"St. Croix Recreational Demonstration Area, St. Croix State Park ccc/ WPA/Rustic Style Historic Resources." National Register Documentation Form. 1995. Minnesota State Historic Preservation Office, Minnesota Historical Society, St. Paul, MN.

"Summary: Minnesota ccc Work, 1933–42." 1941. USDA. U.S. Forest Service. Minnesota Department of Conservation.

"Three Years of Emergency Conservation Work on Minnesota State Forests, 1933–36." 1936. Minnesota ECW.

"Wildlife Investigations and Research Report, 1939–42." Department of Conservation. Monthly Reports. Department of Conservation Records. Minnesota State Archives, Minnesota Historical Society, St. Paul, MN.

ORAL HISTORIES

Oral history interviews. Arrowhead Civilian Conservation Corps Documentation Project. 1981–82. Civilian Conservation Corps Collection. Iron Range Research Center, Chisholm, MN.

Oral history interviews. Minnesota Civilian Conservation Corps Documentation Project. 1993. Civilian Conservation Corps Collection. Iron Range Research Center, Chisholm, MN.

NEWSPAPERS AND JOURNALS

"Camp Contingent Brings Surprises," *Lanesboro Leader*, Jun 29, 1933.

"Colored Boys Moved from Preston Camp," *Preston Republican*, Jul 20, 1933.

"Conservation at Work in Goodhue County." *Goodhue County Historical News*, Nov 1988.

"Five Minnesota Properties Added to the National Register." *Minnesota History Interpreter* 23.5 (May 1995): 1.

Indians at Work. Washington, DC: Bureau of Indian Affairs, GPO, 1933–44.

"Negro Camp is Moved South." *Grand Rapids Herald Review*, May 2, 1934.

"Negroes Filled Day Lake Camp." *Grand Rapids Herald Review*, Dec 13, 1933.

"Orr's Roadside Parking Area Recognized," *The TimberJay*, Oct 5, 2002.

"State ccc Headquarters Comes Here," *Grand Rapids Herald Review*, Aug 25, 1937.

INTERNET RESOURCES

Civilian Conservation Corps Alumni website. http://www.cccalumni.org/states/minnesota1.html.

Kansas Civilian Conservation Corps Newspapers on Microform, Kansas State Historical Society, Topeka. http://www.kshs.org/research/collections/documents/newspapers/ccc_newspapers.htm.

Minnesota Department of Transportation Historic Roadside Development Structures Inventories. http://www.dot.state.mn.us/tecsup/site/historic/files/iforms/CW-GRC-006.pdf; http://www.dot.state.mn.us/tecsup/site/historic/files/iforms/SL-ORC-005.pdf.

"Results of National Register Property Search: Rabideau ccc Camp." http://nrhp.mnhs.org/NRDetails.cfm?NPSNum=76001046.

APPENDIX II: MINNESOTA CCC CAMP NEWSPAPERS

The Badoura Banner
The Baptism Blade
Beacon
The Beantown Bugle
The Bear Facts
The Big Bluff
The Big Lake Breeze
Birch Lake Gazette
Birch Lake Newsette
The Blue Ox
Broken Mirror
Brush Banter
Brush Happy
The Brush Marine
Buckboard Whip
Cabin City Crier
The Caledonia Record
Call of the Wild
The Camp Call
Camp Chips
The Caribou Ripsaw
The CC Seer
The Challenge
The Chippewa Pioneer
The Company Once-Over
The Cottonwood ccc News
Cross River Taps
The Dakota Duster
Dakota Eagle
Dakota Wayside Camper
Day Lake Tattler
Deer Lake Echo
Devil's Track Ripples
Dora Lake Ripples
Duchee Creek Ripples
Dusschee Creek Ripples
Echo Lake Echoes
Echo Trail Echoes
The Flash
Gegoka Newsette
Gitchi Gummi Undertow
Glenwood Gazette
Glenwood Newsette
Gooseberry Times
Gunflint Trail
Gunflint Trailer
Happy Hollow Noos
Isabella Lookout
Isabella Trail-Blazer
Jack Pine Journal
Jackpine Journal
Jay Cooke Arrowhead
Jay Cooke Echo
The Jayhawk
Jumpin Frog
The Jusumpin
Kansas Outburst
Lake Pepin Breezes
The Lakeshore Camp News
The Lakeside Review
The Leader
Lo-Down
The Lone Wolf
Loudspeaker
Loudspeaker of 2709
The Maple Ache
Maple Leaf
The Model C.C.C.
The New Challenge
The New Model
The New Sawbill
Nodak Chippewa Chimes
Nodak Chippewa Times
Nodak Rambler
The North Star
North Star News
Northern Breezes
Northern Hi-Lights
Northern Hi-Lites
Northern Light Beacon
Northern Notes
Northernlight Rays
Ogantz Trail
The Old Hobnail
The Once Over
Owen Lake Sun
Partridge Newsette
The Partridge River Cartridge
The Partridge River Ripsaw
Peat Smoke
Peat Smoke News
Peat Smoke News Flash
Peat Smoke Weekly
Pee Wee Press
Pelican Press
Pepin Breezes
Pepin Newsletter
Pepinette
Pike Bay News
Pike Bay Newsletter
Pike Bay Press
Pike Bay Scandals
Pine Island Press
Pine Knoll Echo
Pine Knots
The Pine Needle Press
Pine Tree Tribune
Pioneer News
Portage River Ripples
The Rambler
Red Wing Duster
Remer Camp News
Remer Rambler
Rice Lake Quacker
Root River Echoes
St. Croix Leader
The Sawbill Journal
The Sawbill Senator
Sawbill Sez-All
Sawbill Smokeater
Sawbill Trails End
Scetch-o-graphs
Schley Tales
The Score of 2704
Sea Gull Times
Sea Gull Weekly Times
Seagull Times
Seagull Weekly Times
The Seagullite
Sibley Speaks
Side Lake Star
The Spotlight
The Spotlite
Spring Creek Crier
Spruce Lake Splash

Steamboat Ripsaw
Stokes Jayhawker
Sturgeon River
Sturgeon River Ripples
The Sturgeon River Star
The Sullivanite
The Sylvan Echo
The Tamarack
Temperance Valley Echo
The Three Bears Camp
The Tiger
Timber Notes
Timber Wolf's Howl
The Tomohawk
Trails End
Tres Lacs
U Name It!
Vermilion River Echoes
The Veterans Voice
The Veteran's Voice
Vet's Call
Vets' Call
Vets Call
The Vet's Voice
Vets Voice
The Voice of Minn-Mo-Dak
The Voice of Plainview
The Walkerite
The Wall Lake Seer
The Wanless Ripsaw
Washburn Lake News
The Washington Post
Weekly Mirror
Whispering Pine
The Whistler
Wildlife
The Woodpecker
Ye Olde Hobnail
Yellow Banks Holler
The 706 Spotlite
The 717 Once Over
The 723 Broken Mirror
The 723 Weekly Mirror
The 1714 Goldbricker
The 1716 Tamarack
2709 Loudspeaker
2709 Reports

The ECW-CCC *Log* contained information and updates about Minnesota's state forest camps.

SOURCES FOR APPENDIX II

Camp Newspaper Files. Civilian Conservation Corps Collection. Iron Range Research Center, Chisholm, MN.

CCC Collections. Carlton County Historical Society, Cloquet, MN.

Civilian Conservation Corps camp papers [microform]. Microfiche Call Number: 1078. Microfilm Call Number: 2051. Minnesota Historical Society, St. Paul, MN.

Rudeen, Marlys, compiler. *The Civilian Conservation Corps Camp Newspapers: A Guide.* Chicago: Center for Research Libraries, 1991.

APPENDIX III: MINNESOTA'S HISTORIC CCC SITES

ccc enrollees worked on the following Minnesota sites listed on the National Register of Historic Places or designated as national historic landmarks and national monuments. The *National Register of Historic Places* is a nationwide list maintained by the National Park Service of districts, sites, buildings, structures, and objects determined to be important to American history, architecture, archaeology, engineering, and culture. Sites on the list are protected under the National Historic Preservation Act of 1966. *National historic landmark* status is conferred on sites of preeminent value to the nation as a whole. A *national monument* is a structure or landmark of historic interest set aside and protected by the federal government. It is similar to a national park but may be designated directly by the president.

COUNTY	SITE	LISTING	DATE
Becker, Clearwater, & Hubbard	Itasca State Park	National Register	May 7, 1973
Beltrami	Rabideau Camp	National Register	Jun 16, 1976
		Historic Landmark	Feb 17, 2006
Brown	Flandrau State Park	National Register	Oct 25, 1989
Carlton	Jay Cooke State Park (including picnic grounds and service yard)	National Register	Jun 11, 1992
Cass	Chippewa National Forest Supervisor's Office	National Register	Jan 31, 1976
Chisago	Interstate State Park	National Register	Jun 11, 1992
Cook	Cascade River Wayside	National Register	Aug 4, 2003
Cook	Grand Portage National Monument	National Monument	1958
		National Register	Oct 15, 1966
Crow Wing	Bridge #5265, Highway 16	National Register	Jun 29, 1998
Dakota & Hennepin	Fort Snelling Historic District	Historic Landmark	Dec 19, 1960
		National Register	Oct 15, 1966
Itasca	Marcell Ranger Station	National Register	May 19, 1994
Itasca	Scenic State Park (including service yard)	National Register	Jun 8, 1992
Kandiyohi	Sibley State Park	National Register	Jan 22, 1992
Lake	Gooseberry Falls State Park	National Register	Oct 25, 1989
Lake	Isabella Ranger Station	National Register	Feb 1, 2006
Lake of the Woods	Norris (ccc) Camp	National Register	Sep 19, 1994
Lyon	Camden State Park	National Register	Apr 19, 1991
Mille Lacs	Bridge #3355, Highway 169	National Register	Jun 29, 1998
Nicollet	Fort Ridgely State Park	National Register	Oct 25, 1989

COUNTY	SITE	LISTING	DATE
Pine	St. Croix RDA (including Yellowbanks CCC camp site)	National Register	Jan 31, 1997
		Historic Landmark	Sep 25, 1997
Pipestone	Pipestone National Monument	National Monument	1938
		National Register	Oct 15, 1966
St. Louis	Civilian Conservation Corps Camp S-52 (Cusson)	National Register	Mar 2, 1989
St. Louis	Kabetogama Ranger Station	National Register	Jun 18, 1993
St. Louis	Orr Roadside Parking Area, Highway 53	National Register	Sep 6, 2002
St. Louis	St. Louis County 4-H Club Camp (including amphitheater built by CCC and WPA in 1934 using prize money awarded by Sears, Roebuck Company for the county's 4-H achievements)	National Register	Mar 4, 1985
Swift	Monson Lake State Park	National Register	Oct 25, 1989
Winona	Whitewater State Park	National Register	Oct 25, 1989

SOURCES FOR APPENDIX III

Benson, David R. *Stories in Log and Stone: The Legacy of the New Deal in Minnesota State Parks.* St. Paul: State of Minnesota, Department of Natural Resources, Division of Parks and Recreation, 2003.

"The National Register of Historic Places Minnesota Listings, January 1, 2003–December 31, 2006." State Historic Preservation Office, Minnesota Historical Society, St. Paul, MN.

Nord, Mary Ann, comp. *The National Register of Historic Places in Minnesota: A Guide.* St. Paul: Minnesota Historical Society Press, 2003.

NOTES

NOTES TO PART I INTRODUCTION

1. Although popularly known as the Civilian Conservation Corps, or CCC, this program's first official name was the Emergency Conservation Work Program, or ECW. The name was not officially changed until June 1937, but because the program was then and still is generally referred to as the Civilian Conservation Corps, the author has chosen to use that name throughout this book.
2. Harvey Richart, interview by Edward P. Nelson, Jan 13, 1994, Iron Range Research Center Collections, Chisholm, MN [hereafter, IRRC]. Guy Osborn, interview by Barbara W. Sommer, Apr 8, 1983, IRRC.

NOTES TO CHAPTER 1

1. William E. Lass, *Minnesota: A History* (New York: W. W. Norton & Co., 1998), 255–56.
2. U.S. Department of Agriculture, Soil Conservation Service, Upper Mississippi Region, "Gilmore Creek Soil Conservation Demonstration Project at Winona, Minnesota" (ca. 1938), Civilian Conservation Corps Collection [hereafter CCC Collection], IRRC, 1.
3. Lass, *Minnesota,* 255–56. Robert "Skip" Drake, "The Conservation Corps: A Brief History," in *It Was A Good Deal: The Civilian Conservation Corps in Northeastern Minnesota,* ed. Edward P. Nelson and Barbara W. Sommer (Duluth, MN: St. Louis County Historical Society, 1987), 9. Kirk Jeffrey, "The Major Manufacturers: From Food and Forest Products to High Technology," in *Minnesota in a Century of Change: The State and Its People since 1900,* ed. Clifford E. Clark, Jr. (St. Paul: Minnesota Historical Society [hereafter, MHS] Press, 1989), 238.
4. John Rabuze, John Cackoski, Russell Sundberg, interview by Edward P. Nelson, Mar 4, 1983; Eino Lahti, interview by Barbara W. Sommer, Apr 27, 1983; Nick Radovich, interview by Edward P. Nelson, Dec 3, 1982, all IRRC.
5. P. J. Halloran, interview by Elizabeth Bright, Mar 1, 1983, IRRC. David A. Shannon, *The Great Depression* (Englewood Cliffs, NJ: Prentice-Hall, Inc. 1960), 30. David Nass, "The Rural Experience," in Clark, ed., *Minnesota in a Century of Change,* 144–45.
6. William T. Cox, "First Biennial Report of the Department of Conservation, State of Minnesota, 1931 and 1932," 23, Department of Conservation Records, Minnesota State Archives [hereafter, MSA], MHS. Drake, "Civilian Conservation Corps," 9.
7. Claude Darst, interview by Barbara W. Sommer, Sep 28, 1993, IRRC.
8. Reinhold Holmer, interview by Edward P. Nelson, Jan 13, 1994. Darst interview. Paul Sersha, interview by Edward P. Nelson, Feb 9, 1994, all IRRC.
9. Darst interview.
10. Clarence Johnson, interview by Stanley A. Johnson, May 18, 1976, Chippewa National Forest Collections, Cass Lake, MN [hereafter, CNFC]. Raymond Noyes, interview by Barbara W. Sommer, Jan 12, 1983, IRRC.
11. Ernest Anderson, interview by Edward P. Nelson, Dec 12, 1982, IRRC.
12. Michael T. Sanchelli, "The Great Depression in Swede Hollow–Part I," Minnesota's Greatest Generation Project, Story ID 168, Aug 11, 2005, MHS, http://people.mnhs.org/mgg/story.cfm?storyid=168 (accessed Jun 29, 2007).
13. Allen Conkright, interview by Barbara W. Sommer, Feb 1, 1983, IRRC.
14. As conditions worsened, payments to the needy in Minnesota rose from $9 million in 1933 to $33 million in 1934. Drake, "Civilian Conservation Corps," 9. David M. Kennedy, *Freedom from Fear: The American People in Depression and War, 1929–1945* (New York: Oxford University Press, 1999), 67.
15. Kennedy, *Freedom from Fear,* 98.

NOTES TO CHAPTER 2

1. Steve Fraser and Gary Gerstle, eds., *The Rise and Fall of the New Deal Order, 1930–1980* (Princeton, NJ: Princeton University Press, 1989), 3.
2. Kennedy, *Freedom from Fear,* 118.
3. John A. Salmond, *The Civilian Conservation Corps, 1933–1942: A New Deal Case Study* (Durham, NC: Duke University Press, 1967), 26. Stan Cohen, *The Tree Army: A Pictorial History of the Civilian Conservation Corps, 1933–1942* (Missoula, MT: Pictorial History Publishing Company, 1980); "Roosevelt's Tree Army: A Brief History of the Civilian Conservation Corps,"

http://www.cccalumni.org/history1.html (accessed Jun 29, 2007); "ccc History: Roosevelt's Tree Army: A Brief History of the Civilian Conservation Corps by the National Association of Civilian Conservation Corps Alumni," http://idahopublictv.com/outdoors/shows/ccc/history/treearmy.html (accessed Jun 29, 2007).

4. Salmond, *Civilian Conservation Corps,* 8.

5. Kennedy, *Freedom from Fear,* 118. Salmond, *Civilian Conservation Corps,* 8. Don Congdon, "The New Deal–Junior Division," in *The Thirties: A Time to Remember,* ed. Don Congdon (New York: Simon and Schuster, 1962), 164. William C. Tweed, Laura E. Soulliere, Henry G. Law, *Rustic Architecture: 1916–1942* (San Francisco, CA: Division of Cultural Resource Management, Western Regional Office, National Park Service, Department of the Interior, 1977), http://www.cr.nps.gov/history/online_books/rusticarch/introduction.htm (accessed Feb 23, 2007). Robert "Skip" Drake, "Environmental Perspectives: People's Attitudes Towards Natural Resources, 1900 & 1934," Forest History Center, MHS, Grand Rapids, MN, n.d., 13–14.

6. Salmond, *Civilian Conservation Corps,* 10, 12, 31. "ccc History: The Civilian Conservation Corps Is Started," http://www.idptv.state.id.us/outdoors/shows/ccc/history/execorder.html (accessed Jun 29, 2007). Robert Fechner, who directed the ccc from its inception in 1933 until his death in December 1939, was a native of Tennessee. Unlike many other heads of New Deal agencies, Fechner was not from an academic or professional background. He quit school at age sixteen and trained as a railroad machinist, joining the International Association of Machinists (IAM) in 1896. After briefly serving in the military, Fechner rose in the ranks of the IAM, becoming general vice president of the union in 1925. Fechner was a lifelong Democrat and an early supporter of Roosevelt's bid for the presidency. Fechner's strong organizational skills, firm labor ties, loyalty to Roosevelt, and reputation for common sense made him an easy choice to head the ccc program.

7. Charles Price Harper, *The Administration of the Civilian Conservation Corps* (Clarksburg, WV: Clarksburg Publishing Company, 1939), 29.

8. Congdon, "New Deal–Junior Division," 164.

9. Harper, *Administration of the Civilian Conservation Corps,* 31, 79.

10. Robert Fechner, "My Hopes for the ccc," American Forests (Jan 1939), available: New Deal Network, http://newdeal.feri.org/forests/af139.htm (accessed Jun 17, 2006).

11. Earl Krause, interview by W. H. Raff, Dec 20, 1982, IRRC. *The Lanesboro Leader,* Sep 26, 1983.

12. John Jacob Saalberg, *Roosevelt, Fechner and the ccc: A Study in Executive Leadership* (Ann Arbor, MI: University Microfilms, Inc., 1964), 31.

13. E. V. Willard to Members of the Conservation Commission, Jun 3, 1933, E. Victor Willard Papers, MSA, MHS, 2–3.

14. Directories of Civilian Conservation Corps Camps, Periods 1–19, Series 13, Camp Directories, 1933–42, Records of the Civilian Conservation Corps, General Records, Record Group 35, National Archives, Washington, DC [hereafter, ccc-NA]. C. N. Alleger, *Civilian Conservation Corps, Minnesota District: That the Work of Young Americans May Be Recorded* (Rapid City, SD: Johnston and Bordewyk, Inc., 1934), 14.

15. These goals illustrate the emphasis on forest conservation work at the start of the ccc. Nationally, close to 63 percent of new camps were in national or state forests. Minnesota, with more forestland than other states in the Seventh Army Corps area, was given a proportionately higher goal for opening new camps. *American Forests: The Magazine of the American Forestry Association* (Jul 1933), see http://newdeal.feri.org/forests/af733.htm (accessed Jun 29 2007). Rosters and directories of ccc camps by period, compiled by the U.S. Forest Service: annual, special, and final reports, 1933–43, ccc-NA. E. V. Willard to Conservation Commission, ca. 1936, Department of Conservation Records, MSA, MHS, 7.

16. Willard to Conservation Commission, ca. 1936, 7.

17. Alleger, *Civilian Conservation Corps,* 12, 57, 96, 137.

18. Camp and company numbers are: Gegoka (F-2, Co.701), Bena (F-13, Co.702), Caribou (F-11, Co.703), Halfway (F-1, Co.704), Pike Lake/Pike Bay (F-12, Co.705), Camp Charles (S-51, Co.719), Side Lake (S-53, Co.717), Owen Lake (S-54, Co.718), Scenic State Park (SP-3, Co.1722), Camp Ripley (SP-4, Co.1723), Lake Itasca (SP-1, Co.1764), Caledonia (PE-88, Co.723), and Houston (PE-89, Co.738). Please see p136 for review of camp designation types.

19. Department of Conservation, *Second Biennial Report, 1933–1934* (St. Paul, MN: Department of Conservation, 1934), 126. Rolf T. Anderson, "Minnesota State Park ccc/WPA/Rustic Style Historic Resources" National Register Multiple Property Documentation Form, II: The Civilian Conservation Corps, State Historic Preservation Office, MHS, 1989, E-13. Harper, *Administration of the Civilian Conservation Corps,* 24.

20. Salmond, *Civilian Conservation Corps,* 23, 76.

21. Robert Fechner to Thomas L. Griffith, Sep 21, 1935, "ccc Negro Selection" file, Box 700, General Correspondence of the Director, Record

Group 35, National Archives, College Park, MD, http://newdeal.feri.org/texts/document_details.cfm?Documentid=823 (accessed Jun 29, 2007). See *New Deal Network,* http://newdeal.feri.org (accessed Jun 12, 2006).

22. Charles Washington to Robert Fechner, Jun 20, 1936, Series 2, General Correspondence, 1933–42, CCC-NA.

23. Minneapolis *Spokesman,* Jul 23, 1937, 2, and Sep 23, 1938, 1, 2. Charles W. Washington to William V. Kelley, Milwaukee Urban League, Nov 14, 1938, Series 2, General Correspondence, 1933–42, CCC-NA.

24. Perry H. Merrill, *Roosevelt's Forest Army: A History of the Civilian Conservation Corps, 1933–1942* (Montpelier, VT: Perry H. Merrill, 1981), 44–45. Calvin Gower, "The CCC Indian Division: Aid for Depressed Americans, 1933–1942," *Minnesota History* 43.1 (Spring 1972): 3–4.

25. Amos Owen interview, Jun 24, 1970, in *To Be an Indian: An Oral History,* ed. Joseph H. Cash and Herbert T. Hoover (1971; repr. ed.: St. Paul: MHS Press, 1995), 141.

26. Gower, "CCC Indian Division," 3. Donald L. Parman, *The Indian Civilian Conservation Corps* (Ann Arbor, MI: University Microfilms, 1967), 28. Clem Bellanger, interview by Barbara W. Sommer, Oct 13, 1993, IRRC. F. J. Scott to James Wind, Jul 22, 1940, Series 212, CCC-ID Subject Correspondence File (1933–44); Records of the Bureau of Indian Affairs, Consolidated Chippewa Agency, Record Group 75, National Archives, Central Plains Region, Kansas City, MO [hereafter, BIA, CCA, NA].

27. Although the terms *Anishinaabe* or *Ojibwe* and *Dakota* are generally used now, the names *Chippewa* and *Sioux* were more commonly used in the 1930s, and these terms will be used in this book. The Minnesota Chippewa Tribe was formed after the Indian Reorganization Act of 1934, with the first constitution signed in 1936. It includes the six reservations served through the Consolidated Chippewa Indian Agency. The Red Lake Band of Chippewa was originally part of the coalition of Minnesota Chippewa tribes but withdrew in 1927. Its first constitution, based at the time on a traditional governing system, was formed in 1918. It is the only reservation in Minnesota on which land was not ceded to the federal government and where allotment was resisted. Land on the reservation is tribally held, with none of the non-Native ownership that characterizes other reservations. Minnesota's Sioux communities include the Lower Sioux at Morton, the Prairie Island Community on Prairie Island at the junction of the Vermillion and Mississippi rivers (settled by the Mdewakanton of the Mississippi Dakota), the Shakopee-Mdewakanton at Prior Lake, and the Upper Sioux in Yellow Medicine County. The Prairie Island and Lower Sioux communities adopted Indian Reorganization Act–style constitutions in 1937. Elizabeth Ebbott for the League of Women Voters of Minnesota, *Indians in Minnesota,* 4th ed. (Minneapolis: University of Minnesota Press, 1985), 23, 31–32, 53–54, 56. Gower, "CCC Indian Division," 7.

28. "The Indian Reorganization Act, June 18, 1934," http://www.infca.org/tribes/IRA.htm (accessed Jun 27, 2007). Edmund Jefferson Danziger, Jr., *The Chippewas of Lake Superior* (Norman: University of Oklahoma Press, 1978), 132.

NOTES TO CHAPTER 3

1. Harper, *Administration of the Civilian Conservation Corps,* 33–34.

2. J. J. McEntee, "Federal Security Agency: Final Report of the Director of the Civilian Conservation Corps, April 1933–June 30, 1942," Series 3, Annual, Special, and Final Reports, 1933–43, CCC-NA, 112. L. R. Beatty, "Five Years for Conservation: A Report of the Conservation and Training Accomplishments of the CCC Camps on the Minnesota State Forests, June 1933–March 1938," Department of Conservation, Forestry Division, Reports and Miscellaneous Records, 1938, Department of Conservation Records, MSA, MHS, 4. Alfred "Irv" Nelson, interview by Stanley A. Johnson, Apr 15, 1976, CNFC.

3. Salmond, *Civilian Conservation Corps,* 55–59.

4. Salmond, *Civilian Conservation Corps,* 57–58. Michael T. Sanchelli, "The Great Depression in Swede Hollow—Part III," Minnesota's Greatest Generation Project, Story ID 171, Aug 11, 2005, MHS, http://people.mnhs.org/mgg/story.cfm?storyid=171 (accessed Jun 29, 2007). W. Frank Persons to Herman J. Aufderheide, Nov 26, 1939, Series 29, Correspondence with State Selecting Agencies, 1933–42, CCC-NA, 33.

5. Minnesota enrollees remembered keeping five dollars per month. The amount enrollees were allowed to keep varied from five to eight dollars per month. Ray Hoyt, *Your CCC: A Handbook for Enrollees* (Washington, DC: Happy Days Publishing Company, Inc., [1940]), 37. McEntee, "Federal Security Agency: Final Report." "Summary and Analysis of 1939 State Plan for CCC Selection," Table 5, Series 11, p20, Procedural Manuals, 1933–43, CCC-NA.

6. Records, Indian Civilian Conservation Work, CCC-ID, Mobile Unit, Fond du Lac, BIA, CCA, NA.

7. Gower, "CCC Indian Division," 7. Conrad L. Wirth, *Civilian Conservation Corps Program of the U.S. Department of the Interior: March 1933 to June 30, 1943* (Washington, DC: Department of the Interior, Civilian Conservation Corps, 1944), 26.

8. *Fifteenth Census of the United States, 1930* (Washington, DC: GPO, 1932), Tables 35 and 41, pp27, 33. Gower, "CCC Indian Division," 5.

9. By September 1934, the war department directed that "colored" enrollees be kept in "colored units within their own states of origin" whenever possible. The policy stated, "In the future, segregation of colored men by company, while not mandatory, will be the general rule and earnest effort will be made to reduce the total number of men in white units." In July 1935, the policy was refined further, making segregation of Blacks and whites complete and mandatory except in states, such as Minnesota, where the Black population was too low to form an entire two hundred–man company. The situation became more restrictive each year. Salmond, *Civilian Conservation Corps,* 88. Olen Cole, Jr., *The African-American Experience in the Civilian Conservation Corps* (Gainesville: University Press of Florida, 1999), 11–12. Paul Wood, interview by Barbara W. Sommer, Oct 7, 1993, IRRC.

10. Conkright interview. Minneapolis *Spokesman,* Oct 28, 1938, 1.

11. Radovich interview. Clarence Johnson interview.

12. Steven Bartek interview by Edward P. Nelson, Feb 24, 1983, IRRC.

13. Radovich interview.

14. Department of Conservation, Land Use and ECW/CCC Camps, 1933–35, Department of Conservation Records, MSA, MHS.

15. Clair Rollings, interview by Stanley A. Johnson, Mar 15, 1977, CNFC. U.S. Department of Agriculture, Forest Service, "E.C.W. Bi-Weekly Camp News," Mar 20, 1934, Department of Conservation Records, MSA, MHS. Camp Report, Co.721, Camp S-63, Finland, Jul 30, 1935, Series 115, Camp Inspection Reports, 1933–42, CCC-NA.

16. Sanchelli, "Great Depression in Swede Hollow–Part III."

17. Noyes interview. Bartek interview.

18. Medical care in the CCC-ID, including physical examinations given upon enrollment and discharge, was provided by regular Indian Service physicians. Use of outside physicians, "either regularly or under contract," was allowed only with special permission. *CCC-ID Handbook* (Washington, DC: GPO, 1941), Section II-1. Conkright interview. Alfred "Irv" Nelson interview.

19. Wood interview.

20. Noyes interview. Alfred "Irv" Nelson interview.

21. Gower, "CCC Indian Division," 9–10. *Indians at Work* 1.10 (Jan 1, 1934): 29.

22. Rollings interview. Salmond, *Civilian Conservation Corps,* 137.

23. Edward Schubert, interview by Amy K. Rieger, Jul 21, 1983, Itasca State Park Collections, Itasca State Park, MN.

24. Clarence "Ole" Allen, interview by W. H. Raff, Dec 12, 1982, IRRC. Ernest Spry, interview by W. H. Raff, Dec 16, 1982, IRRC.

25. Bernard Penner, interview by Barbara W. Sommer, Nov 5, 1982, IRRC.

NOTES TO CHAPTER 4

1. J. C. "Buzz" Ryan, interview by Barbara W. Sommer, Oct 13, 1982, IRRC.

2. Alison T. Otis, William D. Honey, Thomas C. Hogg, Kimberly K. Lakin, *The Forest Service and the Civilian Conservation Corps, 1933–1942* (Washington, DC: Department of Agriculture, U.S. Forest Service, 1986), 72. Radovich interview.

3. Webster Sterba to Ralph T. King, Technical Supervisor, ECW, Jun 14, 1933, Box 2, Folder 23, Collection 940, Division of Entomology and Economic Zoology, University of Minnesota Archives, University of Minnesota, Minneapolis, MN. E. V. Willard telegram to the U.S. Forest Service office, Sep 20, 1933, Department of Conservation Records, MSA, MHS.

4. Cecil A. Levin, Superintendent of Jay Cooke State Park, to the office of National Parks, Buildings and Reservations, Dec 20, 1933, Department of Conservation Records, MSA, MHS.

5. Roster, Emergency Conservation Work Camps, First Period, 1933, and Third Period, Summer 1934, Series 13, Camp Directories, 1933–42, CCC-NA. Darst interview.

6. William Heritage to Commissioner of Indian Affairs, Sep 14 and Nov 1, 1933, Series 212, CCC-ID Subject Correspondence File (1933–44), BIA, CCA, NA.

7. G. M. Conzet to E. V. Willard, Nov 29, 1935, Department of Conservation Records, MSA, MHS.

8. Otis, Honey, Hogg, Lakin, *The Forest Service,* 76, 77–78, 79. One of the few remaining intact CCC camps is a portable camp in Minnesota: the Rabideau Camp in the Chippewa National Forest. It was named to the National Register of Historic Places in 1976 and was designated a national historic landmark on February 21, 2006.

9. Otis, Honey, Hogg, Lakin, *The Forest Service,* 79.

10. Harley Heegard, interview by Amy Rieger, Jul 12, 1993, Itasca State Park Collections, Itasca State Park, MN. Schubert interview.

11. Halloran interview.

12. Noyes interview. John Cackoski, interview by Edward P. Nelson, Dec 13, 1982, IRRC.

13. Victor Pope, interview by Barbara W. Sommer, Aug 10, 1993, IRRC. Ryan interview. Noyes interview.

14. Beatty, "Five Years for Conservation," 8. William J. Fraser, communication to Edward P. Nelson, n.d., CCC Collection, IRRC.

15. Clarence Johnson interview. Alleger, *Civilian Conservation Corps,* 52.

16. Camp Inspection Report, Company 3702, Camp F-25, Luna Lake, Oct 29, 1938, Series 115, Camp Inspection Reports, 1933–42, CCC-NA.

17. J. H. Mitchell to Commissioner of Indian Affairs, May 28 and Jul 11, 1935, Series 212, CCC-ID Subject Correspondence File (1933–44), BIA, CCA, NA.

18. J. H. Mitchell to J. S. Monks, Sep 11, 1935, J. S. Monks to J. H. Mitchell, Oct 4, 1935, both Series 212, CCC-ID Subject Correspondence File (1933–44), BIA, CCA, NA.

19. Norman W. Scherer to Commissioner of Indian Affairs, Feb 3, 1939, Series 212, CCC-ID Subject Correspondence File (1933–44), BIA, CCA, NA.

20. N. W. Scherer, Associate Forester, to Commissioner of Indian Affairs, Jan 11, 1936, J. S. Monks to William Heritage, Jun 12, 1935, both Series 212, CCC-ID Subject Correspondence File (1933–44), BIA, CCA, NA.

21. N. W. Scherer, Associate Forester, to Commissioner of Indian Affairs, Jan 11, 1936, J. S. Monks to William Heritage, Jun 12, 1935, Norman W. Scherer to Commissioner of Indian Affairs, Jun 13, 1939, C. V. Fink to F. J. Scott, Feb 13, 1941, all Series 212, CCC-ID Subject Correspondence File (1933–44), BIA, CCA, NA.

22. Anderson interview. Bartek interview.

23. Don Burcalow, interview by Barbara W. Sommer, Jan 13, 1983, IRRC.

24. McEntee, "Federal Security Agency: Final Report," 20. Company strength ranged from a low of about 75 to a high of about 225 enrollees, depending on general need and enrollment period. Harper, *Administration of the Civilian Conservation Corps,* 43. Department of Conservation, *Second Biennial Report,* 127.

25. Conkright interview. Pete Trygg, interview by Barbara W. Sommer, Jan 6, 1983, IRRC. Willard Nelson, interview by Barbara W. Sommer, Nov 10, 1982, IRRC.

26. Parman, *Indian Civilian Conservation Corps,* 28. Bellanger interview. *CCC-ID Handbook,* VIII-2, 1. George Morrison, communication with Barbara W. Sommer, Oct 23, 1994, CCC Collection, IRRC. Clem Bellanger served in a CCC camp with enrollees from the Seventh Army Corps area including a Nebraska enrollee from the Winnebago reservation.

27. The Sisseton reservation was established in 1867 by Dakota people removed from Minnesota after the U.S.–Dakota War. Thus, these Nett Lake Sisseton enrollees probably had historic ties to Minnesota. Although it was a Consolidated Chippewa camp, it also was the nearest Minnesota CCC-ID camp for them, and they may have enrolled in it for that reason. William Heritage to Commissioner of Indian Affairs, Jan 5, 1934, J. H. Mitchell to Commissioner of Indian Affairs, Aug 12, 1937, both Series 212, CCC-ID Subject Correspondence File (1933–44), BIA, CCA, NA. *Indians at Work* 1.4 (Oct 1, 1933): 29. Scherer to Commissioner of Indian Affairs, Jan 13, 1941, Series 207, CCC-ID Inspection Reports (1933–39), BIA, CCA, NA. William D. Green, *A Peculiar Imbalance: The Fall and Rise of Racial Equality in Early Minnesota* (St. Paul, MN: MHS Press, 2007), 122.

28. Department of Agriculture, U.S. Forest Service Cultural Resource Inventory Form, Forest Service Site #09–09–07–012, 1980, Superior National Forest Collections, IRRC. Captain Eggleston died unexpectedly of a cerebral hemorrhage in February 1934. *Cook County News-Herald,* Feb 8, 1934. David R. Benson, *Stories in Log and Stone: The Legacy of the New Deal in Minnesota State Parks* (St. Paul: Minnesota Department of Natural Resources, 2002), 34. Tofte, Minnesota, Town Clerk Records, Jun 30, 1933, p49, Jul 7, 1933, p49, 50.

29. Halloran interview.

30. Catherine McNicol Stock, *Main Street in Crisis: The Great Depression and the Old Middle Class on the Northern Plains* (Chapel Hill: University of North Carolina Press, 1992), 96–97.

31. *Day Lake Tattler,* Sep 14, 1940, CCC Collection, IRRC.

32. Kinney to the Commissioner of Indian Affairs, Aug 1, 1936, Series 212, CCC-ID Subject Correspondence File (1933–44), BIA, CCA, NA. Anderson, "Minnesota State Park Historic Resources," VII-18. Benson, *Stories in Log and Stone,* 15.

33. Although nationally the CCC was funded through June 30, 1943, the program was active in Minnesota only through the end of 1942, when the last camps shut down. Soil Conservation Service demonstration project work in Minnesota continued until 1944, but for practical purposes the CCC was active in the state only from 1933 to 1942. These figures include the Fort Snelling headquarters camp but do not include CCC-ID camps. Directory, Emergency Conservation Work Camps, Fifth Period, 1935, U.S. Forest Service, Aug 15, 1935, Series 13, Camp Directories, 1933–42, CCC-NA. Anderson, "Minnesota State Park Historic Resources," E-26.

34. *The Big Lake Breeze,* Apr 15, 1937, CCC Collection, IRRC, 12.

NOTES TO CHAPTER 5

1. Halloran interview. Cackoski interview.
2. Wood interview.
3. Alfred Williams, interview by Barbara W. Sommer, Oct 8, 1993, IRRC.
4. Fred Ranger, interview by Edward P. Nelson, Jan 14, 1994, IRRC. R. John Buskowiak, communication to Barbara W. Sommer, Oct 5, 1993, IRRC.
5. Estimate of Cost for the First Six Months, Department of Conservation, Forestry Division, Reports and Miscellaneous Records, Department of Conservation Records, MSA, MHS. Hoyt, *Your CCC*, 32. Lahti interview. *Day Lake Tattler*, Sep 14, 1940, CCC Collection, IRRC, 5. Camp Report, Week Ending Oct 27, 1934, Company 1760, Series 115, Camp Inspection Reports, ECW/CCC, 1933–42, CCC-NA.
6. Parman, *Indian Civilian Conservation Corps*, 70. Morrison communication with Sommer.
7. Richart interview. Darst interview. Camp Inspection Report, Company 703, Camp F-3, Wanless, Jun 12, 1934, Series 115, Camp Inspection Reports, 1933–42, CCC-NA. "Memory of CCC Lives Anew," *St. Paul Pioneer Press*, Mar 7, 1983, 4A.
8. Thanksgiving Day Menu, Company 1720, SCS-2, Caledonia, 1936; Christmas Day Menu, Company 716, F-10, Sawbill, 1934, both CCC Collection, IRRC.
9. Sersha interview. Joe Baratto, interview by Edward P. Nelson, Dec 3, 1982, IRRC. *The Ely Miner*, Jan 2 and 9, 1936, 1.
10. Reuben Berman, "A Memoir" (unpublished manuscript, 1995), CCC Collection, IRRC, 16, 30.
11. Arthur Pryor, interview by Edward P. Nelson, Nov 23, 1982; John Ek, interview by Barbara W. Sommer, Mar 11, 1983, both IRRC. Lahti interview.
12. Frank Ernest Hill, *The School in the Camps: The Education Program of the Civilian Conservation Corps* (New York: American Association for Adult Education, 1935), 9. See "Roosevelt's Tree Army."
13. "Your Camp Regulations, Co.714, SCS-18," ca. 1941, Series 7, Documents Relating to the Organization and Operations of the CCC, 1933–42, CCC-NA, 3. Otis, Honey, Hogg, Lakin, *The Forest Service*, 79. Camp Inspection Report, Company 2770, Camp SCS-9, May 31, 1938, Series 115, Camp Inspection Reports, 1933–42, CCC-NA. "Educational Building Rapidly Progressing" in *Gooseberry Times*, Sep 6, 1938, CCC Collection, IRRC.
14. Conkright interview. Burcalow interview.
15. The CCC camp at Rabideau is still standing. It was placed in the National Register of Historic Places in 1976 and was named a national historic landmark in 2006. Mary Ann Nord, compiler, *The National Register of Historic Places in Minnesota: A Guide* (St. Paul: MHS Press, 2003); "Rabideau CCC Camp," available at http://nrhp.mnhs.org/NRDetails.cfm?NPSNum=76001046 (accessed Jun 29, 2007). Rollings interview.
16. Alfred "Irv" Nelson interview.
17. *The Lanesboro Leader*, Sep 26, 1983. "Your Camp Regulations," 3.
18. Ryan interview.
19. Cliff Nolte, correspondence to Barbara W. Sommer, Aug 11, 1993, CCC Collection, IRRC. Noyes interview. *The CCC at Work: A Story of 2,500,000 Young Men* (Washington, DC: GPO, 1941), 88. McEntee, "Federal Security Agency: Final Report," 112.
20. Allen Mapes, interview by Barbara W. Sommer, Dec 2, 1982, IRRC.
21. Appendix II contains a list of known Minnesota camp newspapers. *The Broken Mirror*, Oct 18, 1937, 2; *The Once Over*, Jan 31, 1937; *Northern Hi-Lights*, Feb 1939, CCC Collection, IRRC.
22. Camp Inspection Reports, Company 3702, Camp F-25, Luna Lake, Jun 30, 1941, and Company 706, Camp SCS-7, Sep 10, 1941, both Series 115, Camp Inspection Reports, 1933–42, CCC-NA.
23. Although occurring about the same time as the CCC educational program, the CCC-ID enrollee program was developed independently from the act of 1937. General provisions for enrollee training in the act ended up helping support the enrollee program. According to statistics compiled by the CCC-ID, three percent of the enrollees could not read or write English, 48 percent had a fourth-grade education, 30 percent had an eighth-grade education, 17 percent were at a high school level, and two percent were at college level. Parman, *Indian Civilian Conservation Corps*, 153–54, 162, 166–67.
24. Published from 1933 to 1945, *Indians at Work* originally was established as the voice of the CCC-ID, but as it grew in popularity it included stories about the Bureau of Indian Affairs along with other information. Mary M. Kirkland and Clarence W. Ringey, "Indians at Red Lake, Minnesota, Meet Problems of a Changing World," *Indians at Work* 6.11 (Jul 1939): 33. Danziger, *Chippewas of Lake Superior*, 144. Parman, *Indian Civilian Conservation Corps*, 172–73.
25. Bartek interview.
26. Conkright interview. Schubert interview.
27. Cackoski interview.
28. Clarence Johnson interview.
29. Baratto interview. J. H. Mitchell to the Commissioner of Indian Affairs, May 17, 1937, Series 212, CCC-ID Subject Correspondence File 1933–44, BIA, CCA, NA.

30. Schubert interview.

31. Cackoski interview.

32. Lorenz R. Lindstrom to Shirley Anderson, ca. 1935, Lorenz R. Lindstrom Letters, MSA, MHS. Cackoski interview. Godfrey Rawlings, interview by Barbara W. Sommer, Oct 7, 1993, IRRC.

33. Robert Engstrom, interview by Edward P. Nelson, Feb 1, 1983, IRRC. Lorenz R. Lindstrom to Shirley Anderson, 1936, Lorenz R. Lindstrom Letters, MSA, MHS.

34. Conkright interview. Cackoski interview.

35. Rollings interview.

36. Schubert interview. Joseph Franzinelli, interview by Edward P. Nelson, Feb 10, 1983, IRRC.

37. Wood interview.

38. The threat of a dishonorable discharge was not to be taken lightly. In 1934, a Black enrollee in a New Jersey camp was given a dishonorable discharge for refusing to stand and fan a white officer. The decision was reversed and he was given an honorable discharge only after the NAACP took up his cause. Omaha *Guide,* Apr 8, 1934. Wood interview.

39. Rawlings interview.

40. Vernon Butcher, interview by Barbara W. Sommer, Jan 12, 1983, IRRC. Don Boxmeyer, "Their Labor Lives on in Forests, Parks, Roads," *St. Paul Pioneer Press,* Jan 9, 2006, 1B.

41. *Day Lake Tattler,* Sep 14, 1940, 5, CCC Collection, IRRC. E. K. "Bud" Mallory, interview by Barbara W. Sommer, Aug 9, 1993, IRRC.

42. Milford Humphrey, interview by W. H. Raff, Dec 13, 1982, IRRC.

43. Mallory interview.

44. Matt Anzelc, interview by Edward P. Nelson, Feb 9, 1994, IRRC. Lahti interview.

45. *The Sullivanite,* Jan 14, 1939, CCC Collection, IRRC.

NOTES TO PART II INTRODUCTION

1. The Division of Forestry was established in the Department of Agriculture in 1881. It became the Bureau of Forestry in 1901 and took on its modern form in 1905. See http://www.lib.duke.edu/forest/Research/usfscoll/policy/Agency_Organization/index.html (accessed Jun 26, 2007).

2. Drake, "Environmental Perspectives," 15, 17.

3. In 1905, Hammond, while studying the effects of rills and gullying on land, first proposed the theory of sheet erosion. He often is called the father of soil conservation. See http://www.nrcs.usda.gov/ABOUT/history/bennett.html (accessed Jan 24, 2007). Hugh Hammond Bennett, *Soil Erosion: A National Menace* (Washington, DC: Department of Agriculture, Circular No. 33, 1928).

4. Donald Worster, *Dust Bowl: The Southern Plains in the 1930s,* 25th anniversary ed. (New York: Oxford University Press, 2004), 213.

5. In October 1994, the Soil Conservation Service changed its name to the Natural Resources Conservation Service. Vic Ruhland, *Through These Eyes: The First Seventy Years of Soil and Water Conservation in Minnesota* (St. Paul: Minnesota State Office, USDA Natural Resources Conservation Service, 2005), 16, 20, 25, 32, 33, 38, 51, 97, appendix B. Herbert Flueck, interview by Tom Copeland, Aug 17, 1977, Minnesota Water Resources Board Oral History Project, MSA, MHS. The state coordinator's office became the state office in 1942, at which time Flueck became the Minnesota State Conservationist. He served from 1942 to 1968. Communications from Vic Ruhland to Barbara W. Sommer, Apr 21, 2003, and Sep 8, 2004. Minnesota's demonstration projects were Gilmore Creek (1934), Deer-Bear Creek (1934), Beaver Creek (1934), Prairie Creek (1935), Twin Valley (1939), Clear Lake (1940), and Storden (1940). A camp in the Fergus Falls area (1941) worked on soil erosion problems but was not part of a demonstration project. U.S. Soil Conservation Service, "A Preliminary Study of Farming and of the Soil Conservation Program in the Deer-Bear Creek Demonstration Area, Fillmore and Mower Counties," CCC Collection, IRRC, 1. CCC Camp work plan, SCS-MN-21, Fergus Falls, MN, 1941, MSA, MHS, 63. The Faribault office became a district/field office in 1942 and continues in this capacity today. Department of Conservation, *Annual Report, 1938, and Fourth Biennial Report* (St. Paul, MN: The Department, 1938), 183.

6. Although the establishment of Camp Release in 1889 is often cited as the beginning of Minnesota's park system, Camp Release is technically a state memorial site, not a state park. And, while the centennial of Minnesota's park system was celebrated in 1989, commemorating the founding of Camp Release, Itasca was in fact the first state park.

7. Lass, *Minnesota,* 244. The Chippewa National Forest was the first national forest to be created by an act of Congress. A tribute to President Theodore Roosevelt's foresight, the Superior National Forest is now the largest ecological community of its kind in the lower forty-eight states. *Golden Anniversary: Chippewa National Forest, 1908–1958* (Washington, DC: Department of Agriculture, U.S. Forest Service, ca. 1958), 1. "Historical Notes on the Chippewa National Forest" in *Factual Information Concerning Minnesota's National Forests* (St. Paul: Minne-

sota Conservation Federation, Jan 1943), 2. See http://gorp.away.com/gorp/resource/US_National_Forest/mn_super.htm (accessed Jun 26, 2007); http://www.fs.fed.us/r9/forests/superior/about/ (accessed Jun 26, 2007).

8. Lass, *Minnesota,* 244. Cox, "First Biennial Report," 93.

9. The 1925 law established the Department of Conservation, but the separate departments retained their autonomy until the 1931 act. In 1971, the name of the department was changed to the Department of Natural Resources. Cox, "First Biennial Report," 95. Department of Conservation, *Second Biennial Report,* 98. Daniel J. Elazar, "A Model of Moral Government" in Clark, ed., *Minnesota in a Century of Change,* 342–43. The divisions were Forestry and Fire Prevention (became Forestry in 1937), Game and Fish, Lands and Minerals, Waters and Drainage (became Drainage and Waters by 1937), Public Relations (became the Information Bureau), and the Tourist Bureau (eliminated by 1957). The Division of State Parks was added in 1935. The Conservation Commission was eliminated in 1937, and its powers were transferred to the Commissioner of Conservation as head of the Department of Conservation. Minnesota Blue Books, 1931, 1933, 1941, 1957–58. Roy W. Meyer, *Everyone's Country Estate: A History of Minnesota's State Parks* (St. Paul: MHS Press, 1991), 84–86. Department of Conservation, *Statistical Report, Biennium Ending June 30, 1940* (St. Paul, MN: Department of Conservation, 1940), 15. "Know Your Conservation Department," An Educational Pamphlet Prepared by the Bureau of Information, Department of Conservation, 1940, Department of Conservation Records, MSA, MHS.

10. Dr. Alway began his career as a professor of chemistry at Nebraska Wesleyan University. He then taught agricultural chemistry at the University of Nebraska–Lincoln before coming to Minnesota as a full professor and head of the Soils Division, a position he held from 1913 to 1942. *Information Manual, University of Minnesota,* compiled by the Department of Relations, 3rd ed., Jan 1987, 66. "Well-Known Men on 'U' Faculties Become 'Emeritus,'" Minnesota Chats 24.1 (May 20, 1942). "Frederick J. Alway, Division of Soils," Frederick Alway file, University of Minnesota Archives, Minneapolis, MN. M. A. Thorfinnson, *History of Soil and Water Conservation Districts in Minnesota, 1929–1965* (St. Paul: U.S. Department of Agriculture, Soil Conservation Service, State Soil Conservation Committee, ca. 1965), 5–6. R. H. Davis, *First Annual Report, Project No. 26.* (La Crosse, WI: Department of Agriculture, U.S. Soil Conservation Service, 1935), 63.

11. Commission of Conservation, *First Biennial Report of the Commission of Conservation, 1931–1932* (St. Paul, MN: Department of Conservation, 1932), 23–24.

12. The Driftless Area encompasses about 15–20,000 square miles in southeast Minnesota, southwest Wisconsin, northeast Iowa, and northwest Illinois that was not covered by the last of the continental glaciers. Theodore C. Blegen, *Minnesota: A History of the State* (Minneapolis: University of Minnesota Press, 1963), 565.

13. Wind erosion, often a symbol of the difficulties of rural people during the Depression, rarely occurred in southeastern Minnesota. It was found in the southwestern and northwestern parts of the state but did not have the impact of the huge dust storms of other states. Department of Agriculture, "Project Monograph, Beaver Creek Project," ca. 1939, 35, and R. H. Musser, "Saving the Soil," (n.d.), 1, both CCC Collection, IRRC. Commission of Conservation, *First Biennial Report,* 49.

NOTES TO CHAPTER 6

1. The twenty-one new and existing state forests were: Beltrami Island, Blackduck, Cloquet Valley, Crow Wing, Finland, Fond du Lac (including the university experimental station), Foot Hills (including Badoura State Forest), George Washington, Grand Portage, Kabetogama, Land O'Lakes, Mille Lacs, Mississippi Headwaters, Paul Bunyan, Pine Island, St. Croix, Savanna, Smokey Hills, Third River, and White Earth. Barbara Bachmann, *A History of Forestry in Minnesota with Particular Reference to Forestry Legislation* (St. Paul, MN: Department of Conservation, 1965), 44–46. L. R. Beatty, *Summary: Minnesota CCC Work, 1933–1941* (St. Paul, MN: Department of Agriculture, U.S. Forest Service, Minnesota Department of Conservation, ca. 1942), 4–28.

2. "The National Forests in Minnesota: Chippewa and Superior," May 1947, Department of Conservation Records, MSA, MHS, 1.

3. Drake, "Civilian Conservation Corps," 10. Grover M. Conzet, *A Forest Policy and Program for the State of Minnesota,* Department of Conservation Records, MSA, MHS, 1931, 1. Grover Conzet, "General Summary of Land Classification Reports for the Establishment of State Forests and Conservation Areas," Department of Conservation Records, MSA, MHS, 1933, 8–12. Commission of Conservation, *First Biennial Report,* 25–29. Today, Minnesota has fifty-eight state forests encompassing four million acres. *Minnesota Laws 1931,* Chapter 124, refers to the following state forests prior to the CCC: Badoura, Beltrami

Island, Cloquet Valley, Fond du Lac, Foot Hills, George Washington, Kabetogama, Koochiching, Pillsbury, Pine Island, St. Croix, Savanna, Sturgeon River, and White Earth. Bachmann, *History of Forestry,* 61. Rolf T. Anderson, "Federal Relief Construction in Minnesota, 1933–1941," National Register of Historic Places Continuation Sheet, II. The Civilian Conservation Corps, State Historic Preservation Office, MHS, 1989, E-16. Department of Conservation, *Second Biennial Report,* 73–80, 82.

4. Drake, "Civilian Conservation Corps," 11. Harper, *Administration of the Civilian Conservation Corps,* 57–59. Circular Letter dated Jan 2, 1934, from G. M. Conzet to ECW Camp Superintendents and MFS District Rangers, Department of Conservation Records, MSA, MHS. Department of Conservation, *Second Biennial Report,* 129. Ryan interview.

5. Conzet to ECW Camp Superintendents and MFS District Rangers. Luke Walker, communication to Barbara W. Sommer, Jul 4, 1993, CCC Collection, IRRC.

6. Conzet to ECW Camp Superintendents and MFS District Rangers. Department of Conservation, *Third Biennial Report,* 1935–1936 (St. Paul, MN: Department of Conservation, 1936), 9.

7. Department of Conservation, Summary of Reconnaissance Program in Minnesota State CCC Camps, ca. 1939, Department of Conservation Records, MSA, MHS, 1. William Webb to Chief (Ralph T. King, Technical Supervisor, ECW), Apr 10, 1935, Box 2, Folder 24, Collection 940, Division of Entomology and Economic Zoology, University of Minnesota Archives, University of Minnesota, Minneapolis, MN.

8. Pryor interview. Clarence Johnson interview.

9. Forrest Stillwell, interview by Barbara W. Sommer, Jan 27, 1983, IRRC.

10. Anderson interview. Lahti interview.

11. Webb to Chief, Apr 10, 1935.

12. Lahti interview. Lorenz R. Lindstrom to Shirley Anderson, Summer 1938, Lorenz R. Lindstrom Letters, MSA, MHS. Wood interview.

13. Noyes interview.

14. Minnesota Forest Service, Forest Planting Record, George Washington Memorial Forest, Oct 8, 1935, Department of Conservation Records, MSA, MHS.

15. Lorenz R. Lindstrom to Shirley Anderson, May 13, 1936, Lorenz R. Lindstrom Letters, MSA, MHS. Chester Erickson, interview by W. H. Raff, Nov 30, 1982, IRRC.

16. "Planting Manual for CCC Enrollees," Larsmount Camp S-98, CCC Company 720, Wilton, MN, CCC Collection, S1179, box 72, Carlton County Historical Society, Cloquet, MN.

17. Department of Conservation, *Second Biennial Report,* 86. Department of Conservation, *Third Biennial Report,* 9. J. W. Trygg, "Six Years of CCC Progress on Superior National Forest," *The Ely Miner,* Apr 22, 1939. *Deer Lake Echo,* Aug 1938, CCC Collection, IRRC, 5.

18. *Deer Lake Echo,* Aug 1938, CCC Collection, IRRC, 5.

19. Anderson interview.

20. Walker communication to Sommer. Wood interview.

21. U.S. Department of Agriculture and Minnesota Department of Conservation, *Blister Rust Control Handbook,* 1936, p1–2, and "History of White Pine Blister Rust Control in Minnesota," ca. 1947, p27, both Department of Conservation Records, MSA, MHS. Burcalow interview.

22. "A Special Tree, A Long-Fought Battle," *Minneapolis Star and Tribune,* Sep 24, 1992. Gower, "CCC Indian Division," 9.

23. "Five Properties Added to the National Register," *The Minnesota History Interpreter* 23.5 (May 1995), 1. Ruhland, *Through These Eyes,* 37–38.

24. Clarence Johnson interview. Heegard interview. CCC enrollees built the last twenty miles of the trail, adding to construction that began around 1875. John Henrickson, *Gunflint: The Trail, The People, The Stories* (Cambridge, MN: Adventure Publications, Inc., 2003), 19, 21. Rawlings interview.

25. Claude Ingram, interview by W. H. Raff, Nov 19, 1982, IRRC.

26. Gower, "CCC Indian Division," 9.

27. Clarence Johnson interview.

28. Noyes interview.

29. Anderson interview. Michael Sanchelli, "Forest Fire, Friday, April 13, 1934, Isabella, Minn., Camp 1721, C.C.C.," MSA, MHS.

30. Department of Conservation, *Third Biennial Report,* 106–7.

31. Anderson, "Minnesota State Park Historic Resources," E-21.

32. State Historic Preservation Office, "Chippewa National Forest Superior's Office Headquarters Building" National Register of Historic Places Inventory—Nomination Form, State Historic Preservation Office, MHS, 1974.

33. Forests established in 1933 were Beltrami Island, Cloquet Valley, Finland, Fond du Lac, Foot Hills, Grand Portage, Kabetogama, Land O'Lakes, Pine Island, Savanna, Third River, White Earth, and lands in Becker and Mahnomen counties. Forests established in 1935 were Blackduck, Buena Vista, Crow Wing, Hay Lake, Mille Lacs, Mississippi Headwaters, Nemadji, Northwest Angle, Paul Bunyan, Pillsbury, Rum River, Smoky Hills, and Waskish. Foot Hills,

Land O'Lakes, and White Earth were enlarged at this time. Bachman, *History of Forestry*, 44, 46. Both national forests were extensively planted during the CCC years, with harvesting beginning about thirty years later. Production at the Cass Lake nursery, serving the Chippewa National Forest, was increased to four million seedlings annually during the CCC years to help keep up with the demands made by planting in that national forest. In the Superior National Forest, the first timber crop planted by the CCC was harvested in the Isabella Ranger District (junction of State Highway 1 and County Road 2) on June 1, 1967. *Golden Anniversary, Chippewa National Forest,* 3. See http://www.fs.fed.us/r9/forests/superior/about/ (accessed Jun 26, 2007). Walt Okstad, communication with Barbara W. Sommer, Jun 24, 2004.

NOTES TO CHAPTER 7

1. Grover Conzet had a WPA camp named for him. It was located on the present site of Magney State Park and was also known as the Hobo Camp. Pat Zankman, "The Grover Conzet Transient Camp," *Overlook* (Winter 2000–2001): 3–4. The state parks in existence at the time of this legislation were Alexander Ramsey, Camp Release, Charles A. Lindbergh, Fort Ridgely, Horace Austin, Interstate, Itasca, Jay Cooke, John Latsch, Lake Shetek Monument, Minneopa, Scenic, Sibley, Sleepy Eye, Toqua Lakes, Traverse de Sioux, and Whitewater. Bachman, *History of Forestry,* 40. Department of Conservation, *Second Biennial Report,* 98. Department of Conservation, *Statistical Report, Biennium Ending June 30, 1942* (St. Paul, MN: Department of Conservation, 1942), 106.
2. Department of Conservation, *Second Biennial Report,* 23. Harold W. Lathrop, Monthly Report to E. V. Willard, Jan 1935, Department of Conservation Records, MSA, MHS, 8. Meyer, *Everyone's Country Estate,* 87, 103, 142. Willard to Conservation Commission, ca. 1936, 8. John C. Paige, *The Civilian Conservation Corps and the National Park Service, 1933–1942: An Administrative History* (Washington, DC: GPO, 1985), 40, 67.
3. Harlan D. Unrau and G. Frank Willis, *Administrative History: Expansion of the Park Service in the 1930s* (Denver, CO: National Park Service Denver Service Center, 1983), 79. Anderson, "Minnesota State Park Historic Resources," E-5, 6. Reuben Law, interview by Amy Rieger, Ben Thoma, Ron Miles, Jun 23, 1993, Itasca State Park Collections, Itasca State Park, MN.
4. Wirth's program, which started as part of the National Park Service Branch of Planning, soon was designated the State Park Division of the Emergency Conservation Work Program. After the CCC, Wirth stayed with the National Park Service and served as its director from 1951 until 1964. Anderson, "Minnesota State Park Historic Resources," E-4. Paige, *Civilian Conservation Corps and National Park Service,* 39. Penner interview. Harper, *Administration of the Civilian Conservation Corps,* 68–72.
5. Noyes interview. Schubert interview.
6. Edward Barber, interview by Ben Thoma and Gladwin Lynne, May 8, 1994, Itasca State Park Collections, Itasca, MN.
7. Noyes interview. Schubert interview. Weikko Seppo, interview by Barbara W. Sommer, Jan 30, 1983, IRRC.
8. Frederick Johnson, interview by Barbara W. Sommer, Aug 8, 1993, IRRC.
9. The term *rustic* refers to a movement in American architecture associated specifically with a single government agency: the National Park Service. Considered a "natural outgrowth of the new romanticism about nature" and the growing interest in conservation that began in the early 1900s, it is a unique architectural style in which a building or structure (such as a bridge) is considered an accessory to nature while "giving the feeling of having been executed by pioneer craftsmen." It was the dominant form of national park architecture and the guiding principle for Minnesota state park design during the CCC years. Tweed, Soulliere, Law, *Rustic Architecture.* Barber interview. Anderson, "Minnesota State Park Historic Resources," E-5–7, 17, 37. Paige, *Civilian Conservation Corps and National Park Service,* 40. Parks not in existence in 1931 were formed during the CCC years in response to availability of funding and labor along with recommendations in some cases from the National Park Service. In addition to CCC labor, state parks benefited from the work of enrollees in two other New Deal relief programs: the WPA and the National Youth Administration. Meyer, *Everyone's Country Estate,* 103–45. Department of Conservation, *Statistical Report, Biennium Ending June 30, 1942,* 254.
10. Frederick K. Johnson, "The Civilian Conservation Corps: A New Deal for Youth," *Minnesota History* 48.7 (Fall 1983): 298. The fur post replica reconstruction was directed by Harold Lathrop using plans developed by Edward Barber and logs provided by John Fritzen of the state forest service. Theodore Blegen, superintendent of the Minnesota Historical Society, supported the project. "Rebuilt Post Presents Picturesque View at Fond du Lac," *Duluth Herald,* Aug 2, 1935. "The Trading Post at Fond du Lac," *Duluth News-Tribune,* Aug 22, 1935. "Astor Trading Post," *Duluth News-Tribune,* Sep 23, 1935. "Sticker to Swing in '90," *Duluth News-Tribune,* Sep 28, 1989.

"Then and Now," *Duluth News-Tribune,* Oct 2, 2002. Law interview.

11. Penner interview. Benson, *Stories in Log and Stone,* 66.

12. Benson, *Stories in Log and Stone,* 63. Noyes interview.

13. Benson, *Stories in Log and Stone,* 68.

14. In 1953, Udert W. Hella was named director of the Minnesota Department of Conservation Division of State Parks. Throughout his career he was called "the Inspector" by many coworkers because of his work with the CCC. Patricia Murphy, *The Public Buildings of the State of Minnesota: An Architectural Heritage* (St. Paul, MN: State Historic Preservation Office, 1986), 36. See http://rptsweb.tamu.edu/Pugsley/Hella.htm (accessed Feb 23, 2007).

15. Benson, *Stories in Log and Stone,* 68, 92. State Historic Preservation Office, "Rustic Style Resources in Minnesota State Parks," see http://www.mnhs.org/places/nationalregister/stateparks/ (accessed Jun 27, 2007). Department of Conservation, *Second Biennial Report,* 104.

16. Department of Conservation, *Second Biennial Report,* 107. State Historic Preservation Office, "Rustic Style Resources."

17. *Hibbing Daily Tribune,* May 5, 1937. Meyer, *Everyone's Country Estate,* 26. State Historic Preservation Office, "Rustic Style Resources."

18. Murphy, *Public Buildings of Minnesota,* 36–37. Anderson, "Minnesota State Park Historic Resources," E-8, 9.

19. "CCC Reunion Held at St. Croix," *The Hinckley News,* Jul 30, 1992.

20. Anderson, "Minnesota State Park Historic Resources," E-8–10. Department of Conservation, *Second Biennial Report,* 131.

21. "Roadside Development on Minnesota Trunk Highways, 1920–1960," see http://www.dot.state.mn.us/tecsup/site/historic/files/narrative.pdf (accessed Jun 27, 2007), 32–33. Anderson, "Minnesota State Park Historic Resources," E-22–3.

22. Murphy, *Public Buildings of Minnesota,* 36. National Park Service, "Expansion of the National Park Service in the 1930s: Administrative History," ch. 4, "New Initiatives in the Field of Recreation and Recreational Area Development," at http://www.cr.nps.gov/history/online_books/unrau-williss/adhi4f.htm (accessed Jun 27, 2007).

23. Wirth, *Civilian Conservation Corps Program,* 30, 31. Department of Conservation, *Statistical Report, Biennium Ending June 30, 1942,* 238. Anderson, "Minnesota State Park Historic Resources," E-31, 37, and individual park nomination forms.

24. Anderson, "Minnesota State Park Historic Resources," E-17. Department of Conservation, *Statistical Report, Biennium Ending June 30, 1942,* 254.

NOTES TO CHAPTER 8

1. Ruhland, *Through These Eyes,* 25. The Dust Bowl was an area of about 150,000 square miles in the southern Great Plains states. "Topsoil Losses in Minnesota," *Northfield News,* Jul 28, 1938. Department of Conservation, *Second Biennial Report,* 24. U.S. Soil Conservation Service, "Preliminary Study of Farming and of the Soil Conservation Program," 3–4.

2. The projects were done on the J. C. Gengler farm near Caledonia and the George Fischer farm near Lewiston. Thorfinnson, *History of Soil and Water Conservation Districts,* 4.

3. Ruhland, *Through These Eyes,* 19.

4. The *Rochester Post-Bulletin* noted the temperature was ninety-seven degrees at 3:20 PM that day. "Thousands Applaud President on 90-Mile Tour through Southeastern Minnesota," *Rochester Post-Bulletin,* Aug 8, 1934. Darst interview.

5. The program was run by regional director and Minnesota state coordinator R. H. Davis and the state's first soil conservationist, Herbert Flueck, from offices in La Crosse, WI, until 1937. At that time, Minnesota's soil conservation coordinator's office opened in St. Paul with Flueck as acting state coordinator. Davis and Flueck worked closely with F. W. Peck, director of the Minnesota State Extension Service at the University of Minnesota, to "coordinate the efforts . . . in Soil erosion control; to avoid duplication, confusion of methods, and overlapping of work, to the end that a unified program combining all known methods of attack on erosion may be effectively carried out." Ruhland, *Through These Eyes,* 20, 33. "Memorandum of Understanding Between the Minnesota Agricultural Extension Service and the Soil Conservation Service, United States Department of Agriculture, Relative to Soil Conservation Work in the State of Minnesota," Feb 1936, Box 44, Soil Conservation: Agreement–Soil Conservation Agricultural Extension (University), 1936–1946, Collection 922, Institute of Agriculture, University of Minnesota Archives, University of Minnesota, Minneapolis, MN. Department of Conservation, *Annual Report, 1938, and Fourth Biennial Report,* 182.

6. Minnesota's loss of topsoil was lower than in many Dust Bowl states; it was in the southeastern part of the state that the problem was "most severe." Department of Agriculture, "Project Monograph: Beaver Creek Project," 31. Department of Agriculture, "Project Monograph 2, Beaver Creek Project," ca. 1939, CCC Collection, IRRC, 5, 19, 40, fig. 3. USDA, "Gilmore Creek Demonstration Project," 1–4. Department of Agriculture, "Annual Report, Gilmore Creek Project, 1937–1938," ca. 1938, CCC Collection, IRRC, 2–3.

7. Today, the Gilmore Creek project does not receive the attention it did during the CCC years. Many people look to the Coon Creek project in Wisconsin as the historic model demonstration project in the Minnesota-Wisconsin area. USDA, "Gilmore Creek Demonstration Project," 1, 8.

8. Ruhland, *Through These Eyes,* 31. R. John Buskowiak, "My Days in the C.C.C.'s," unpublished manuscript, 1993, MHS, 2.

9. The work plan for SCS-21 at Fergus Falls stated camp work sites were limited to areas that could be reached in "travel time of about 45 minutes at a speed of 25 miles per hour," which was estimated to be an eighteen-mile radius from camp. CCC Camp Work Plan, Camp SCS-MN-21, Fergus Falls, Minnesota, Department of Conservation Records, MSA, MHS, 1.

10. Eldor Rahn, interview by Barbara W. Sommer, Aug 10, 1993, IRRC. Pope interview.

11. Darst interview.

12. Department of Conservation, *Third Biennial Report,* 63. Communication from Vic Ruhland to Barbara W. Sommer, Sep 9, 2004.

13. Beatty, "Five Years for Conservation," 8. Willard to Conservation Commission, ca. 1936, 7. Department of Conservation, *Annual Report, 1938, and Fourth Biennial Report,* 182.

14. Wirth, *Civilian Conservation Corps Program,* 13, 14.

15. Wirth, *Civilian Conservation Corps Program,* 36. Cohen, *The Tree Army,* 93.

16. "Wildlife Investigations and Research Report for the Month of May, 1939," Department of Conservation, Conservation Department Monthly Reports, Jun 12, 1939, Department of Conservation Records, MSA, MHS. *Deer Lake Echo,* Aug 1938, CCC Collection, IRRC, 5.

17. Darst interview. Pope interview. Buskowiak, "My Days in the C.C.C.'s," 2.

18. Buskowiak, "My Days in the C.C.C.'s," 2, 4. Jim Flaherty, letter to Barbara W. Sommer, Jul 9, 1993, CCC Collection, IRRC. Pope interview.

19. "CCC Camp Members Held Reunion Last Weekend," *The Lanesboro Leader,* Sep 26, 1983. Lorenz R. Lindstrom to Shirley Anderson, Aug 1936, Lorenz R. Lindstrom Letters, MSA, MHS.

20. Pope interview.

21. "Soil Conservation Service to Plant 1,390,600 Trees," Scrapbook of the Prairie Creek Project–Faribault, Rice County Historical Society, Faribault, MN. Ruhland, *Through These Eyes,* 26. Rahn interview.

22. Worster, *Dust Bowl,* 219. Harper, *Administration of the Civilian Conservation Corps,* 53, 74. Ruhland, *Through These Eyes,* 35–36, 37. Each Soil Conservation District was, and continues to be, governed by an elected group of five supervisors. Following the pattern developed when they were organized, operations are structured through an annual comprehensive work plan that defines local conservation priorities, resource treatment needs, and construction schedules. The districts are authorized to conduct survey and demonstration projects, develop public information activities, and implement practices within their boundaries. The Burns-Homer-Pleasant District became part of the Winona County district in 1986. Herbert Flueck, "Soil and Water Conservation in Minnesota—A Review" in Presentations Made at Minnesota Chapter SCSA 1985 Annual Meeting, Jan 25, 1985, MSA, MHS, 5.

23. Gower, "CCC Indian Division," 7.

24. George Morrison with Margot Fortunato Galt, *Turning the Feather Around: My Life in Art* (St. Paul: MHS Press, 1998), 46. *Indians at Work* 1.13 (Feb 15, 1934): 22.

25. R. W. Hellwig, assistant forester, to William Heritage, Dec 14, 1938; Hellwig to Scherer at the Lake States Regional Office, Apr 5, 1939; Heritage to Commission of Indian Affairs, Jan 5, 1934; Collier to Burns, May 10, 1934, Series 212, CCC-ID Subject Correspondence File (1933–44), BIA, CCA, NA. Tsegaye Nega and Wei-Hsin Fu, *Wild Rice Management at Bois Forte Indian Reservation: History and Current Perspectives* (Nett Lake, MN: Bois Forte Tribal Council, Department of Natural Resources, 2001), 15.

26. See http://www.nps.gov/grpo/ (accessed Jun 28, 2007). The site became part of the Grand Portage (Chippewa) Indian Reservation when the reservation was established through the Treaty of 1854. William Heritage to Commissioner of Indian Affairs, Sep 14, 1933; Kinney to Commissioner of Indian Affairs, Aug 1, 1936; Heritage to Commissioner, Oct 1, 1936, Series 212, CCC-ID Subject Correspondence File (1933–44), BIA, CCA, NA. Carolyn Gilman, *The Grand Portage Story* (St. Paul: MHS Press, 1992), 128.

27. Morrison communication with Sommer.

28. William Heritage to Commissioner, Oct 1, 1936, Series 212, CCC-ID Subject Correspondence File (1933–44), BIA, CCA, NA. Agency Cost Analysis, Emergency Conservation Work, Feb 1, 1937, Series 207, CCC-ID Inspection Reports (1933–39), BIA, CCA, NA.

29. Scherer to Commissioner, Oct 26, 1936; Kinney to Commissioner, Oct 8, 1938; Scherer to Commissioner, Feb 3, 1939, Series 212, CCC-ID Subject Correspondence File (1933–44), BIA, CCA, NA. A description of this study, taken from Alan R. Woolworth's report based on Brown's original notes, is found in Erwin N. Thompson, *Grand Portage National Monument: Great Hall Historic Structures Report History Data Section* (Washington, DC: Department of the Interior, National Park Service, 1970), 29–33. The report also contains eight illustrations from the MHS/CCC excavations following page 120. Gilman, *Grand Portage Story*, 128–30. The work of the CCC-ID helped pave the way for the establishment of the Grand Portage National Monument in 1960.

30. Ron Cockrell, *Grand Portage National Monument, Minnesota: An Administrative History* (Washington, DC: Department of the Interior, National Park Service, 1982). Danziger, *Chippewas of Lake Superior*, 156.

31. Buskowiak, "My Days in the C.C.C.'s," 4.

NOTES TO CHAPTER 9

1. "Enrollees Favor CCC's," *The Company 17 Once-Over* (spring 1936): 1.

2. Salmond, *Civilian Conservation Corps*, 146–47, 153, 156.

3. Directory, Emergency Conservation Work Camps, Fifth Period, 1935, U.S. Forest Service, Aug 15, 1935, Series 13, Camp Directories, 1933–42, CCC-NA; Series 29, Correspondence with State Selecting Agencies, 1933–42, CCC-NA. Calvin Drews, "How The CCC Has Helped Me," n.d., Series 101, Success Stories, 1936–41, CCC-NA. Mapes interview.

4. Salmond, *Civilian Conservation Corps*, 160. See "Roosevelt's Tree Army."

5. One group of enrollees in the late 1930s was different from the rest: in July 1939, enrollees included the New Ulm high school football team. After their "conditioning period" working on conservation projects, they were given honorable discharges to go back to school in September. Telephone conversation between C. S. Rondestvedt, Supervisor of CCC enrollments for the State Relief Agency, with Dean Snyder, Administrative Assistant to W. Frank Persons at the Department of Labor, Nov 2, 1939. "Report for the Months of July, August and September, 1941," Department of Conservation, Conservation Department Monthly Reports, Department of Conservation Records, MSA, MHS. Camp Inspection Report, Company 1724, Camp F-34, Jun 9, 1941; Camp Inspection Report, Company 3707, Camp F-53, Feb 10–11, 1942, both Series 115, Camp Inspection Reports, 1933–42, CCC-NA. Arnold R. Alanen noted in "Years of Change on the Iron Range" that iron mine production for World War II was two and one-half times that of the Depression years. Alanen, "Years of Change on the Iron Range," in Clark, ed., *Minnesota in a Century of Change*, 158.

6. Anderson, "Minnesota State Park Historic Resources" E-26. "Report for the Months of January, February, March, 1942," Department of Conservation, Conservation Department Monthly Reports, Department of Conservation Records, MSA, MHS. Camp Inspection Report, Company 721, Camp F-8, Jul 21, 1941; Supplemental Report, Camp F-10, Co. 716, Tofte, MN, Jul 8, 1941; Supplemental Report, Camp F-13, Co. 702, Bena, MN, Feb 19, 1942, all Series 115, Camp Inspection Reports, 1933–42, CCC-NA.

7. Camp Report, Company 712, Camp F-5, Gunflint, Jul 24, 1935; Supplemental Report, Camp F-5, Company 712, Grand Marais, MN, May 18, 1942, both Series 115, Camp Inspection Reports, 1933–42, CCC-NA. McEntee, "Federal Security Agency: Final Report," 33.

8. Radovich interview. Sanchelli, "Great Depression in Swede Hollow–Part III."

9. Former CCC-ID enrollees joined the armed forces in significant numbers. Charles E. Trimble, a member of the Oglala Lakota Tribe, founder of the American Indian Press Association (1969), and executive director of the National Congress of American Indians (1972–78), noted that "Following Pearl Harbor in 1941, Indians came forth in such great numbers [to enlist in the armed forces] that to accommodate the onslaught" some tribes even set up offices for recruiters on the reservations. "Midlands Voices: Nation Should Honor Our Indian Veterans," *Omaha World-Herald*, Nov 11, 2005. Native Americans have traditionally served in the U.S. armed forces in greater numbers proportionally than any other racial group in the country. Barbara W. Sommer and Mary Kay Quinlan, *Native American Veterans Oral History Initiative Planning Document* (Omaha, NE: Red Willow Institute, 2002), 11. J. W. Palmer to Commissioner of Indian Affairs, May 12, 1942, Box 1, Miscellaneous Correspondence, Series 212, CCC-ID Subject Correspondence File (1933–41), BIA, CCA, NA. Parman, *Indian Civilian Conservation Corps*, 239.

10. Danziger, *Chippewas of Lake Superior*, 156. John Collier, "The Spirit of CCC Will Last Forever," *Indians at Work* 9. 9–10 (May-Jun 1942): 35. Wirth, *Civilian Conservation Corps Program*, 25–26. Gower, "CCC Indian Division," 9.

11. Johnson, "Civilian Conservation Corps," 302.

12. Burcalow interview. Darst interview.

13. Department Reflections, unsigned and undated, ECW Committee, Dec 19, 1934, Department of Conservation, Division of Forestry, Department of Conservation Records, MSA, MHS.

14. "National Forests in Minnesota," 1, 5.

15. Beatty, *Summary: Minnesota CCC Work*, 4–28.

16. Drake, "Civilian Conservation Corps," 14. Beatty, *Summary: Minnesota CCC Work*, 2–3. Merrill, *Roosevelt's Forest Army*, 141.

17. Drake, "Civilian Conservation Corps," 14. Beatty, *Summary: Minnesota CCC Work*, 2–3. Merrill, *Roosevelt's Forest Army*, 141. Anderson, "Minnesota State Park Historic Resources" E-24. J. C. "Buzz" Ryan, "Just Who Benefited from the CCC," in Nelson and Sommer, eds., *It Was a Good Deal*, 5.

18. H. O. Anderson and P. E. McNall, *A Dozen Years of Conservation Farming, 1935–1949* (Madison, WI: Department of Agriculture, U.S. Soil Conservation Service with the State Soil Conservation Service and the Agricultural Extension Service, University of Wisconsin, Madison, 1949), 1. Herbert Flueck, interview by Tom Copeland, Aug 17, 1977, Minnesota Water Resources Board Oral History Project, MSA, MHS.

19. Robert Fechner, "My Impressions of the IECW," *Indians at Work* 2.2 (Oct 1, 1934): 16.

20. Congdon, "New Deal–Junior Division," 164–65. Johnson, "Civilian Conservation Corps," 302.

21. Department of Conservation, *Third Biennial Report*, 44.

22. In all, from 1933 to 1942, Minnesota had 74,688 CCC enrollees (including veterans) and 2,536 Native Americans in the CCC-ID. An additional 7,187 camp officers and supervisory personnel were employed by the CCC. McEntee, "Federal Security Agency: Final Report," 108. Salmond, *Civilian Conservation Corps*, 129. Anderson, "Minnesota State Park Historic Resources," E-24. The CCC-ID figure was less than four percent of CCC expenditures in Minnesota for the same period. Gower, "CCC Indian Division," 12.

23. Richart interview. Sanchelli, "Great Depression in Swede Hollow–Part III."

24. C. S. Rondestvedt, Supervisor of CCC Selection, to Dean Snyder, Administrative Assistant to W. Frank Persons, Dec 14, 1938; C. S. Rondestvedt, Superintendent of CCC Selection, to Neal E. Guy, Civilian Conservation Corps, Mar 30, 1940, both Series 29, Correspondence with State Selecting Agencies, 1933–42, CCC-NA. "Quarterly Report of Former CCC Enrollees Who Have Attained Outstanding Success in Private Life," Jun 1, 1939, Series 56, Success Stories, 1939, CCC-NA. See http://www.ecmpostreview.com/2006/October/18shandiovthma.html (accessed Jun 28, 2007). "State Artist George Morrison Dies," *[Minneapolis] Star Tribune*, Apr 18, 2000, A1, A9.

25. "Norman E. Borlaug, Biographical Sketch," n.d.; Curriculum Vitae, Dr. Norman E. Borlaug, "Brief Biographical Sketch," ca. 1970; "Curriculum Vitae, Dr. Norman E. Borlaug," 1982; NEB Background Material, 1982; Norman Borlaug, interview by William C. Cobb for the Rockefeller Foundation, Jun 12, 1967, oral history transcript 1967 (1), p130, all Box 1, Borlaug Collection, University of Minnesota Archives, University of Minnesota, Minneapolis, MN. "Living History Interview with Dr. Norman E. Borlaug," *Transnational Law and Contemporary Problems* 1.2 (Fall 1991): 541. Dr. Norman Borlaug was awarded the 1970 Nobel Peace Prize for a lifetime of work in improving agriculture production, especially in Third World countries. His work is often referred to as the "Green Revolution." "Nourishing Inspiration" in *Newsletter* of the Vesterheim Norwegian-American Museum 25.2 (Summer 1990): 1, 5.

26. Lahti interview.

27. Darst interview. Frank Chernivec, interview by Kathy Kainz, Oct 18, 1982, IRRC. Halloran interview.

28. Halloran interview. Rawlings interview. William J. Fraser, communication with Edward P. Nelson, n.d., CCC Collection, IRRC.

29. Morrison communication with Sommer. Mike Vuksech, interview by Barbara W. Sommer, Jan 17, 1983, IRRC. Noyes interview. Osborn interview.

ORAL HISTORY SOURCE NOTE

An oral history interview is a primary source document created in an interview setting with a witness to or a participant in a historical event. Its purpose is to collect and preserve the person's firsthand information—and make it available to others.

The oral histories in this book are primarily from the Arrowhead Civilian Conservation Corps Documentation Project (ACCCDP) and the Minnesota Civilian Conservation Corps Documentation Project (MCCCDP). The ACCCDP was organized in 1982 by Edward P. Nelson, archivist at the Iron Range Research Center in Chisholm, to document the work of the CCC in northeastern Minnesota. Completed in June 1983 in time for the fiftieth anniversary of the founding of the CCC, it focused on the Arrowhead region of Minnesota. The MCCCDP, a smaller project done by the author and funded by a grant from the Minnesota Historical Society, followed the ACCCDP by about ten years. It focused on collecting information on the work of the CCC in southeastern Minnesota and on documenting the experiences of African American and Native American enrollees.

The ACCCDP used a team of interviewers working from the same basic question format. This gave the project uniformity while allowing for adaptation for specific needs. Interviews generally followed a chronological order, beginning with a description of the narrator's life prior to joining the CCC and ending with "thought questions" about what the CCC meant to each. The body of the interview focused on life in the camps and on work projects.

Although the bulk of the interviews were with CCC enrollees, the ACCCDP also interviewed military personnel, camp administrators, work project supervisors, and LEMS. Thus, narrators represented nearly all aspects of CCC camp life and work. Interviews gave narrators the chance to put on record their views about a program that, for most, had a profound impact on their lives.

MCCCDP interview questions followed the same format as the ACCCDP for uniformity, with specific questions developed as needed. As with the ACCCDP, abstracts were developed for all interviews and a select number were fully transcribed. Together, the ACCCDP and MCCCDP resulted in 109 interviews, each between one and two hours long.

These interviews are held at the Iron Range Research Center. Excerpts from the interviews are used throughout this book. Combined with other primary source information and with secondary sources, they help tell the story of not only what happened but how and why.

Practitioners of oral history often use the interview format to collect information from adults about adult experiences. However, historians are increasingly realizing that documenting events that occurred during childhood can provide unique insights. The interviews in this book were recorded with men as they reached or passed retirement age, but the events discussed occurred for many during their teenage and young adult years. When they spoke of the disintegration of families during the Great Depression or of not having enough to eat, narrators were describing situations they faced not as grown men but as teenagers and young adults. Food was important: the lack of it at home and the types and amounts served in the CCC camps. For many, it was a symbol of the difficulties at home and the relative security of camp life. Their comments in the interviews reflected this.

General statements about the camps also can provide insight into the CCC experience. At first glance, many descriptions sound alike. But when one examines and compares the comments of white, African American, and American Indian enrollees, even general statements can be quite revealing. In some cases, they transcend race and ethnicity, helping us understand the universality of the Depression and CCC experiences. In other cases, they bring to light the racial intolerance and segregation patterns of the times.

For the most part, narrators in both oral history projects spoke positively of the CCC. In the interest of objectivity, criticisms and concerns are included wherever indicated by the research, sometimes with comments from the narrators as a balance. The discussion of the treatment of African American enrollees is the most critical in this book, reflecting local views in some cases along with the standard U.S. Army segregation policy of the time and its enforcement by district commanders overseeing Minnesota camps.

Oral history projects often end up collecting more than just the spoken word. This was true of the ACCCDP and the MCCCDP. Both projects unearthed a wealth of photographs, camp newsletters, cookbooks, memory books, and other documents related to camp organization and life—thousands of them at last count. Many of these are now part of the CCC Collection at the Iron Range Research Center and the Minnesota CCC History Center, both of which are located on the grounds of the Ironworld Discovery Center at Chisholm, Minnesota. The Iron Range Research Center also is the repository for a microfilmed collection of camp newsletters held by the Newberry Library in Chicago and for archival collections from the Superior and Chippewa national forests. All of these varied sources, gathered through the course of the ACCCDP, MCCCDP, and follow-up work, help give us a broader understanding of the CCC and its impact on the land and the people of Minnesota.

Following are the names of those who participated in oral history projects—including the ACCCDP, MCCCDP, and others—whose information helps to teach us about the CCC in Minnesota. Unless otherwise stated, interviews were undertaken as part of the ACCCDP or MCCCDP.

Allen, Clarence "Ole," December 12, 1982.

Anderson, Ernest, December 12, 1982.

Anderson, Osmos, December 7, 1982.

Anzelc, Matt, February 9, 1994.

Arndt, George, October 6, 1993.

Ball, John, February 28, 1983.

Baratto, Joseph, "Joe," December 3, 1982.

Barber, Edward W., May 8, 1994.
Itasca State Park, MN.

Bartek, Steven, "Steve," February 24, 1983.

Bellanger, Clement, "Clem," October 13, 1993.

Bernard, Louis, November 6, 1982.

Buffington, Virgil, September 28, 1993.

Burcalow, Donald, "Don," January 13, 1983.

Buskowiak, R. John, September 28, 1993.

Butcher, Vernon, January 12, 1983.

Cackoski, John, December 13, 1982, and March 4, 1983.

Carter, Melvin Whitfield, Sr., February 19 and November 28, 2003. Rondo Oral History Project, Ramsey County Historical Society, St. Paul, MN.

Cavanaugh, Harry, April 21, 1983.

Chernivec, Frank, October 18, 1982.

Christians, Kenneth, September 10, 1982.

Conkright, Allen, February 1, 1983.

Couillard, Alvin, January 11, 1983.

Crnkovich, Tony, September 30, 1982.

Darst, Claude G., September 28, 1993.

Davey, Glenn, November 5, 1993.

Donnell, Leo, October 13, 1993.

Eastlund, Alfred, October 6, 1993.

Ek, John, March 11, 1983.

Engstrom, Robert, February 1, 1983.

Erickson, Albert, April 11, 1974.
Chippewa National Forest, Cass Lake, MN.

Erickson, Chester, November 30, 1982.

Erickson, Leroy, August 11, 1993.

Fesnick, Robert, Sr., December 6, 1982.

Flueck, Herbert, August 17, 1977.
Minnesota Historical Society, St. Paul, MN.

Forsmark, Donald, January 24, 1983.

Franzinelli, Joseph, February 10, 1983.

Fredrickson, Ted, December 6, 1982.

Gagne, Bill, September 10, 1982.

Gary, Earl, November 10, 1982.

Greer, Harold, October 6, 1993.

Hall, Melvin, May 5, 1983.

Halloran, P. J., March 1, 1983.

Haneca, John J., October 6, 1993.

Harvivarz, Veikko, December 8, 1982.

Heegard, Harley, July 12, 1993.
Itasca State Park, MN.

Holmer, Reinhold, January 13, 1994.

Holter, Arne, August 6, 1993.

Humphrey, Milford J., December 13, 1982.

Huseby, Willard, August 9, 1993.

Ingram, Claude, November 19, 1982.

Johnson, Clarence, May 18, 1976.
Chippewa National Forest, Cass Lake, MN.

Johnson, Frederick, August 8, 1993.

Johnson, Jim, December 14, 1982.

Kaukila, Eino, October 7, 1982.

Keuhn, Kenneth, December 5, 1982.

King, Jim, August 9, 1993.

Krause, Earl, December 20, 1983.

Krueger, Delbert, "Del," October 6, 1993.

Kruse, Gerald, December 2, 1983.

Lahti, Eino, April 27, 1983.

Laudenschlager, Robert, August 9, 1993.

Law, Reuben, June 23, 1993.
Itasca State Park, MN.

Lekatz, John, November 10, 1982.

Lekatz, Paul, October 5, 1982.

Lyght, John R., October 11, 1993.

Mahelich, Edward, December 8, 1982.

Malisheske, Severin, October 4, 1982.

Mallory, E. K., "Bud," August 9, 1993.

Mapes, Allen, December 2, 1982.

Matson, Ray, March 30, 1977.
Chippewa National Forest, Cass Lake, MN.

Matteson, Robert, December 7, 1982.

Matthews, Walter, November 22, 1982.

Miller, Walter, December 7, 1982.

Morrison, George, October 23, 1994.

Nelson, Alfred, "Irv," April 15, 1976.
Chippewa National Forest, Cass Lake, MN.

Nelson, Willard, November 10, 1982.

Nickovich, Mike, September 30, 1982.

Niebeling, Lawrence J., October 6, 1993.

Noyes, Raymond, January 12, 1983.

Osborn, Guy, April 8, 1983.

Owen, Amos. June 24, 1970.
American Indian Research Project
(AIRP), University of South Dakota,
Vermillion, SD.

Palmer, Donald, November 23, 1982.

Partington, George, October 6, 1993.

Pavolich, John, December 6, 1982.

Penner, Bernard, November 5, 1982.

Phillips, Marvin, December 2, 1982.

Pope, Victor, August 10, 1993.

Pryor, Arthur, November 23, 1982.

Psyck, Al, May 5, 1983.

Quaife, Morris, "Morey," December 3, 1982.

Rabuze, John, March 4, 1983.

Radovich, Nicholas, "Nick," December 3, 1982.

Rahn, Eldor, August 10, 1993.

Ranger, Fred, January 14, 1994.

Rawlings, Godfrey, October 7, 1993.

Reimann, J. A., "Jack," August 11, 1993.

Richart, Harvey, January 13, 1990.

Roberts, Donald, December 14, 1982.

Rollings, Clair T., March 15, 1977.
Chippewa National Forest, Cass Lake, MN.

Ryan, James C., "Buzz," October 13, 1982.

Saari, Uno, September 28, 1982.

Sanchelli, Michael T., August 11, 2005.
Minnesota's Greatest Generation Project,
Minnesota Historical Society.

Schubert, Edward, July 21, 1993.
Itasca State Park, MN.

Schulte, Walter, "Wally," December 10, 1982.

Scott, John, October 8, 1993.

Seppo, Weikko, January 30, 1983.

Sersha, Paul, December 14, 1982, and
February 9, 1994.

Shea, David P., October 6, 1993.

Smith, James G., October 6, 1993.

Smith, Jewell, December 12, 1982.

Spry, Ernest, December 16, 1982.

Stillwell, Forrest, January 27, 1982.

Stimac, Albert, February 8, 1983.

Sundberg, Russell, March 4, 1983.

Takkinen, Leonard, November 11, 1982.

Tillman, Henry, November 4, 1982.

Todd, George H., October 7, 1993.

Trygg, Pete, January 6, 1983.

Vuksech, Michael, "Mike," January 17, 1983.

Wagner, Willard, January 14, 1983.

Wiese, James, June 14, 1983.

Williams, Alfred, October 8, 1993.

Wood, Paul L., October 7, 1993.

Zobitz, Edward, December 14, 1982.

BIBLIOGRAPHY

Abbreviations

IRRC Iron Range Research Center, Chisholm, MN

MHS Minnesota Historical Society, St. Paul, MN

MSA Minnesota State Archives, St. Paul, MN

UM University of Minnesota Libraries, University of Minnesota, Minneapolis, MN

PRIMARY SOURCES

ARCHIVAL COLLECTIONS

Civilian Conservation Corps Camp Papers [Microform]. Microfiche 1078 and Microfilm 2051. MHS.

Civilian Conservation Corps Collection. IRRC.

College of Forestry Records. UM.

Company 719 CCC S-51, Camp Charles Alumni Records. Northeast Minnesota Historical Collections. Kathryn A. Martin Library. University of Minnesota Duluth.

Department of Conservation Records. MSA. MHS.

Division of Entomology and Economic Zoology Records. UM.

E. Victor Willard Papers. MSA. MHS.

Frederick Alway File. UM.

Institute of Agriculture Records. UM.

Lindstrom, Lorenz R. Civilian Conservation Corps Camp Letters to Shirley Anderson, 1935–38. MSA. MHS.

Norman Ernest Borlaug Papers. UM.

Records of Civilian Conservation Corps. U.S. National Archives and Records Administration, General Services Administration. Record Group 35. Washington, DC.

Records of the Bureau of Indian Affairs. U.S. National Archives and Records Administration–Central Plains Region. Record Group 75. Kansas City, MO.

Scrapbook. Prairie Creek Project. Rice County Historical Society. Faribault, MN.

Town Records, 1933–34. Tofte, MN.

MANUSCRIPTS

Berman, Reuben. "A Memoir." Sep 1995. CCC Collection. IRRC.

Burcalow, Donald W. "Vocational Opportunities in the CCC." Radio talk given over WHLB. Virginia, MN. Dec 12, 1938. IRRC.

Buskowiak, R. John. "My Days in the C.C.C.'s." Oct 1993. MHS.

Cheyney, E. G. "History of Forestry in Minnesota." n.d. IRRC.

Daubner, Nathan. "The History of the WPA and the CCC in Winona County." May 3, 1933. MHS.

Drake, Robert. "Environmental Perspectives: People's Attitudes Towards Natural Resources, 1900 & 1934." n.d. Forest History Center, MHS. Grand Rapids, MN.

Hoyum, Wanda. "Camp Rabideau—Civilian Conservation Corps." Chippewa National Forest. 1996. IRRC.

Knoblauch, D. J. "Recollections of C.C.C. Days on the Chippewa." Chippewa National Forest. n.d. IRRC.

Lauer, Wilfred H., and Sillman, William T. "Pasture Management for Erosion Control." Radio talk given over KWNO, Winona, MN. Mar 6, 1939. IRRC.

Pederson, Harold C. "Conservation Review Reveals Growth." 1957. IRRC.

Sanchelli, Michael. "Forest Fire, Friday, April 13, 1934, Isabella, Minn., Camp 1721, C.C.C.s." n.d. MSA. MHS.

Swenson, Paul Arthur. "Family and Personal History." n.d. MSA. MHS.

Woolworth, Alan R. "Archeological Excavations at the North West Company's Fur Trade Depot, Grant Portage, Minnesota, in 1936–1937 by the Minnesota Historical Society." 1963.

———. "The Grand Portage Textbook" (ms). The Minnesota Chippewa Tribe, 1983.

GOVERNMENT PUBLICATIONS

Anderson, H. O., and P. E. McNall. *A Dozen Years of Conservation Farming, 1935–1949.* Madison, WI: U.S. Department of Agriculture, Soil Conservation Service, State Soil Conservation Committee, Agricultural Extension Service, University of Wisconsin, Madison, 1949.

Bachman, Barbara. *A History of Forestry in Minnesota with Particular Reference to Forestry Legislation.* St. Paul: Minnesota Department of Natural Resources, Division of Forestry, 1965.

Beatty, L. R. *Summary: Minnesota CCC Work, 1933–1941.* St. Paul: U.S. Department of Agriculture, Minnesota Department of Conservation, ca. 1942.

Bennett, Hugh Hammond. *Soil Erosion: A National Menace.* Washington, DC: U.S. Department of Agriculture, Circular No. 33, 1928.

Benson, David R. *Stories in Log and Stone: The Legacy of the New Deal in Minnesota State Parks.* St. Paul: Minnesota Department of Natural Resources, 2002.

Bergoffen, William W. *100 Years of Federal Forestry.* Information Bulletin #402. Washington, DC: U.S. Department of Agriculture, Forest Service, 1976; reissued 1990.

Blister Rust Control Handbook. St. Paul: U.S. Department of Agriculture and Minnesota Department of Conservation, ca. 1935.

Breining, Greg. *Managing Minnesota's Natural Resources: The DNR's First 50 Years, 1931–1981.* St. Paul: Minnesota Department of Natural Resources, 1981.

Brown, Mark H., and Iver J. Nygard. *Erosion and Related Land Use Conditions.* Washington, DC: U.S. Department of Agriculture, Soil Conservation Service, 1941.

Carhart, Arthur H. *Preliminary Prospectus: An Outline Plan for the Recreational Development of the Superior National Forest.* Washington, DC: U.S. Department of Agriculture, Forest Service, ca. 1920.

Civilian Conservation Corps. Washington, DC: U.S. Department of Agriculture, Forest Service, Region 9, 1935.

Cockrell, Ron. *Grand Portage National Monument, Minnesota: An Administrative History.* Washington, DC: U.S. Department of the Interior, National Park Service–Midwest Regional Office, 1982–83.

Conzet, G. M. *A Forest Policy and Program for the State of Minnesota.* St. Paul: Minnesota Department of Conservation, State of Minnesota Forest Service, 1931.

———. *Land Classification Report: Cloquet Valley State Forest Project.* St. Paul: Minnesota Department of Conservation, 1932.

Gateways to Forestry: Book I, Introduction. Washington, DC: U.S. Department of Agriculture, Forest Service, North Central Region, ca. 1933.

Geiger, Robert L., and Georgie A. Keller. *Organization and Development of the Soil Conservation Service: A Reference for Employees.* Washington, DC: U.S. Department of Agriculture, Natural Resources Conservation Service, 1970.

Golden Anniversary: Chippewa National Forest, 1908–1958. Washington, DC: U.S. Department of Agriculture, Forest Service, 1958.

Grand Portage National Monument/Minnesota: Final General Management Plan/Environmental Impact Statement. Washington, DC: U.S. Department of the Interior, National Park Service, 2003.

Helms, Douglas. "Coon Valley, Wisconsin: A Conservation Success Story." *Readings from the History of the Soil Conservation Service.* Washington, DC: U.S. Department of Agriculture, Soil Conservation Service, 1992.

Highlights in the History of Forest Conservation. 1948. Rev. ed., Washington, DC: U.S. Department of Agriculture, Forest Service, 1964.

Karamanski, Theodore J. *Saving the St. Croix: An Administrative History of the St. Croix National Scenic Riverway.* Omaha, NE: U.S. Department of the Interior, National Park Service–Midwest Region, 1993.

Kieley, James F., ed. *A Brief History of the National Park Service.* Washington, DC: U.S. Department of the Interior, National Park Service, 1940.

"Know Your Conservation Department." St. Paul: Minnesota Department of Conservation, 1940.

Lowdermilk, Walter C. *The Eleventh Commandment.* Washington, DC: U.S. Department of Agriculture, Soil Conservation Service, 1939.

———. *Reflections in a Graveyard of Civilization.* Washington, DC: U.S. Department of Agriculture, Soil Conservation Service, 1944.

McClelland, Linda Flint. *The Historic Landscape Design of the National Park Service, 1916–1942.* Washington, DC: U.S. Department of the Interior, National Park Service, 1993.

McEntee, J. J. *Woodsmanship for the Civilian Conservation Corps.* Washington, DC: Federal Security Agency, 1941.

Mackintosh, Barry. *The National Park Service: A Brief History.* Washington, DC: U.S. Department of the Interior, National Park Service, 1999.

Mather, Stephen T. *Ideals and Policies of the National Park Service: Handbook of Yosemite National Park.* Washington, DC: U.S. Department of the Interior, National Park Service, 1921.

Matson, Keith W. "The Civilian Conservation Corps on the Chippewa National Forest. 1933–1942." 1985. Rev. ed., Washington, DC: U.S. Department of Agriculture, Forest Service, 2002. Document on file at Supervisor's Office, Cass Lake, MN.

Nega, Tsegaye, and Wei-Hsin Fu. *Wild Rice Management at Bois Forte Indian Reservation: History and Current Perspectives.* Nett Lake, MN: Bois Forte Tribal Council, Department of Natural Resources, Jul 2001.

Olsen, Russ. *Organizational Structure of the National Park Service—1917 to 1985—Administrative History.* Washington, DC: U.S. Department of the Interior, National Park Service, 1985.

Organization and Development of the Soil Conservation Service. Washington, DC: U.S. Department of Agriculture, Soil Conservation Service, Jul 1970.

Otis, Alison T., William D. Honey, Thomas C. Hogg, Kimberly K. Lakin. *The Forest Service and the Civilian Conservation Corps: 1933–1942.* Washington, DC: U.S. Department of Agriculture, Forest Service, 1986.

Paige, John C. *The Civilian Conservation Corps and the National Park Service, 1933–1942: An Administrative History.* Washington, DC: GPO, 1985.

Pfaff, Christine. *The Bureau of Reclamation and the Civilian Conservation Corps, 1933–1942.* Washington, DC: U.S. Department of the Interior, Bureau of Reclamation, 2000.

Ritter, L. B. *White Pine Blister Rust Control, Minnesota, 1935.* St. Paul: U.S. Department of Agriculture, Minnesota Department of Conservation, 1936.

Ruhland, Vic. *Gilmore Creek Soil Erosion Control Project Revisited. Winona County, Minnesota.* St. Paul: U.S. Department of Agriculture, Natural Resources Conservation Service, Minnesota State Office, Jun 2001.

———. *Through These Eyes: The First Seventy Years of Soil and Water Conservation in Minnesota.* St. Paul: Minnesota State Office, USDA Natural Resources Conservation Service, 2005.

Soil Erosion Sentinel: Upper Mississippi Valley Region. La Crosse, WI: U.S. Department of Agriculture, Soil Erosion Service, ca. 1935.

Stewart, Donald M. *White Pine Blister Rust Control.* St. Paul: U.S. Department of Agriculture, Minnesota Department of Conservation, 1938.

The Superior National Forest. Washington, DC: U.S. Department of Agriculture, Forest Service, ca. 1935.

Supervisor's Handbook—Soil and Water Conservation District. St. Paul: Minnesota Board of Water and Soil Resources, n.d.

Thoma, Ben. *The Civilian Conservation Corps and Itasca State Park.* Itasca: Minnesota Department of Conservation, Division of State Parks, Itasca State Park, 1984.

Thompson, Erwin N. *Grand Portage National Monument: Great Hall Historic Structures Report History Data Section.* Washington, DC: U.S. Department of the Interior, National Park Service, 1970.

Thorfinnson, M. A. *History of Soil and Water Conservation Districts in Minnesota 1929–1965.* St. Paul, MN: U.S. Department of Agriculture, Soil Conservation Service, State Soil Conservation Committee, ca. 1965.

Tweed, William C., Laura E. Soulliere, Henry G. Law. *Rustic Architecture: 1916–1942.* San Francisco, CA: Division of Cultural Resource Management, Western Regional Office, National Park Service, Department of the Interior, 1977.

Two Years Afield With the C.C.C. Washington, DC: U.S. Department of Agriculture, Forest Service, ca. 1935.

U.S. Federal Security Agency and the Civilian Conservation Corps. *The CCC at Work: A Story of 2,500,000 Young Men.* Washington, DC: GPO, 1941.

———. *CCC-ID Handbook.* Washington, DC: GPO, 1941.

Unrau, Harlan D., and G. Frank Willis. *Administrative History: Expansion of the Park Service in the 1930s.* Denver, CO: U.S. Department of the Interior, National Park Service, 1983.

White, Bruce M. *Grand Portage as a Trading Post: Patterns of Trade at "the Great Carrying Place."* Grand Marais, MN: U.S. Department of the Interior, National Park Service, Grand Portage National Monument, 2005.

Wirth, Conrad L. *Civilian Conservation Corps Program of the United States Department of the Interior.* Washington, DC: U.S. Department of the Interior, Civilian Conservation Corps, 1944.

SECONDARY SOURCES

BOOKS AND PAMPHLETS

Aby, Anne J., ed. *The North Star State.* St. Paul: Minnesota Historical Society Press, 2002.

Alleger, C. N., comp. *Civilian Conservation Corps, Minnesota District: That the Work of Young America May be Recorded.* Rapid City, SD: Johnston and Bordewyk, Inc., 1934.

Barone, Michael. *Our Country: The Shaping of America from Roosevelt to Reagan.* London: Collier Macmillan Publishers, 1990.

Cash, Joseph H., and Herbert T. Hoover, ed. *To Be an Indian: An Oral History*. 1971. 2nd ed., St. Paul: Minnesota Historical Society Press, 1995.

Clark, Clifford, Jr., ed. *Minnesota in a Century of Change: The State and Its People since 1900.* St. Paul: Minnesota Historical Society Press, 1989.

Cohen, Stan. *The Tree Army: A Pictorial History of the Civilian Conservation Corps, 1933–1942.* Missoula, MT: Pictorial History Publishing Co., 1980.

Cohen, Wilber J., ed. *The Roosevelt New Deal: A Program Assessment Fifty Years After.* Austin: Lyndon B. Johnson School of Public Affairs, University of Texas, 1986.

Cole, Olen, Jr. *The African-American Experience in the Civilian Conservation Corps.* Gainesville: University Press of Florida, 1999.

Congdon, Don, ed. *The Thirties: A Time to Remember.* New York: Simon and Schuster, 1962.

Conkin, Paul K. *The New Deal.* 2nd ed. Arlington Heights, IL: AHM Publishing Co., 1975.

Dana, S. T., J. H. Allison, R. N. Cunningham. *Minnesota Lands.* Washington, DC: American Forestry Association, 1960.

Danziger, Edmund Jefferson, Jr. *The Chippewas of Lake Superior.* Norman: University of Oklahoma Press, 1978.

Davis, Kenneth S. *FDR: The New Deal Years, 1933–1937.* 3rd ed. New York: Random House, 1986.

Gilman, Carolyn. *The Grand Portage Story.* St. Paul: Minnesota Historical Society Press, 1992.

Goldston, Robert. *The Great Depression: The United States in the Thirties.* Indianapolis, IN: The Bobbs-Merrill Co., Inc., 1968.

Graubard, Stephen R. *Minnesota, Real & Imagined: Essays on the State and Its Culture.* St. Paul: Minnesota Historical Society Press, 2000.

Harby, Samuel F. *A Study of Education in the Civilian Conservation Corps of the Second Corps Area.* Ann Arbor, MI: Edwards Brothers, Inc., 1938.

Harper, Charles Price. *The Administration of the Civilian Conservation Corps.* Clarksburg, WV: Clarksburg Publishing Co., 1939.

Helms, Douglas, and Susan L. Flader, eds. *The History of Soil and Water Conservation.* Washington, DC: Agricultural History Society, 1985.

Henrickson, John. *Gunflint: The Trail, The People, The Stories.* Cambridge, MN: Adventure Publications, Inc., 2003.

Hill, Edwin G. *In the Shadow of the Mountain: The Spirit of the* CCC. Pullman: Washington State University Press, 1990.

Hill, Frank Ernest. *The School in the Camps: The Educational Program of the Civilian Conservation Corps.* New York: American Association for Adult Education, 1935.

Holland, Kenneth, and Frank Ernest Hill. *Youth in the* CCC. Washington, DC: American Council on Education, 1942.

Hoyt, Ray. *"We Can Take It": A Short Story of the C.C.C.* New York: American Book Co., ca. 1935.

———. *Your* CCC: *A Handbook for Enrollees.* Washington, DC: Happy Days Publishing Co., Inc., ca. 1940.

Kennedy, David M. *Freedom from Fear: The American People in Depression and War, 1929–1945.* New York: Oxford University Press, 1999.

Lacy, Leslie Alexander. *The Soil Soldiers: The Civilian Conservation Corps in the Great Depression.* Radnor, PA: Chilton Book Co., ca.1976.

Lass, William E. *Minnesota: A History.* 2nd ed. New York: W. W. Norton and Co., 1998.

Leipold, L. E. *Cecil E. Newman: Newspaper Publisher.* Minneapolis, MN: T. S. Denison and Co., Inc., 1969.

Lowitt, Richard, and Maurine Beasley. *One Third of a Nation: Lorena Hickok Reports on the Great Depression.* Urbana: University of Illinois Press, 1981.

McEntee, James J. *Now They Are Men: The Story of the* CCC. Washington, DC: National Home Library Association, ca. 1940.

Marsh, G. P. *Man and Nature.* 1864. Annotated reprint, Cambridge, MA: Harvard University Press, 1965.

Merrill, Perry H. *Roosevelt's Forest Army: A History of the Civilian Conservation Corps, 1933–1942.* Montpelier, VT: Self-published, 1981.

Meyer, Roy W. *Everyone's Country Estate: A History of Minnesota's State Parks.* St. Paul: Minnesota Historical Society Press, 1991.

Minnesota Chats 24.1. May 20, 1942.

Morrison, George, with Margo Fortunato Galt. *Turning the Feather Around: My Life in Art.* St. Paul: Minnesota Historical Society Press, 1998.

Nelson, Edward P., and Barbara W. Sommer. *It Was a Good Deal: The Civilian Conservation Corps in Northeastern Minnesota.* Duluth, MN: St. Louis County Historical Society, 1987.

Nord, Mary Ann, comp. *The National Register of Historic Places in Minnesota: A Guide.* St. Paul: Minnesota Historical Society Press, 2003.

Oliver, Alfred C., and Harold M. Dudley. *This New America: The Spirit of the Civilian Conservation Corps.* New York: Longmans, Green, and Co., 1937.

Parman, Donald L. *The Indian Civilian Conservation Corps.* Ann Arbor, MI: University Microfilms, 1967.

Perkins, Van L. *Crisis in Agriculture: The Agricultural Adjustment Administration and the New Deal, 1933.* Berkeley: University of California Press, 1969.

Raff, W. H. *CCC Days in Cook County, 1933–1942.* Grand Marais, MN: Cook County Historical Society, 1983.

Rudeen, Marlys, comp. *The Civilian Conservation Corps Newspapers: A Guide.* Chicago: Center for Research Libraries, 1991.

Ryan, J. C. "Just Who Benefited from the C.C.C.?" in *It Was a Good Deal: The Civilian Conservation Corps in Northeastern Minnesota.* Edward P. Nelson and Barbara W. Sommer, eds. Duluth, MN: St. Louis County Historical Society, 1987.

Saalberg, John Jacob. *Roosevelt, Fechner and the CCC: A Study in Executive Leadership.* Ann Arbor, MI: University Microfilms, Inc., 1964.

Salmond, John A. *The Civilian Conservation Corps, 1933–1942: A New Deal Case Study.* Durham, NC: Duke University Press, 1967.

Shannon, David A. *The Great Depression.* Englewood Cliffs, NJ: Prentice-Hall, Inc., 1960.

Sherman, Hila. *Bayport: Three Little Towns on the St. Croix, 1842–1976.* Hudson, WI: Star-Observer Publishing Co., 1976.

Simmons, Dean B. *Swords into Plowshares: Minnesota's POW Camps during World War II.* St. Paul, MN: Cathedral Hill Books, 2000.

Simms, D. Harper. *The Soil Conservation Service.* New York: Praeger, 1970.

Sitikoff, Harvard, ed. *Fifty Years Later: The New Deal Evaluated.* Philadelphia, PA: Temple University Press, 1985.

Steen, Harold K. *The U.S. Forest Service: A History.* Seattle: University of Washington Press, 1976.

Taylor, David Vassar. *African Americans in Minnesota.* St. Paul: Minnesota Historical Society Press, 2002.

Tweton, D. Jerome. *The Civilian Conservation Corps, The National Youth Administration, and the Public Schools.* Washington, DC: Educational Policies Commission, ca. 1942.

———. *Conserving Social and Natural Resources.* Minnesota District Civilian Conservation Corps, ca. 1938. Photo album. MSA. MHS.

———. *Factual Information Concerning Minnesota's National Forests.* Minneapolis: Minnesota Conservation Federation, 1943.

———. *Historic Roadside Development on Minnesota Trunk Highways, 1920–1960.* St. Paul: Minnesota Department of Transportation, 2000: http://www.dot.state.mn.us/tecsup/site/historic/files/narrative.pdf.

———. *The New Deal at the Grass Roots: Programs for the People in Otter Tail County, Minnesota.* St. Paul: Minnesota Historical Society Press, 1988.

———. *Problems and Progress of Forestry in the United States; Part I: The Forest Situation in the United States.* Washington, DC: Society of American Foresters, 1947.

ARTICLES

Anderson, Johan Emil. "Nature's Last Stand." *The Minnesota Conservationist* (Sep 1935): 11, 23–24.

Beatty, Leslie R. "A Forest Ranger's Diary." *The Conservation Volunteer* 25.146–31.180 (Mar-Apr 1962/Jul-Aug 1968).

Beatty, Robert O. "The Conservation Movement." *Annals of the American Academy of Political and Social Science* (May 1952): 10–19.

Bennett, Hugh H. "Planning for Soil Conservation." *Soil Conservation Magazine* 1.7 (Jan 1946): 6–12.

———. "There's But One Way to Do the Job." *Soil Conservation Magazine* 11.6 (Dec 1945): 1–5.

Berg, Shary Page. "Civilian Conservation Corps Initiative: Cultural Resources in Massachusetts Forests and Parks." *APT Bulletin* 31.4 (2000): 47–52.

Brown, Ralph D. "Archeological Investigation of the Northwest Company's Post, Grand Portage Minnesota, 1936." *Indians at Work* 4.18–19 (May 1937): 38–43.

Burns, Mark L. "Indians and the New Deal." *Indians at Work* 2.9 (Dec 15, 1934): 42–45.

Carlson, E. J. "Indian Rice Camps at the White Earth Reservation." *Indians at Work* 2.7 (Nov 15, 1934): 16–23.

Cole, Olen, Jr. "African-American Youth in the Program of the Civilian Conservation Corps in California, 1933–1942: An Ambivalent Legacy." *Forest & Conservation History* 35 (Jul 1991): 121–27.

Collier, John. "The Spirit of the ccc Will Last Forever." *Indians at Work* 9.9–10 (May-Jun 1942): 35.

Doughty, Tom. "From Bleakness to Greatness." *The Farmer* 105.20 (Nov 21, 1987): 38.

Drake, Robert M. "Being Careful with Natural Resources, or Before and After Earth Day 1970." *Roots* 18.1 (Fall 1989): 3–10.

———. "A Prideful Recollection of the Old ccc." *The Minnesota Volunteer* 46.269 (Jul-Aug 1983): 2–9.

Fechner, Robert. "The Civilian Conservation Corps Program." *Annals of the American Academy of Political and Social Science* 194 (Nov 1937).

———. "My Impressions of the IECW." *Indians at Work* 2.2 (Oct 1, 1934): 15–16.

Flueck, Herbert. "Soil and Water Conservation in Minnesota: A Review." Fifty Years of Soil and Water Conservation: Presentations Made at Minnesota Chapter SCSA Annual Meeting. January 25, 1985.

Gower, Calvin W. "The ccc Indian Division: Aid for Depressed Americans, 1933–1942." *Minnesota History* 43.1 (Spring 1972): 3–13.

———. "The Struggle of Blacks for Leadership Positions in the Civilian Conservation Corps: 1933–1942." *Journal of Negro History* 61.2 (1976): 123–35.

Helms, Douglas. "SCS: 50 Years Young." *The Farmer Magazine* (Mar 16, 1985).

Howell, Lyle E. "Training Fire Fighters." *Indians at Work* 5.3 (Nov 1, 1937): 20–21.

Johnson, Frederick. "The Civilian Conservation Corps: A New Deal for Youth." *Minnesota History* 48.7 (Fall 1983): 295–302.

———. "The Civilian Conservation Corps: Public Works or Panacea?" *Public Works* 3.10 (Oct 1980): 80–81, 117.

Kirkland, Mary M., and Clarence W. Ringey. "Indians at Red Lake, Minnesota, Meet Problems of a Changing World." *Indians at Work* 6.9 and 6.11 (May and Jul 1939): 30–34.

Mitchell, J. H. "The Pipestone Quarry or Restoring an Ancient Indian Shrine." *Indians at Work* 2.8 (Dec 1, 1934): 25–28.

Mitchell, J. H., and Charles I. Dunaven. "Red Lake Indians in Semi-Technical Positions." *Indians at Work* 2.5 (Oct 15, 1934): 21–22.

Mitchell, J. H., and Charles H. Racey. "Indian Emergency Conservation Workers Restore the Historic Grand Portage Trail." *Indians at Work* 1.4 (Oct 1, 1933): 22–24.

Nelsen, Alfred L. "The CCC and Minnesota's Resources." *Crusade for Conservation* (Mar-Apr 1956): 1–3.

Nute, Grace Lee. "Grand Portage." *Indians at Work* 4.17 (Apr 15, 1937): 26–32.

Paddock, Nancy. "Soil Conservation, A Sometime Priority." *Roots: Caring for Minnesota—Its Forests, Rivers, and Land* 18.1 (Fall 1989): 25–33.

Rice, Anna M. "General Christopher C. Andrews: Leading the Minnesota Forestry Revolution." *The History Teacher* 36.1 (2002): 91–115.

Richardson, Elmo R. "Was There Politics in the Civilian Conservation Corps?" *Forest History* 16.2 (Jul 1972): 12–21.

Rolvaag, Karl F. "New Horizons in Conservation." *Conservation Volunteer* (Sep-Oct 1964).

Salmond, John A. "The Civilian Conservation Corps and the Negro." *Journal of American History* 52.1 (Jun 1956): 75–88.

Searle, R. Newell. "Christopher C. Andrews." *Roots* 18.1 (Fall 1989): 11–16.

———. "Minnesota Forestry Comes of Age: Christopher C. Andrews, 1895–1911." *Forest History* 17.2 (Jul 1973): 14–25.

Young, Dwight. "Marvelous Army: The Work of the Civilian Conservation Corps Lives All Around Us." *Preservation* 56.1 (Jan/Feb 2004): 64.

Zankman, Pat. "The Grover Conzet Transient Camp." *Overlook* (Winter 2000–2001): 3–4.

———. "An IECW Camp in a Tamarack Swamp—Nett Lake—And a Program for the Coming Winter." *Indians at Work* 2.6 (Nov 1, 1934): 14–15.

———. "Nourishing Inspiration." *Newsletter* of the Norwegian-American Museum 25 (Summer 1990).

INDEX

ILLUSTRATION CREDITS

pages ii–iii, 58, 75, 91, 130—National Archives
pages 3, 5, 68 bottom—Chippewa National Forest
pages 15, 25, 51, 67—Bill Raffe Photographic Collection, Iron Range Research Center (IRRC)
pages 19, 20, 50— CCC Collection, Carlton County Historical Society
pages 29, 35—Uno Saari Oral History, IRRC
page 34—Eino Lahti Photographic Collection, IRRC
pages 37, 68 top, 132—Robert Engstrom Collection, IRRC
pages 41, 42 top right, 59, 112, 133—Nick Radovich Collection, IRRC
page 42 top left—John Cackoski Photographic Collection, IRRC
page 42 bottom— Alfred "Irv" Nelson Collection, Chippewa National Forest
page 44—Paul Sundberg Collection, IRRC
pages 45, 60—John Rabuze Collection, IRRC
page 47—Kenneth Aery Collection, IRRC
pages 55, 69 bottom—Howard Paakkonen Collection, IRRC
pages 56, 101, 103, 105, 128—Copyright Minnesota, Department of Natural Resources
page 61—Joseph Bombich Collection, IRRC
page 69 top—John Kramerich Collection, IRRC
page 76 top— Frances Benjamin Johnston Collection, Library of Congress
page 84—Osmos Anderson Collection, IRRC
page 86—Photograph courtesy of Northeast Minnesota Historical Center, Duluth
pages 88 top, 124, 134—Kathy Kainz Photographic Collection, IRRC
page 88 bottom—Mrs. William Wipf Photographic Collection, IRRC
page 110—USDA Soil Conservation Service
page 113—Edward Mehelich Collection, IRRC
page 135—CCC Collections, IRRC
page 206—Francis Carroll

Maps on pages 54, 80, 81 by Map Hero—Matt Kania
All other images from MHS collections

To learn more about the history of the ccc in Minnesota, visit the Minnesota Civilian Conservation Corps History Center at the Ironworld Discovery Center in Chisholm, Minnesota. Developed as a partnership between Ironworld USA, the Iron Range Research Center, and Chapter 119 of the National Association of ccc Alumni, its exhibits tell the story of the life and work of the Minnesota ccc. At Gooseberry Falls State Park, the *ccc Worker* statue honors Minnesota's enrollees and all who were a part of the ccc in the state. Dedicated on August 9, 2007, it stands along a trail near the park's visitor center, facing a ccc-built stone retaining wall.

This pin was given to an enrollee from the Big Lake Camp at Cloquet.

Hard Work and a Good Deal was designed and set in type at Cathy Spengler Design, Minneapolis. The book was printed at Friesens, Altona, Manitoba. The typefaces are LinoLetter, Gill Sans, and Gomorrah.

CPSIA information can be obtained
at www.ICGtesting.com
Printed in the USA
BVHW011325030422
633235BV00005B/22

9 781681 342344